# INTEGRATING SUSTAINABILITY INTO MAJOR PROJECTS

# INTEGRATING SUSTAINABILITY INTO MAJOR PROJECTS

## Best Practices and Tools for Project Teams

Wayne McPhee, M.Eng., P.Eng., MBA

Sabrina M. Dias, MES, P.Eng.

WILEY

*Registered Office*
John Wiley & Sons, Inc., 111 River Street, Hoboken, NJ 07030, USA

*Editorial Office*
John Wiley & Sons, Inc., 111 River Street, Hoboken, NJ 07030, USA

For details of our global editorial offices, customer services, and more information about Wiley products visit us at www.wiley.com.

Wiley also publishes its books in a variety of electronic formats and by print-on-demand. Some content that appears in standard print versions of this book may not be available in other formats.

*Library of Congress Cataloging-in-Publication Data is Available:*

ISBN 9781119557906 (hardback)
ISBN 9781119557920 (ePDF)
ISBN 9781119557890 (ePub)

Cover Design: Wiley
Cover Images: Shanghai Road intersection © ansonmiao/Getty Images,
Open pit mining © Fertnig/Getty Images,
Windmills © Santiago Urquijo/Getty Images,
Dam Pond Hydroelectric Production Dam Of Cavallers © makamuki0/Pixabay

Set in 10/14pt, ElectraLTStd by SPi Global, Chennai, India.

Printed in the United States of America

V10016864_011020

# Contents

**Chapter 4**

## Understanding What Is Important   51

**Chapter 5**

## Project Management   71

**Chapter 6**

## Stakeholder Engagement   89

**Chapter 7**

## Managing Risk and Opportunity   107

# About the Authors

Wayne McPhee, M.Eng., P.Eng., MBA is a sustainability specialist who has 30 years experience as a technology developer, consultant, team leader, and senior manager. Wayne has led the development and management of cross-disciplinary project sustainability programs within global engineering firms. His experience includes a wide range of major projects, including new mines, highways, LNG terminals, wind farms, hazardous waste removal, and brownfield redevelopment. His work has included sustainability planning and strategy, risk workshops, sustainability management systems, water and energy management, regulatory approvals, and stakeholder engagement. He has lectured on integrating sustainability into project management and written papers on strategy and sustainable decision making.

Sabrina Dias is the founder and CEO of SOOP Strategies Inc., a highly specialized mining and sustainability brand delivering intelligent sustainability performance solutions. She is a regular guest lecturer at universities and industry conventions. Her field work includes Tanzania, Madagascar, Australia, New Caledonia, Papua New Guinea, northern Canada, the United States, and South America. Sabrina has 20 years of experience in the extractives sector, achieving high levels of sustainability performance. A licensed Professional Engineer of Ontario, Sabrina holds a Bachelor's Degree of Ceramic Engineering and Society (McMaster University), Master's Degree of Environmental Studies (York University), and Graduate Diploma in Business and Environment (Schulich School of Business).

# Acknowledgments

Many major projects around the world are built on indigenous lands and impact indigenous peoples. We acknowledge this and will continue to learn from indigenous peoples about true sustainable development. The authors would like to thank the indigenous communities with whom we have worked over the years for sharing their traditional knowledge and the wisdom of generational thinking for sustainability.

The authors would like to thank the team at Wiley, in particular Margaret Cummins and Kalli Schultea, who have provided guidance and support for the development of the book, from approach and strategy through to production and marketing.

Wayne would like to thank his wife, Eileen, who not only provided enthusiastic support for the book but also provided design guidance, editing of the early draft, and design of the figures in the book. Also, thanks to my three daughters, Lucy, Hannah, and Theresa, for their support in the ongoing challenge of integrating sustainability into every part of our life. I would like to thank all of the sustainability colleagues who have shared their experiences and knowledge, especially Alan MacDonald, who provided invaluable insights and feedback on the initial book concept. And thank you to all of the many people I have worked with on project teams over the last 30 years for sharing their insights, experiences, and knowledge. My opinions are my own and not those of my employer.

Sabrina is most thankful to her husband, Jeffrey, and son, Theophil, whose unconditional support and patience while writing this book continues to provide endless reasons for gratitude. I have much appreciation for colleagues I have worked with and learned from over the years, and lovely friends who guided and encouraged my writing practice. I especially want to thank Jacques Gérin and David Wheeler, mentors and friends who were early champions of sustainable development and consistently demonstrate how to live and work with integrity. And finally, immense gratitude to Benoit Taillon, who, with one conversation and a cup of tea, changed the trajectory of my career – for the better.

# INTEGRATING SUSTAINABILITY INTO MAJOR PROJECTS

# CHAPTER 1

# Introduction

Sustainability books typically start with dire warnings about the future of the planet and a "call to arms" to fix all of the world's problems. In considering a book about sustainability for major projects, we have purposefully decided to take a pragmatic project management view of sustainable development and provide a set of processes and tools that can help project teams create better, more sustainable projects: projects with a smaller environmental footprint, projects that maintain support from the local community, and projects that achieve financial goals now and in the future. And, over time, a collection of better projects around the world can help to ensure a more sustainable future for the planet.

Integrating sustainability into major projects is still an emerging field of practice. No two projects are the same, so using scorecards and checklists can only get you so far. Project teams need to explore all the sustainability tools and tricks of the trade to create custom solutions that fit the location, the technology, the industry, owners of the project, and the groups of people who have a vested interest in the project.

We have tried to provide a logical and structured approach for integrating sustainability into project delivery that can be used to build alignment across an entire project team. In addition to the typical goal of getting government approvals for the project, good sustainability programs can help ensure that budgets and schedules are met, projects risks are understood and managed, and projects can obtain the necessary development financing.

It is important to understand that sustainability should not be a standalone discipline off to the side, separated from the rest of the project organization. Rather, sustainability must be integral to every aspect of project delivery. We have made every effort to demonstrate how sustainability is a team sport where everyone on the project team contributes.

This book will lead project teams through the various types of major projects, explain how sustainability can be integrated into traditional project management functions, and demonstrate how sustainability can play a critical role throughout the project lifecycle.

## 1.1   Terminology

There are many ways to describe the integration of environmental, social, and economic development challenges and opportunities into a project. Here are some of the most common terms:

- Sustainability
- Sustainable development
- Responsible development
- Corporate citizenship
- Corporate social responsibility
- Creating shared value

Although there are subtle differences in definition, all of the terms are basically capturing the same concepts. This book uses the term "sustainability," but project teams can and should use whatever terminology allows them to create a better project. If your organization or industry primarily uses other terminology, then it is best to stick with what is familiar and accepted. Managing sustainability on major projects is hard enough without trying to introduce new terminology to your organization or industry.

### DEFINITION: SUSTAINABILITY

We cannot discuss sustainability for major projects without clarifying what we mean by the term. We use "sustainability" as the shortened version of "sustainable development," a term classically defined by the World Commission on Environment and Development:

> Sustainable development is development that meets the needs of the present without compromising the ability of future generations to meet their own needs.

## 1.2   Creating Value by Integrating Sustainability

Value creation on major projects is traditionally assessed by a strict financial analysis: Was the project delivered on-budget? These days, most organizations and financial institutions are evolving how they see "value." And they are now incorporating concepts of brand and reputation, risk minimization, and responsible investing into the evaluation of an organization's or project's success.

Project sustainability efforts are often seen as an additional cost, a negative line item on the project budget. If managed properly, however, sustainability becomes a critical component of creating value out of the project.

Sustainability programs can:

- Drive innovation that can reduce overall project costs.
- Reduce the risk of project delays that can increase budgets and delay revenue generation from the finished project.
- Help secure and maintain community support that can streamline approvals.
- Reduce project risks, which can improve access to capital and lower financing costs.
- Create a better, more attractive project that draws potential buyers and increases project valuation.

## Attracting Investors

One of the most powerful tools to gain executive-level support for integrating sustainability into major projects is to demonstrate how sustainability can have a positive impact on project financing. This is true for industrial projects that rely on stocks, bonds, and debt financing, as well as government projects where financing could come from project-specific bonds, green bonds, or financing strategies like public-private partnerships (P3s). A strong sustainability program will help improve the project's access to capital, reduce the cost of borrowing money, and improve overall project profitability. Studies have shown that industrial firms "with better sustainability who disclosed their strategies to pivotal stakeholders enjoyed higher stakeholder trust and lower capital access restraints."[1]

Globally, financial institutions have recognized that one of the largest risks for major projects is environmental, social, and governance (ESG) risks and this has led to the adoption of standards for sustainability and ESG management. Financial institutions often perform extensive due diligence prior to providing capital to develop a project. It is now becoming increasingly common for institutions to require an ESG review as part of due diligence and to include regular audits after financing has been approved. This helps to ensure that ESG commitments are being met and that project risks are being managed on an ongoing basis.

A strong sustainability program and project team is essential to addressing ESG risks and providing concrete evidence to financial institutions and their auditors that these risks are being managed. A traditional view of projects may see sustainability and environmental programs as an unnecessary cost or an annoying delay in getting construction started. But most projects require outside financing, and with financial institutions requiring strong risk and sustainability management before making an investment, a well-integrated sustainability program is essential for many projects to proceed.

## Attracting Buyers

Many projects (resource extraction projects, in particular) are developed with the intent of selling the asset once it has been built and commissioned. Whether the acquiring organization is a larger organization, a pension fund, or a stock market investor, the project will need to demonstrate that there is strong community support for the project and that environmental and social risks are being managed effectively.

Project teams should develop their sustainability program not just to meet the minimum needs of local approvals, but also to consider how the sustainability program will fit with the requirements of the potential future owners. Like most elements of good project management, it is better to structure the project correctly at the beginning than it is to try to fix it at the end.

## Developing Future Projects

Whether the organization is considering a future expansion to the current project or developing other projects in the future, it is critical to maintain a strong reputation and build community support. With the expansion of social media to all corners of the world, issues at one site can damage the ability of the organization to pursue projects at new locations. Communities located near a new project site might not know the organization but can quickly find out how they have performed on other projects. With this knowledge they can take action either to protect their community by blocking the new project or to welcome an organization that has proven it can develop sustainable projects.

A strong sustainability program can ensure that the project helps the organization build credibility and a reputation to support the success of the current project and to ensure that the organization is well-prepared for future projects.

## Avoiding Rework

Integrating sustainability into project planning and engaging with local stakeholders can help the team understand design constraints and potential issues early in the project development, which can avoid rework and redesign later in the project. People who live and work in the area of the proposed site can help the project team understand the context of the local area, local regulatory requirements, and potential social and environmental impacts. Engaging with local communities can help the team get a sense of whether the project will be supported and, if not, how they can revise and improve the design and development plans early in the project. Engaging with local communities can also create value by accessing local knowledge that can be used to improve designs and reduce costs.

## Improving Productivity

Lost productivity is a potential and often overlooked cost to a project, whether it is due to dissatisfied employees, high turnover, or community blockades that delay construction. Integrating sustainability into the project, especially into construction management, can help to keep the local workforce engaged and productive. If there are unresolved issues with the local community then the project could experience a disengaged or angry local workforce that has high absenteeism, low productivity, and high turnover, all of which lead to higher costs of project delivery.

# 1.3   Creating a Sustainability Focus

There are a number of different ways to think about sustainability. Some people understand sustainability to be only about renewable energy or green buildings. Others think sustainability is about engaging with the local community or philanthropic donations to a local charity. In our approach we think about sustainability as a focus on creating the maximum positive impact and the minimum negative impact from a project. This goes beyond meeting regulatory requirements and involves all elements of the project.

This section examines some of the models that the project team can use to create a sustainability focus across the entire project. We look at the evolution of organizations from being compliance focused to being sustainability focused, how project teams can focus on managing sustainability, and how to think about complexity and social capital.

## Sustainability versus Compliance

We believe that an impactful focus for project teams is to move beyond a compliance culture and pursue sustainability in design, procurement, and construction. Creating a better, more sustainable project reduces overall risks, improves financial performance, and ensures that the project leaves a positive legacy that everyone on the team can be proud of.

A simple but effective diagram is the sustainability versus compliance graphic (see Figure 1.1), by Wheeler, Colbert, and Freeman (2002).[2] This clearly shows how an organization can shift from a culture of compliance to a culture of relationship management, and eventually to a culture of sustainability where maximum value is created.

This model can be applied to the evolution of delivering major projects. Traditionally, organizations and project teams have focused on getting the required permits for a project with limited engagement with stakeholders and local communities. More recently, projects have moved to a relationship management

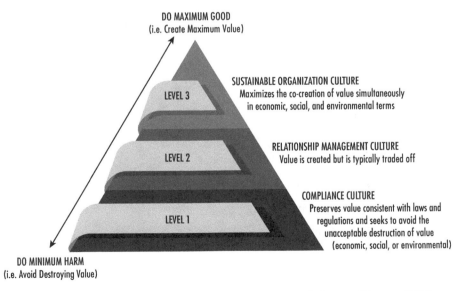

Figure 1.1   Sustainability versus compliance. Adapted from Wheeler, Colbert, and Freeman (2002) reproduced with permission of the *Journal of General Management.*

approach where stakeholder engagement is considered a necessary requirement for major projects. However, the engagement is still typically performed by a small team focused on getting project approvals rather than creating long-term relationships with the local community. Integrating sustainability into major projects is focused on building a culture of sustainability across the entire organization where the team looks at building value for both the project owners and the local community.

## Sustainable Project Management

Another way to think about project sustainability is outlined in Figure 1.2, which shows how projects can be considered sustainable in two ways. A project is plotted based on its underlying sustainability features (x-axis) where some projects, such as a wind farm, are typically considered to be "sustainable projects" and thus are placed further to the right on the x-axis. On the other hand, nonrenewable resource extraction projects, such as a mine, are considered unsustainable by their fundamental nature (i.e. removing a resource from the earth that will not be replaced) and so are placed further to the left on the x-axis.

An alternative view (on the y-axis) is to look at how the project is managed to improve its overall sustainability. For example, a typical mine that extracts a nonrenewable resource may not be considered fundamentally sustainable, but if development can be managed to mitigate environmental impacts, reduce energy requirements, and create benefits for local communities, then it can still create a positive benefit. In this case, the mining project would move from a low position on the graph to a higher, more sustainable position.

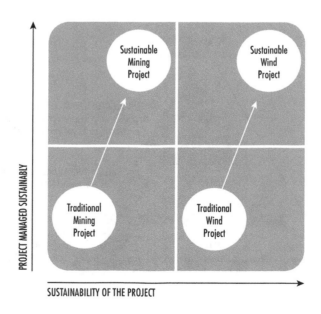

Figure 1.2   Sustainable project management model.

Conceptually, the sustainability focus for the project team should be on how they can move the project as far as possible to the upper right of the graph while maintaining the underlying organizational objectives.

Project teams rarely have control over the underlying sustainability features of the project that they are working on. But they do have the ability to improve project management and delivery to reduce negative impacts and improve benefits. One of the core themes of this book is to help project teams define what sustainability means for their project and then provide tools and systems to help them achieve that vision and focus.

## Complexity Is the New Reality

Managing major projects is a messy and complex business. It is getting even more complex with competing priorities for budget, schedule, quality, safety, environment, security, and community. Project teams need to develop the skills, tools, workflows, and thought processes to manage these competing priorities, make informed decisions, and create new solutions that help meet often contradictory project goals. These challenges are also opportunities for innovation, for new approaches, and for collaboration to solve problems.

A key starting point in developing a mindset about sustainability is to be aware that there will be both competing and complementary objectives between the traditional technical and financial goals, and the sustainability goals. Project teams need to embrace this complexity and view sustainability as an opportunity to create a better project, rather than as an annoyance and additional cost. In *Reconstructing Value: Leadership Skills for a Sustainable World*, the authors refer to this approach as a "sustainability Mindset," where there is a synthesis of these competing challenges rather than just a compromise:

> A sustainability mindset holds that the key challenge is in advancing human development in areas such as prosperity, justice and human rights, while at the same time preserving nature and respecting the regenerative limits of the biosphere.[3]

The sustainability mindset understands that new major projects are essential to human development but also looks to ensure that the work is done with respect for the environment and the local communities impacted by the project.

Sustainability is creating more complex business and technical environments, and project teams cannot manage increasing project complexity with the same processes and tools that have been used for years. Project teams need to look for ways to improve existing tools and processes to incorporate sustainability. They need to introduce new tools that help manage the increasing complexity, shift roles and responsibilities, and diversify project teams to bring in new and varying skills sets to ensure that sustainability challenges are managed.

By our nature, we are more comfortable solving problems that are familiar. However, with the rapid changes occurring in the world, project teams are often faced with new problems that don't have proven solutions. If we are going to meet the challenges of this new reality, we will need to adapt and find new ways of collaborating and working together to solve problems.

When we face changes that encompass several disciplines, there is a need for collaboration with multidisciplinary teams that can bring a broad range of experience and expertise to the problem. These multidisciplinary project teams are comprised not just of technical specialists, but may include new team members who have valuable knowledge of the challenges facing the project, including socioeconomic and geopolitical experts, academics, stakeholders, and a facilitator who can bring the team together. Complexity is the new reality and project teams need to find ways of working together and with key stakeholders to meet this challenge and create better, more sustainable projects.

## Co-Creating Value

As projects move toward a sustainability focus, stakeholder engagement is shifting from compliance and risk mitigation to looking for opportunities that create positive relationships that can uncover the project's potential to co-create value for both the organization and local communities. This has been named "Creating Shared Value" by Porter and Kramer.[4]

Opportunities for collaborating and co-creating value can be evaluated by answering a number of initial questions aimed at understanding both the planned or current project impacts and the potential for value creation, but also the potential for new activities that can create shared value that neither player could achieve on their own. These questions are:

1. What impact(s) does the project and its activities have on each element of the society?
2. What impacts could we change or improve if we changed how the project was delivered?
3. What impacts could the element of society have on the project?
4. What benefits could we co-create if we work together to address impacts and challenges?

The initial questions are intended as only a first step. True co-creation cannot be achieved by one side of the relationship acting alone. It requires ongoing dialogue and interaction to create understanding and new ideas.

One model for co-creating value is the DART model,[5] which we have adapted from a business model for working in developing economies. DART, which stands for Dialogue, Access, Risk Assessment, and Trust/Transparency, suggests that you need to focus on the four elements to fundamentally change the traditional relationship between the project and the local community, as shown in the sidebar.

---

### TIP: "DART" MODEL FOR CO-CREATING VALUE

The four elements of the DART model are:

**Dialogue:** Dialogue includes two-way communication (rather than a one-way flow of information), shared learning, and collective problem solving. Project teams need to approach stakeholders as partners in problem identification and problem solving, and not as barriers to be managed. Communities need to engage in the process to create value for their community.

**Access:** Ensure that stakeholders have access to the project team and, in particular, to the right people in the team. This includes active engagement through meetings and participation in the local community. One of the keys to ensuring good access is to ask stakeholders how they would like to communicate and offer them opportunities to try out different methods.

**Risk Assessment:** Risk encompasses not just the potential for harm to the local community but the perception of potential harm. Everyone on the project team should understand that the community's perception of risk is important and should be treated with respect, rather than dismissed as a lack of understanding.

**Trust and Transparency:** The project team controls most of the information about the project, so the local community may feel that they are being misled about the potential negative impacts of a project. Establishing trust requires transparency and honesty so that all players can understand the potential impacts and work together to co-create solutions to these challenges. To ignore or downplay potential impacts not only damages trust but also shuts down any potential for creating solutions and shared value.

## Understanding Community Support

Historically, formal approval for major projects meant convincing government regulators that the project was in the best interest of the government. As local communities and stakeholders gain more influence, it is becoming essential for projects to demonstrate that they have the support of the local community and can maintain that support to successfully deliver the project.

There are a number of different terms that are used to capture this idea of establishing stakeholder support. Depending on your organization or industry you may need to use one or all of these terms, including:

- Social capital
- Good will
- Public support
- Community support
- Social license to operate (SLO)

"Social license to operate" implies that there is an actual license or signed document to demonstrate the project has required support to move forward, but there is no such formal license. SLO is simply shorthand to indicate that there is a positive relationship with the local community and that they support the project, at least at the present time. "Securing an SLO" essentially means earning the trust of the project's local communities and building strong, mutually respectful relationships with them. It is important to understand that SLO is not a legal document and that stakeholders can "revoke" their project support (i.e. the SLO) at any time and without notice.

Social capital and good will are terms that suggest that you can place an economic value on relationships with stakeholders and local communities. Good will can be used in a social context to mean that a person is trusted. In the accounting context it is used to represent the intangible assets that an organization has, such as brand value, reputation, and intellectual property.

In the context of a major project, social capital and good will relate to the value that exists in the strength of the relationships with the local community, which can be leveraged to help make the project a success.

Strong relationships mean a high level of mutual respect and trust and much of this value is based on how the local community perceives the project and how they feel they are being treated by the project team.

Having a high level of social capital helps projects in many ways, including fewer project delays due to community disputes, faster permitting, and a more engaged local work force. Social capital provides value if there is a problem or an unforeseen environmental or social incident. With strong social capital, the project will be able to address the problem with limited negative backlash and perhaps local support to resolve issues faster.

## TIP: MANAGING YOUR SOCIAL CAPITAL BANK ACCOUNT

Discussing the concept of social capital with a traditional project team can be a challenge. The concept of social capital may seem vague or may be seen as irrelevant to the team members focused on design and construction activities.

One analogy we have found to be effective is the metaphor of a "Social Capital Bank Account," which holds the project's trust and reputation with the local community. Maintaining a healthy bank account can help to avoid delays and secure approvals on time. When your bank account is full, local stakeholders will not stand in the way of permits/approvals and may even vouch for your project with the local government and regulators.

Every time the team does something positive for the local community, such as taking time to listen and treating people with respect, you are putting "money" into the bank. Every time you mismanage a spill or ignore a complaint, you are losing "money" from the bank. Lose enough and all the social capital is gone.

Each project department should understand that they have a role in filling the Social Capital Bank Account, whether it is engineering who must consider alternate roads to preserve a local sacred site, or construction who must reconsider shift schedules to accommodate local hunting seasons. Everyone on the team has the potential to help fill the bank or to break the bank. The collective objective of the team is to maintain a full Social Capital Bank Account over time so that the project can move ahead smoothly.

The terms "public support" and "community support" focus the idea of social capital on the local community rather than on the broader concepts of support from external stakeholders, including governments and non-governmental organizations (NGOs). With the growth of social media and shifting social expectations, the support of the local community is becoming more and more important for major projects. Traditionally, major projects could get built without community support as long as they had government approvals, but that is no longer possible in most places around the world. To reflect this change, we refer primarily to community support as the focus for building social capital.

## 1.4   Sustainability Is a Team Sport

As managing sustainability becomes increasingly important to project success and the complexity of meeting such targets increases, sustainability must be embraced by all members of the project team. It cannot be delegated to a separate sustainability department or completely outsourced to external consultants. Meeting sustainability goals and creating a better project requires input from every member of the team and every person on a project.

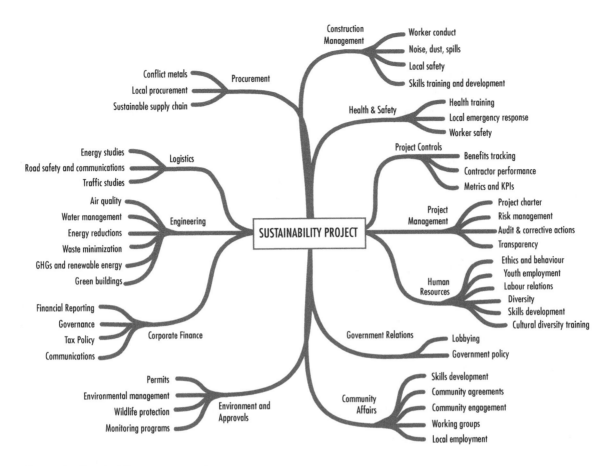

Figure 1.3  Sustainability as a team sport.

The diagram in Figure 1.3 shows how sustainability can fit into the entire project. Each department can influence sustainability issues and have a positive effect on the project. The diagram is by no means complete and will change from project to project but shows how sustainability is truly a team sport and not just the responsibility of the sustainability team.

It is also important to remember that sustainability issues are not specific to one group or department. In many cases, more than one group across the project team may need to be involved to have an influence on activities and issues. Take, for instance, providing training and skills development to the local community in order to increase the opportunity to hire as many local workers as possible. This objective can be influenced by:

- Human resources, which develops training programs
- Construction management, which runs the job training
- Health and safety, which gets involved in improved health or safety training

- Procurement, which incorporates training requirements into contractor Request for Proposals (RFPs) and contracts
- Indigenous affairs, which ensures local indigenous communities get training in transferable skills that create benefits for the community
- Project controls, which would be tasked with tracking training metrics as part of project key performance indicators (KPIs)

One effective way to create the sustainable team sport diagram for your project team is to hold a series of meetings with each of the departments or groups to discuss the basic concept and overall project sustainability objectives. Each group is then encouraged to find creative ways that they can contribute to the sustainability of the project.


## 1.5   Who Is This Book For?

With the rapidly changing social and environmental responsibilities that major projects are facing, project teams need to have the background knowledge, strategic insights, and skills to ensure that their organization is proactively managing sustainability.

This book is intended for the project leadership team responsible for all aspects of the project, the sustainability team responsible for managing the project's sustainability program, and for the entire project team involved in delivering aspects of the sustainability program.

This book will help everyone involved in the delivery of major projects, including:

- **Project owners** who want to manage risks and optimize project value
- **Project directors and managers** responsible for creating a successful project that meets budget, schedule, and sustainability objectives
- **Engineering** discipline leads and teams tasked with creating designs
- **Procurement** teams responsible for bringing the best contractors and suppliers to the project
- **Construction** management teams that want to ensure their workforce is engaged and that there are no unexpected delays in their schedule
- **Sustainability, environment, and communications** teams that want to improve their engagement with the entire project team
- **Financing agencies** that want to ensure the projects they invest in can manage risks, achieve institutional requirements, and deliver projects that will not make the news and damage the financial institute's brand
- **Consultants and contractors** who need to understand how their work can support the project team with delivering a successful project
- **Government regulators** who want to understand the challenges of delivering major projects
- **Students** who are looking for careers in project management and project delivery

Although this book is intended for major development projects, many of the processes and tools are also helpful for smaller projects. For example, the decision support tools are useful for upgrades to operating facilities and corporate decision making.

## 1.6   How to Use This Book

This book is divided into four parts and follows project development from concept to commissioning. Part 1 (Chapters 1 and 2) provides an overview of managing sustainability on major projects and outlines the importance of managing sustainability and how sustainability fits into the structure of major projects.

In Part 2 (Chapters 3 and 4), we show how each project is unique and how sustainability programs need to be customized to reflect the challenges and goals for each project. This part provides an overview of the numerous sustainability guidelines and systems that are available, as well as tools and processes to focus the sustainability program on material issues and opportunities.

As managing sustainability on major projects becomes more complex, it is critical to integrate sustainability into project management rather than have a separate group or program that is stuck on the side of the project. Part 3 (Chapters 5 to 9) provides concepts, tools, and processes that help sustainability to be integrated directly into project management and project execution plans, risk management, stakeholder and community engagement, and managing commitments and regulatory requirements.

Part 4 (Chapters 10 to 14) explores tools and processes to integrate sustainability into each of the main components of project delivery: engineering design, procurement, construction, commissioning, and eventual closure.

Project teams might not need all the tools and processes provided in the book. However, it is important to review the available tools and decide which are required for your project and which can help to capture opportunities to create a better project.

We acknowledge that this book is not a complete solution to sustainability challenges of major projects. Many components of sustainability management are well-developed fields of practice on their own, such as health and safety, risk management, impact assessments, skills development training, and environmental management systems. We will show how these fields fit into the overall sustainability management process but will not provide details on how each of these fields should be managed.

The book also provides additional resources for the project team, including models, sustainability diagrams, and sample tools. A website has been developed that provides useful templates and tools for readers, to reduce the level of effort required to get started with integrating sustainability into your project. As more major projects are executed with integrated sustainability programs, the tools and processes will continue to evolve and improve. We welcome your experiences, your lessons learned, and advice on your favorite tools and processes. Please visit our website (www.integratingsustainability.com) to get updates and share your experiences to help others create better projects.

We have based this book our own practical experiences, as well as drawing on the wisdom and experience from professionals we have had the privilege of working with on project teams. We hope this book will provide a solid foundation and starting point for individuals and project teams and look forward to hearing your experiences and insights that can help all of us develop better, more sustainable major projects.

# Endnotes

1. Turner, Lauren, "Two Ways Sustainability Drives Access to Capital, Network for Business Sustainability," September 12, 2016, accessed at https://nbs.net/p/two-ways-sustainability-drives-access-to-capital-973e115d-0141-4251-8a05-5739d5fd9cb4 on March 1, 2019.
2. Wheeler D., Colbert, B., and Freeman, R.E., "Focusing on Value: Reconciling Corporate Social Responsibility, Sustainability and a Stakeholder Approach in a Network World," *Journal of General Management* 28, no. 2 (Spring 2003).
3. Kurucz, E.C., Wheeler, D., and Colbert, B.A., *Reconstructing Value: Leadership Skills for a Sustainable World* (Rotman-UTP Publishing, 2013).
4. M.E. Porter and Kramer, M.R., "Creating Shared Value," *Harvard Business Review*, January–February 2011.
5. C.K. Prahalad and Ramaswamy, V., *The Future of Competition: Co-Creating Unique Value with Customers* (Harvard Business Press, 2004).

# CHAPTER 2

# Overview of Major Projects

Before we dive into discussing integrating sustainability into major projects, it is important to explore some of the concepts around major projects so that we establish a shared understanding and language for this book. This starts with a review of what makes a project "major" and how that creates unique challenges and opportunities for project managers and teams, especially related to sustainability concepts. The discussion will also consider different challenges for a broad range of major projects that include resource extraction, energy, industrial, infrastructure, or linear infrastructure, as well as projects that could have elements of more than one type of major project, like an energy facility that includes a transmission line, or a new mine with an access railroad and a new port facility.

The next step is to understand the key players on major projects. We will be discussing the project owner and overall project team, government employees, and local communities. It is important not only to discuss who is involved but how they interact with one another. Most project teams have a good understanding of the people and groups involved in the design and delivery of the project, and many understand financial players and government regulators. But they may not have as much experience considering local communities as key players and contributors to the success of a major project.

It is also important to consider how each of the key players perceives and interacts with the project by their sense of space (location of the project) and time (how long they will be engaged with the project), and their perception of risk and reward.

The typical timeline that a project takes to move from concept to construction and commissioning will be discussed with a focus on the three main parallel paths that include 1) design and delivery, 2) sustainability, and 3) financial management. Each of these three paths has hurdles that need to be crossed for the project to be successfully delivered. This requires project teams to understand the three paths and how everyone can contribute to the project's progress toward becoming reality.

This overview of the major projects includes some common management structures of major projects from EPCM (engineering, procurement, and construction management) to DBFOO (design-build-finance-own-operate), with a focus on how the choice of project structure can influence the team's ability to integrate sustainability into project management. Project structures that separate the organization's financial performance from the long-term efforts to maintain community support and manage social and environmental impacts can potentially create conflict between the key players on the project. These organizations should consider using strategies that help balance objectives and reduce the risk of conflict.

## 2.1   What Is a Major Project?

The discipline of project management includes a wide range of project types, from software system installation, to a house renovation, to the construction of a new mine or nuclear power plant. There is no good definition of what makes a project a "major" project. For the purposes of this book, a major project typically:

- Involves the construction of a physical structure
- Is large enough to require a separate team of specialists to deliver the project
- Is managed and structured outside of an existing operation
- Gets financing outside of the normal organizational cash flow
- Is located in a new geography or involves an expansion of the footprint of an existing facility
- Engages new stakeholders or impacts existing stakeholders in a new way

Smaller projects can also get significant benefits from improved sustainability management. The broad definition of major projects is provided to give some context to the discussion in the book, but the insights, models, and tools that we have provided can also be used on smaller projects. Smaller projects may not need all of tools but many of the concepts will still be useful for identifying project-specific challenges and opportunities, managing communications with the local community, and creating better projects.

## 2.2   Types of Major Projects

There are many types of major projects, from nuclear power plants to highways to mines, and all of these major projects have similar sustainability challenges and opportunities. When evaluating how to integrate sustainability into their specific project, teams should think more broadly about major projects rather than just looking at their own industry sector. Cross pollination of ideas across industries has helped to build the tools and processes collected in this book and will continue to allow improved sustainability of major projects across industries and geographies.

The main types of major projects are discussed below with a review of the unique challenges that each type of project can have for the team.

## Infrastructure

Infrastructure projects include a wide range of facilities that generally support a large number of local users and include:

- Airports
- Marine facilities
- Landfills and waste disposal
- Water and waste water treatment plants
- Hospitals

Infrastructure projects are often developed as public projects that are managed by governments or government agencies but can also be privately built projects that make money from user fees or tolls. Or they can be developed as public-private partnerships (P3). Infrastructure projects have unique challenges, including managing multiple users of the facility and the potential for safety and security concerns associated with the public use of the facilities.

Sustainability can be a challenge for these projects because they will provide a public benefit for the public at large, and so project teams tend to assume that the broader and long-term benefits counterbalance the short-term construction pains. It is often assumed that public good will be sufficient to overcome the resistance of the people living closest to the facility. Developing strong sustainability programs for infrastructure can be important in avoiding a not-in-my-backyard (NIMBY) response from the local community.

## Linear infrastructure

Linear infrastructure projects are a specific type where the facility is built to connect locations together, including:

- Roads, highways, and bridges
- Power lines
- Pipelines (water, sewage, oil)
- Rail lines
- Public transportation (subways, rapid transit)

In many ways, linear infrastructure projects are similar to standard infrastructure projects except that they will have multiple stakeholders and a greater reach of environmental and social impacts along the route. This raises the complexity of integrating sustainability into the project because many communities will be impacted, and there will be both winners and losers along the route of the infrastructure. They can bring a flow of goods, services, and people that stimulate the local economy. At the same time, linear infrastructure can bring social disruptions, noise, and pollution. Integrating sustainability into these projects can help to better manage both negative and positive impacts.

## Energy Facilities

Another type of infrastructure project is an energy facility that is used to create electricity for the grid or thermal energy for district heating, including:

- Thermal power plant (coal, oil, natural gas)
- Renewable energy (wind or solar farm)
- Hydroelectric facility
- Nuclear power plant

Energy facilities have unique challenges related to location selection. There is a balance between putting the facility near the people who will use the energy but far enough away to mitigate impacts from the energy production. The selection of an ideal project location could look at the best location from an energy production perspective (close to water for cooling or best wind/ solar resource), minimization of energy transmission requirements, availability of local labor, environmental impacts, risk and disaster response, and climate resilience.

Energy facility projects will often include a related linear infrastructure project, such as power lines. These further complicate the challenges of integrating sustainability. Like infrastructure projects, energy facility project teams need to keep in mind the difference between the overall benefit of the energy facility versus the local impacts to the environment and people living in the local community.

## Industrial Facilities

The development of large industrial facilities has many of the same challenges as infrastructure projects but has the additional challenge in that the project is typically for the benefit of a corporation rather than a government project that will provide a public benefit. The wide range of industrial facilities include:

- Chemical plants
- Refineries
- Smelters
- Large manufacturing facilities

Industrial facilities have a number of unique challenges, such as choosing a location that balances access to infrastructure (roads, rail lines, ports, water, and power), availability of skilled local labor, environmental impacts, and climate resilience. Large industrial facilities often include their own infrastructure projects within the overall project such as pipelines, road and rail transport, marine ports, water treatment, power plants, and landfills.

## Resource Extraction

Resource extraction can include both nonrenewable and renewable resource projects where there is a large impact on the local community and environment, such as a new forestry development. Resource projects include:

- Mining and quarrying
- Off-shore oil and gas facilities
- On-shore oil and gas drilling and fracking
- Forestry

Resource extraction projects have a number of unique challenges associated with the depletion of finite resources, royalties for access to the resources, and managing within the constraints of the location of the resource as opposed to being able to select a location for the facility. Project sites are often in remote areas where the potential for large impacts on the local community is high both from a positive perspective (jobs, skills development, and economic development) and from a negative perspective (social disruption, environmental damage, waste management, and impacts on health).

Resource extraction projects often include their own infrastructure projects within the overall project such as pipelines, road and rail transport, marine ports, water treatment, power plants, waste disposal, and landfills. Resource extraction may also incorporate large industrial projects like mineral processing facilities at a mine site.

# 2.3   Types of Project Structures

Major projects are typically delivered by a large team of employees, external consultants, and contractors who work together to design and deliver the project. There are a variety of project structures that can be used to organize the team and manage who is responsible for which task.

The "owner" (also called the proponent) of a major project is the organization that is ultimately responsibility for the successful delivery of the project and controls the project financials. The owner could be a government, a development agency, a corporation, a partnership, or a cooperative of organizations.

The owner will decide on the project structure that is best suited for project delivery. Depending on the structure, the project team will span different organizations with varying goals and objectives. The project structure will have a significant impact on overall project success and will have a significant influence on how sustainability is managed and how successful it will be. There is no single answer, but each project structure will have advantages and disadvantages that need to be managed to create the most successful project.

Some of the common project structures include:

- Self-perform
- Engineering, procurement, and construction management (EPCM)
- Engineer-procure-construct (EPC) or design-build
- Design-build-own-operate (DBOO)
- Design-finance-build-own-operate (DFBOO)
- Public-private partnership (P3)
- People-public-private partnership (P4)

## Self-Perform

In a self-perform structure, the owner manages all aspects of the project themselves and hires contractors and consultants as required to deliver specific pieces of work that the owner's team cannot handle themselves. This structure is typical where the project is an expansion of an existing facility or a new facility for a large organization that has a strong capacity for project delivery.

A self-perform project structure can be positive from a sustainability integration perspective as there is little to no disconnect between the goals of the owner and the goals of the project delivery team. The down side is that self-perform project teams can become isolated from emerging trends and may not be fully up to speed on new technologies and new ways of delivering projects. Self-perform teams should be open to innovation from contractors and suppliers so that they can deliver successful projects.

## Engineering, Procurement, and Construction Management (EPCM)

One of the most common project delivery structures is engineering, procurement, and construction management (EPCM), where the owner hires an engineering consulting firm to complete the major design and delivery of project components but maintains control over financial management, earning, and maintaining local community support, and most of the sustainability management activities related to regulatory approvals. The EPCM consultant will typically work in close alignment with the owner's team, which provides final approval of major decisions and deliverables.

The EPCM structure can create good alignment between the owner and the EPCM firm for design and finance activities but is not often well-aligned for integrating sustainability. Traditionally, the EPCM firm does not get involved in the initial project approvals and community engagement activities, yet they need to integrate the results of these activities into local procurement, local employment, and communications during construction.

For an EPCM project to successfully integrate sustainability it is important to clearly identify how both organizations are responsible for meeting project commitments and how sustainability will be incorporated into all project activities. Involvement of the EPCM firm typically ends when commissioning is finished. Project contracts should build incentives into project delivery that optimize long-term performance, secure community support, and help to build local capacity in order to maximize local employment and procurement. In other words, identify and utilize innovative solutions that are not part of the EPCM firm's typical, off-the-shelf design solutions.

## Engineering, Procurement, and Construction (EPC)

The engineer, procurement, and construct (EPC) project structure, also known as design-build, is a variation on EPCM where the owner hires a consulting firm to complete the full project delivery of the project, including full control over the project construction, and then hands the project over to the owner for operations during commissioning. In the traditional EPC contract, the owner is still responsible for financing and sustainability activities but has less control over procurement and selection of contractors. This is especially true when the EPC contract is structured as a fixed-price contract that provides a strong incentive for the EPC firm to minimize overall costs with no incentive to build or maintain community support.

From a sustainability perspective the EPC project structure can be difficult to integrate environmental and social goals into project delivery. For example, renewable power systems that have a large capital cost but low operating costs may be rejected in favor of traditional hydrocarbon power plants that come with lower capital costs and lower short-term risks. As with EPCM contracts, it is important to clearly identify who is responsible for meeting project commitments, how sustainability will be incorporated into all project activities, and how incentives will be used to optimize long-term performance, maintain community support, build a strong local workforce, and utilize innovative solutions.

## Design-Build-Finance-Own-Operate (DBFOO)

There are a number of different project types that use variations on the concept of design-build-finance-own-operate (DBFOO) contracts depending on who provides financing and how the operations and maintenance contract is structured. DBFOO is often used for infrastructure projects where the owner can hand over all activities to the DBFOO firm to both deliver the project and operate the project over a specified period of time. In a DBFOO contract the owner is still responsible for financing the project and pays the firm in specified installments over the life of the project. The DBFOO firm provides initial project financing and the owner provides a set annual operations payment throughout the operations. The DBFOO firm recovers its investment from these operations payments.

In these contracts, the owner also hands over significant control of project delivery to the DBFOO firm. Therefore, a clear understanding of who will be responsible for sustainability and community engagement is important. The owner and the DBFOO firm need to have a common understanding of the sustainability requirements and expectations so that project success can be realized for both parties. The DBFOO firm may need only a bare minimum of community support to build and operate the project to recover their investment, but the owner may be looking for a higher level of community engagement and acceptance.

One of the key advantageous of a DBFOO contract is that it shifts the time horizon of the typical EPC structure. Now the project development firm has a strong incentive to manage long-term operating costs and community support since they will also be operating the project for a set period of time. The time horizon for DBFOO contracts is longer than EPC contracts but it is still important for the owner to specify project conditions at exit of the contract. This is to prevent the risk that the DBFOO firm will reduce their attention to key environmental and social aspects toward the end of the contract, lose community support, and leave the owner with an asset that requires significant investment to repair and maintain.

## Public-Private Partnership (P3)

The use of public-private partnerships (P3s) gained popularity in the 1990s as a way for governments to reduce the tax investment required for infrastructure projects. Similar structures have also been used in resource projects where governments share in the investment in access roads or ports for resource areas and then recover the investment from user fees or tolls on the roads.

Although in theory creating a partnership between the private and public sectors should create the best potential for a well-integrated sustainability program, the public piece of the partnership was typically the government rather than the local community or the general public. As we will discuss later in this chapter, the government and the local community are often two distinct players with diverging interests in the project. In some cases, P3 projects have led to poor sustainability outcomes and in extreme cases a loss of community support, lawsuits, and protests. P3 project teams need to integrate sustainability into project delivery to ensure that they have local community support, ensure that positive opportunities are achieved, and create better projects.

P3 contracts should clearly identify who is responsible for meeting project commitments, how sustainability will be incorporated into all project activities, and how incentives will be used to optimize long-term performance, maintain community support, build a strong local workforce, and utilize innovative solutions.

## People-Public-Private Partnership (P4)

As discussed above, the "'public" in a P3 agreement is not typically the general public or local community, but the government. As projects continue to evolve and incorporate social responsibility, some projects are adding a fourth "p" representing the local people and creating P4: a people-public-private partnership structure. This type of project structure would help ensure participation and support from the local communities. P4 structures provide an approach that improves attention to and discussion regarding community concerns and potential benefits (i.e. steady revenue from infrastructure, long-term employment for local communities), and provides good risk management for the government, operators, and financial organizations by ensuring that the local community has a seat at the table.

P4 strategies are not well developed yet but they represent a possible solution for economic development infrastructure projects and for portions of resource projects, especially infrastructure (roads, water treatment, and power). P4 structure could provide benefits for the project owner, the government, and the local community.

# Summary of Project Structures

There is no project structure that works specifically to ensure sustainability is effectively integrated into project delivery. Each structure has advantageous and disadvantageous that can make integration easier or harder, but each system still requires a well-organized program to integrate sustainability into project management and delivery.

Figure 2.1 summarizes some of the sustainability strategies that can be implemented to counterbalance the difficulties with each of the main project structures discussed above. The table is arranged with the project structures that provide the owner with the highest level of control over the sustainability program at the top and the least control at the bottom. The types of challenges to managing sustainability in each structure are provided, as well as some high-level strategies to help integrate sustainability into the project.

| STRUCTURE | DESCRIPTION | CHALLENGES | SUSTAINABILITY STRATEGIES |
|---|---|---|---|
| Self-Perform | Owner manages project delivery. | • Owner's team may not be familiar with latest approaches or innovative solutions. | • Request innovative solutions from consultants and contractors<br>• Ensure sustainability requirements are included in all contracts and subcontracts |
| EPCM | Owner hires consultant to complete engineering and procurement and manage construction. Owner maintains financial control and pays construction contractors. | • Not clear who is responsible for sustainability.<br>• Short-term focus of project team | • Establish clear goals and responsibilities<br>• Ensure sustainability requirements are included in all contracts and subcontracts<br>• Tie sustainability performance to bonuses or penalties |
| P3 | Government (public) and project delivery firm (private) jointly own and develop the project. | • Local community not included in the project<br>• Not clear who is responsible for sustainability | • Establish clear goals and responsibilities<br>• Establish sustainability steering committee<br>• Tie sustainability performance to bonuses or penalties |
| EPC | Owner hires consultant to complete engineering, procurement and complete the construction often for a fixed price. | • Owner has limited control over sustainability<br>• Short-term focus of project team | • Specify commissioning handoff requirements<br>• Tie sustainability performance to bonuses or penalties |
| DFBOO/DBOO | Owner engages project firm to design, build, and operate the project for a specified amount of time. Project firm may also own and finance the project. | • Owner has limited control over sustainability.<br>• Owner and project firm have different sustainability objectives. | • Specify end of contract handoff requirements<br>• Establish sustainability steering committee<br>• Tie sustainability performance to bonuses or penalties |

*DECREASING OWNER CONTROL*

Figure 2.1    Sustainability strategies for different project structures.

## 2.4  Key Players

This section explores what we see as three categories of key players in a major project, and how they can interact throughout the project life to establish a framework for understanding some of the challenges and opportunities to integration of sustainability into projects. The key players involved in major projects can be divided into three broad categories: the organization, the government, and the local community.

The organization includes any group involved in the delivery of a project, including the owner organization, project delivery team, consultants, suppliers, contractors, and employees. Government includes the broad range of government departments such as economic development, taxation, regulatory approval, health, environment, and education. And the community includes the people that live in the area surrounding or near the project or are affected by the project's downstream impacts or transportation routes.

Traditionally, these three key players interacted in a basic linear structure (see Figure 2.2) where the organization engaged with the government over regulatory approvals and taxation, and the government and the community engaged through elections (if the project was located in a democracy), law enforcement, social services, and taxation. The organization and the community had some engagement (typically around local employment) but, overall, they had only limited formal engagement with each other.

Over time, as local communities have gained more understanding of project development and more influence (i.e. through social media), the relationship between the three players has evolved into a more complex structure where the organization, the government, and the community are all interacting as active players with each other, as illustrated in Figure 2.3. Obviously, this is still a gross oversimplification of the situation but understanding project development as a three-player model allows us to gain useful insights into the variety of interactions and the potential for conflict faced by each of the players.

At the core of this understanding is that organizations now require both official approvals and permits from the government and informal permission from the community to develop and operate the project. In the traditional linear model, an organization would seek permits from the government and then rely on the government to ensure that the local community does not prevent the project from being developed. In the new model, an organization still must engage with the government to get the required official permits, but now must also engage with the local community to gain and maintain community support. Too many organizations still rely on government approvals alone, and then are forced to delay project construction due to legal challenges or protests from an unsupportive local community.

This can be most challenging when the organization developing the project is led by a government entity where there may be a sense that they do not need to engage local communities and earn their support,

Figure 2.2    Traditional organization, government, and community relationship.

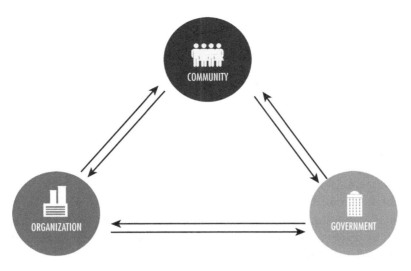

Figure 2.3    Modern organization, government, and community relationship.

since they are already representatives of the public. In these cases, the organization needs to understand the difference between the general public that the government represents (i.e. national or regional) and the local communities that are directly experiencing project impacts.

The proposed approach, where the project organization embraces the three-player model and ensures that the community has input into the project, can help ensure that the local community has a seat at the negotiating table. In this model, the community benefits from the project and maintains a strong position of influence with both the organization and the government. Actively bringing the local community into the project development process may seem counterintuitive but local engagement can reduce project costs, provide a broader set of options for developing and operating the project facility, and reduce overall project risk.

## 2.5  Managing Time and Space

One of the key challenges with understanding how other groups and people will respond to your project is to understand their perception of the project in space (location) and time. Projects are typically short-term in duration (i.e. 3 to 10 years), which is usually at odds with sustainability goals that can be multigenerational. The brief time frame can create a very transactional, short-term approach to project delivery as opposed to a cooperative, longer-term approach that focuses on the full life–cycle impact of project development, operations and maintenance, and eventual decommissioning.

Project teams need to understand that they have a very different set of objectives than governments and local communities (see Table 2.1). To create better projects, teams need to expand their traditional short-term thinking to look beyond capital cost and construction schedule to consider long-term impacts on the environment and the local community, as well as the long-term relationships with project stakeholders.

Table 2.1  Time and space for players Involved in major projects.

| Player | Time Involved in the Project | Space |
| --- | --- | --- |
| Project team | 2 to 3 years | Visit the project site |
| Government workers | 5 to 10 years | Visit the region |
| Local community | 25+ years | Live near the project site |

## Understanding Time

For project teams the timespan that they consider is essentially the time for project delivery from initial studies to commissioning and handover to the operations team, which typically takes between 5 and 10 years. In addition to this, individual team members may only work on the project for short periods of time, finish their piece of the design or construction, and then move on to the next project. Major projects may also start and stop with changes in personnel on the project team or a change in consulting firms, so that the typical person on a project team might spend only 2 to 3 years on a major project.

The timespan that government personnel will be involved in a project will vary depending on the government and government agency. Civil servants may spend a large part of their career with a single government agency, but politicians work on different timelines depending on when elections are scheduled, so the typical government employee might spend 5 to 10 years involved on a project.

Local communities have a much longer timespan of experience and engagement with a project. Although there may be short-term focus on jobs and economic benefits, there is also a longer-term focus on community success over generations so that their children and grandchildren also see positive benefits from the project.

## Understanding Space

The sense of space, location, and geography is also very different between the key players involved in a project. Project teams will typically not be from the local region and in many cases may never even visit the site but complete their design work from maps and drawings of the project site. The project team will have little personal stake in the project outcome other than to build on their experience and have a good project to add to their resume for their next job.

Government workers are usually more connected to the geographical location of the project site but being in the same country or region is not the same as living in the community.

And the local community, by contrast, will experience the project directly through impacts to the economy, traffic, noise, environmental damage, and other social disruptions.

## Managing Time and Space

These differences in perception of space and time can have a significant influence on how the project is perceived by each of the key players. For example, changing the timespan and location can affect the perception of risk and the balance between risk and reward. A government agency may view the economic rewards to an entire region or country from jobs and taxes generated by the project as a justification for the project risk. However, the local communities who bear the risk of social disruption and environmental damage may not see the risk-reward balance in quite the same way.

The impact of different perceptions of space can often be seen on major projects that have more than one location and where the project benefits and risks are not evenly distributed across each of the locations. In a linear infrastructure project, for example, the positive impacts are created where the urban center is located but the negative impacts could be felt by communities along the highway or commuter rail route that receives the noise and potential environmental impacts from spills, without getting any of the economic benefits.

The difference in the perception of time can create a difference between a typical transactional (often litigious) approach to relationships seen in major construction projects, where the project team, contractors and consultants are often focused on maximizing their share of a fixed project budget (a zero-sum game) and a cooperative approach to relationships where the project team and the local community focus on building trust-based relationships for long-term, mutually beneficial outcomes.

There is no way to eliminate the differences in perceptions of the project in time and space. At a minimum, project teams must understand the large disconnect between the key players on the project and use that understanding to adjust their approach.

## 2.6   Project Lifecycle

There are three main pathways in a project lifecycle that are interconnected and interdependent:

- Design and delivery
- Sustainability
- Financial management

The design and delivery pathway has always been well integrated with the financial management pathway. They are closely linked in all aspects from decision making and design to procurement and construction. The sustainability pathway is newer and therefore not as well integrated, but it is becoming more and more critical in the project lifecycle to understand and integrate project sustainability into the overall project lifecycle. Projects have required regulatory approvals for many years, but the big change is the need for community support, not just to ensure regulatory approval but also to de-risk the project and gain project financing.

The transition from two major pathways to three major pathways has left a gap in project planning and project management. The idea that the sustainability pathway can be managed solely by an outside consultant or a junior regulatory specialist is no longer tenable nor sufficient for delivering successful projects. Projects require senior sustainability leadership that can deliver critical sustainability elements and ensure that sustainability issues and challenges are addressed.

**THREE PATHWAYS FOR SUCCESSFUL PROJECT DELIVERY**

| ① DESIGN AND DELIVERY | ② SUSTAINABILITY | ③ FINANCIAL MANAGEMENT |
|---|---|---|
| Concept / Scoping | Stakeholder Mapping and Early Engagement | Seed Financing |
| Pre-Feasibility Study | Community Engagement | Second-Round Financing |
| Feasibility Study | Approvals and Social License | Project Finance |
| Detailed Design and Procurement | Permits & Community Agreements / Local Skills Development | Institutional Financing |
| Construction | Tracking & Reporting / Communications & Complaints | Financial Management |
| Commissioning | Transition to Operations | Holdbacks and bonuses |

Figure 2.4    Three pathways for successful project delivery.

The three pathways each have their own set of approvals and stages to move toward project completion (see Figure 2.4), including project owner approval to move through each stage of the design and delivery pathway, raising financing from internal and external sources, and sustainability approvals that includes permits and community agreements.

Over the life of the project, complex relationships can develop between the three main pathways. There needs to be clear communication among the team members. Everyone needs to understand the challenges and opportunities that other teams face in order to help overcome hurdles and move the entire project forward. A hurdle for one pathway is a hurdle for the entire project, and teams need to understand that everyone is responsible – not just the teams leading each of the pathways. All three pathways need to be part of the same project planning and project scheduling so that everyone understands the potential impacts.

Each of the three pathways are dependent on the other pathways. Having a solid strategy and team for one or two of the pathways is not going to create a successful project without the third stream also producing the required results. In the same way that poor financial management can kill a project with no cash to spend, or a poor design can kill a project with feasibility studies that owners or investors disagree about investing in, poor sustainability management can kill a project with failure to achieve community support, which can lead to protests, lawsuits, and blocked construction sites.

The project team will also change and grow as the project moves along the three pathways. As projects move from feasibility to design and construction, the project team will grow, so it is important to put in place management systems and communication tools to prevent information from getting lost. As the project develops there can also be time gaps between each of the stages and changes in personnel, contractors, and consultants working on the project. Installing systems such as commitments tracking, stakeholder engagement, and managing complaints between project stages is imperative to maintaining project success. See Chapter 8 for details on project management systems and tools.

## 2.7  Summary

No two major projects are alike, and each project requires a customized approach that fits the type of project, organization, industry, location, and stakeholders. The tools, processes, and best practices outlined in the rest of the book provide a structure that project teams can adapt to build a sustainability program that makes sense for their unique situation. The different types of major projects have unique challenges, and all require a custom sustainability program. Public infrastructure projects in an urban setting will have different requirements than a resource extraction project in a developing economy.

And unfortunately, as of writing this book, there is not yet a project structure that specifically integrates sustainability into project delivery. Each structure, from self-perform to design-build-finance-own-operate to public-private partnership (P3) has advantages and disadvantages. But each structure still requires a well-organized strategy to create a successful, sustainable project.

In this book we discuss techniques that project teams can use to integrate sustainability into project delivery in order to manage the complex requirements of governments and local communities, that have very different perceptions of the project in time and space. Some of these techniques include:

- Developing a project charter and goals (Chapter 5) that looks beyond project completion and short-term cost and schedule targets
- Decision making that incorporates social and environmental impacts (Chapter 10)
- Procurement workshops that bring local community engagement into supporting local economic development (Chapter 11)
- Engaging operations team members early in the process to bring longer-term thinking to the project team (Chapter 13)
- Designing for closure and progressive reclamation to reduce long-term impacts beyond the lifecycle of the project. (Chapter 14)

The tools and best practices collected in this book and the discussion in this and the following chapters will help project teams understand how to fulfill sustainability requirements, rather than allowing them to become unexpected barriers to project success.

CHAPTER **3**

# Standards and Guidelines

Although sustainable development is becoming part of the dialogue in organizations, it is not yet formally regulated by governments. Nongovernmental organizations (NGOs) have emerged as strong influencers in developing standards and guidelines for measuring and managing sustainability performance. The United Nations (UN) and the International Finance Corporation (IFC), for example, provide guidance for corporations and governments on operating standards, performance metrics, and operating principles for sustainability. Many of these guidelines, including the UN's Sustainable Development Goals and the IFC's Performance Principles, are considered effective in helping corporations and governments address global issues including poverty, human rights abuses, and changing climate, through their business plans and operational practices. By developing practices that adhere to guidelines for sustainable development, organizations can improve the sustainability performance of their projects and operations.

Depending on the level of commitment your organization or project has in becoming a high performer in sustainability, you may have a number of standards and guidelines that your project is looking to follow, or perhaps no decisions have been made about which standards or guidelines to follow. This chapter provides an overview of some of the main standards and guidelines that can help the team integrate sustainability into project planning and development.

In this chapter, we provide an overview of many of the popular sustainability standards and guidelines that are used by many organizations today. We start with international standards and guidelines and then present industry specific ones. And finally, we discuss the role the investment community plays in monitoring and supporting the integration of sustainability by offering specific benchmarks and indices based on the sustainability performance for project financing and publicly traded companies and investment instruments like green bonds.

Projects are not typically required to follow specific standards and guidelines, but the structure and direction included in the guidelines can provide a number of advantages to the project, including:

1. Generating a comprehensive list of various issues the project might face as it is developed

2. Improving the reputation of the project owner

3. Participating in an industry association that has an obligation to follow a particular guideline in order to be a member

4. Meeting the requirements of a financing company that might require projects be developed to a certain standard

5. Building support with local communities and stakeholders who will appreciate that the project is being built using a recognized standard

## 3.1 Getting Started

If your organization has not yet identified any standard or guideline that the project is going to follow, then you are essentially starting from scratch, which provides you with the opportunity to select standards and guidelines that best fit your project.

The first step is to identify if your organization has other operations or projects and review the standards and guidelines that are used for other projects, which you might be able to find in your organization's annual Sustainability Report, if one is produced. You can also look for any corporate policy statements or commitments in the areas of social, environment, and governance or whether the organization has publicly stated support for any international standards, like the Paris Agreement, for example. This type of information will help you decide which guidelines should be applied to the project and, in turn, support the organization's overall commitment to sustainability.

Most importantly, a sustainability standard or guideline should add tangible benefit to project development. It should help the project team consider sustainability issues during project design and execution, and lead to better solutions. Standards and guidelines should help the team identify innovative solutions to standard project dilemmas by asking questions that are not typically posed during the traditional project planning processes. If a particular standard does not have the potential to create value for the project, then it should not be applied. Consider each standard and guideline carefully for its applicability, potential effectiveness, and usefulness.

## 3.2 International Standards and Guidelines

There are number of international sustainability standards that have been developed for governments and corporations over the last 30 years. Although these standards are not enforceable by law, they can give the

As part of the application for IFC investment, a proposed project site would undergo an environmental and social due diligence by the IFC, which is integrated into their overall due diligence of the project, which includes a financial and risk review. IFC weighs the costs and benefits of the proposed project and records its rationale and project-specific conditions for the proposed activity. These are then provided to IFC management for approval.

If already a client of the IFC, the organization is responsible for identifying and taking responsibility for managing its own environmental and social risk as defined by the IFC Environmental and Social Performance Standards. The project would also be subject to an audit to ensure compliance with the Performance Standards.

## The World Bank Group Environmental, Health, and Safety Guidelines

The World Bank Group Environmental, Health, and Safety Guidelines are technical reference documents containing examples of Good International Industry Practice (GIIP), as described in the IFC Performance Standards. They contain the performance levels and measures that are normally considered acceptable for Projects in Non-Designated Countries, and achievable in new projects by existing technologies. Two sets of guidelines are used: General Environmental, Health, and Safety Guidelines, and Industry Sector Guidelines.

General Environmental, Health, and Safety Guidelines contain information on environmental, health, and safety issues that may be applicable to all industry sectors and all major projects. They are divided into these sections: Environmental, Occupational Health and Safety, Community Health and Safety, Construction, and Decommissioning. They should be used together with the relevant Industry Sector Guideline(s).

Industry Sector Guidelines contain information on industry-specific impacts and performance indicators, plus a general description of industry activities. They are grouped as follows: Agribusiness/Food, Production, Forestry, Chemicals, General Manufacturing, Infrastructure, Mining, Oil and Gas, and, Power. Most major projects will fall under at least one of these Sector Guidelines.

## Global Reporting Initiative (GRI)

The Global Reporting Initiative (GRI) is an international organization, considered to have pioneered sustainability reporting since 1997. They are currently the most commonly used set of sustainability reporting standards across almost all industries. GRI takes the viewpoint that through reporting, an organization can better understand and communicate their impact on sustainability issues, including human rights, governance, and climate change. Although GRI is focused on reporting, the concepts they present are useful to consider when project planning.

The most recent version of the guidelines is the 2016 GRI Standards. Organized into modules, the structure ensures that there is crossover and mutual support between the modules. It includes three universal standards that all organizations producing a sustainability report must use. There are three series of standards that focus on specific areas of sustainable development: environmental, economic, and social. From these standards, a project team can select the topic-related standards that are relevant to their project.

Typically, oversight of the GRI is at the organization's leadership level and applied to all projects and operations or facilities. Project teams would track progress through a set of measurable sustainability indicators as agreed upon by the organization, and then feed this data to corporate for inclusion into the annual sustainability report.

GRI offers a common language for organizations and stakeholders with which to communicate and understand the economic, environmental, and social impacts their projects and operations. Its value lies in that it is a useful tool for benchmarking and comparing your sustainability impacts within an organization, and with similar organizations by industry or region. This opportunity for global comparability and quality of information then enables improvements in project strategy and collaboration.

A key part of the GRI process is the up-front materiality phase where a project reviews, through internal and external stakeholder engagement (whenever possible), its project execution plans and identifies their social and environmental impacts. The result of the materiality process is a list of issues that are relevant to the organization and to stakeholders, especially the local community. The use of the GRI materiality assessment is discussed in more detail in Chapter 4.

## Carbon Disclosure Project (CDP)

The Carbon Disclosure Project (CDP)[5] is a nonprofit organization that operates a system for companies and governments worldwide to measure and disclose their greenhouse gas (GHG) emissions and environmental footprint. It is the largest collection of self-reported environmental data globally. Much like the GRI, CDP approaches its work from the belief that a strong awareness about sustainability is achieved through measurement and disclosure, which is essential for effectively managing GHG emissions and climate risks. Its approach is to partner with companies and governments to measure their footprint in order to reduce it. CDP provides support and guidance, making it easy for organizations to participate. The collected data is analyzed and assessed, providing member companies with current data with which to make informed decisions.

An organization can volunteer or be requested (by a regulator, investor or customer) to participate in annual CDP reporting. The CDP started with a focus on carbon reporting but has added two other focus areas for water and forest footprints. This is out of consideration that addressing water security and deforestation are critical business risks and keys to sustainable development.

CDP currently requests information on climate risks and low carbon opportunities from more than 650 signatories. CDP takes the data submitted by participants and members and conducts a detailed analysis on potential environmental impacts and opportunities. Institutional investors use the data and insights to make better-informed investment decisions.

CDP offers three streams of participation:

1. Investor membership means access to information and data pertinent to financial decision-making.

2. Supply chain members strive to manage risks and opportunities in their supply chain, and through CDP they can access the tools to capture vital data on climate change, deforestation, and water security within their supply chains.

3. Reporter services membership means open access to tools for data analysis, support, and insights into what gaps and opportunities mean in your report.

**Table 3.3**  ISO standards applicable to integrating sustainability into a major project.

| ISO number | Title | Description/applicability |
|---|---|---|
| ISO 14001 | Environmental Management Systems | Intended for use by an organization seeking to manage its environmental responsibilities in a systematic manner that contributes to the environmental pillar of sustainability. |
| ISO 26000 | Guidance on Social Responsibility | Intended to assist organizations in contributing to sustainable development by promoting a common understanding in the field of social responsibility. It is currently a guidance document and cannot be audited or certified. |
| ISO 37101 | Sustainable Development in Communities | When used, this standard helps communities set their sustainability objectives and define their sustainable development strategy at a local level. |
| ISO 20400 | Sustainable Procurement | For identifying a standard of practice for sustainable procurement so that the (local) economy, environment, and society benefit from the organization's purchasing practices. |
| ISO 50001 | Energy Management Systems | Helps organizations establish an energy management system in order to establish and implement efficient energy-use practices. |
| ISO 37001 | Anti-Bribery Management Systems | Bribery is one of the world's most challenging issues and reduces quality of life, increases poverty, and erodes public trust. This ISO standard helps organizations fight bribery and promote an ethical business culture. |

## The International Organization for Standardization (ISO)

The International Organization for Standardization (ISO) is an independent, non-governmental organization that develops and publishes international standards of performance in a wide variety of areas including the popular quality, health and safety, and environment standards. At the time of publication, ISO has over 22,000 published standards and related documents that cover almost every conceivable sector from technology to food safety, agriculture to healthcare.

The two primary objectives of the ISO Standards are to 1) improve global safety, and 2) improve efficiency. Although there is no ISO standard specifically for sustainability, per se, ISO has developed a variety of standards that support many of the key elements of sustainable development.

An organization that commits to ISO performance in any area means they have declared that the project or operation or facility (or product) in question meets specific requirements and is assured by a third-party ISO auditor. Upon approval, certification is awarded by an independent body in the form of written assurance.

A few key standards most relevant to integrating sustainability into your project are listed in Table 3.3. This is not a limiting list and it can be expanded significantly, depending on your project. We strongly recommend reviewing the ISO website or contacting the standards body representing ISO in your home country or the country in which you are developing a major project.

## 3.3 Industry Guidelines

Sustainability is now a generally accepted concept that the general public is well aware of and expects from the performance of their governments and the business community. Support for sustainability initiatives is not limited to non-governmental organizations. Industry associations are also collaborating and engaging with stakeholders to create sustainable development guidance for organizations working in their industry. Their goal is to help organizations improve their sustainability performance in order to earn the support of the local community and improve public perception of the industry sector, which can help all of the organizations obtain regulatory approvals and project financing. Following are a few examples of industry associations dedicated to making their sector a more sustainable one.

## Extractives Sector

The extractives sector, which includes the oil and gas, mining and metals, and aggregate sectors, faces some of the biggest challenges in developing projects, managing environmental impacts, and working with local communities. As a result, these sectors have developed a number of guidelines and materials that can provide support for projects in the extractive sector and in other sectors. Some of the well-known programs are described in the following sections.

### International Council on Mining and Metals (ICMM)

The International Council on Mining and Metals (ICMM) is an international organization that brings together almost 30 mining and metals companies from over 30 regions that are all dedicated to achieving and maintaining a safe, fair, and sustainable mining and metals industry. Their collaborations provide guidance and research to mining and metals companies on how to strengthen social and environmental performance. Through their efforts, ICMM members believe they can serve as a catalyst for changing the mining sector's contribution to society by helping eliminate poverty and improve quality of life for local communities. The ICMM's publications, research papers, and webinars are available to anyone.

ICMM member companies commit to a set of 10 principles[6] and eight supporting position statements through which the industry as a collective will contribute to global sustainable development. Members must also practice sustainability reporting annually in accordance with GRI Guidelines, and must obtain annual third-party assurance as a demonstration of transparency.

### Voluntary Principles on Security and Human Rights

The Voluntary Principles Initiative is a collaboration between governments, multinational extractive sector companies, and NGOs that has developed the Voluntary Principles on Security and Human Rights, which is a very specific guideline designed for the mining and energy sectors. The goal is to help ensure that the human rights of employees and local communities are respected while managing projects, operations, and facilities. It provides members with support and guidance on how to conduct a comprehensive human rights risk assessment, maintain the safety and security of their sites and surrounding communities, and operate within a framework that ensures human rights are respected.

Companies, governments, and NGOs who participate in the Voluntary Principles commit to implementing the guidelines. The principles can provide support for major projects that are being developed in regions considered to be a security risk or where human rights for local stakeholders has been identified as an issue.

## Initiative for Responsible Mining Association

Initiative for Responsible Mining Association (IRMA) is a voluntary certification for social and environmental performance at mine sites. The system uses an internationally recognized standard that has been developed in consultation with a wide range of stakeholders. The standard defines good practices for what responsible mining should look like at the industrial scale, and provides a list of expectations that independent auditors use as the benchmark for responsible mines.

The standard includes the following four elements:

1. Business integrity
2. Planning for positive legacies
3. Social responsibility
4. Environmental responsibility

## International Petroleum Industry Environmental Conservation Association

The International Petroleum Industry Environmental Conservation Association (IPIECA) is a nonprofit association that develops and promotes good practice and knowledge to help the oil and gas sector to improve its environmental and social performance. Membership consists of corporations, associations, and sector industries that supply or service oil and gas companies. Their areas of focus are:

1. Climate and energy
2. Environment
3. Social
4. Reporting

IPIECA has formed several strategic partnerships in order to promote sustainability and better support their members for integrating sustainability into projects and operations, including partnerships with the United Nations Development Programme (UNDP) and the International Finance Corporation (IFC). IPIECA developed the SDGs Atlas, a shared understanding of the implications of the UN SDGs for the oil and gas industry and how the industry can most effectively contribute. The SDGs Atlas guides organizations working in the oil and gas industry to effectively support the achievement of the SDGs by 2030.

## Hydropower

### *International Hydropower Association*

The International Hydropower Association (IHA) is a nonprofit organization of over 100 members who are committed to advancing sustainable hydropower. They are the official management body for the Hydropower Sustainability Assessment Protocol, which was developed to support training and hydropower project assessments. The protocol provides a framework for assessing hydropower projects against a comprehensive range of social, environmental, technical, and economic criteria.

IHA also produces a variety of publications on the role of hydropower in the world, as well as tracking and assessing new trends and developments in the hydropower sector. Their Hydropower Sustainability Guidelines, of which there are 26, provide guidance on the processes and outcomes relating to good sustainability practices in the planning, operation, and implementation of hydropower projects.

## Infrastructure

Infrastructure projects create facilities that support and influence our daily lives. Designing and constructing sustainable infrastructure projects means creating them in ways that maximize the public benefit and do not negatively impact the social, economic, and environmental aspects of the local communities. There is a significant amount of support for sustainable infrastructure, and organizations that provide guidance and resources for making infrastructure more sustainable. Several of the larger organizations are listed below and there are also a number of country and regional level organizations that project teams can use, depending on the location of their project.

### *International Institute for Sustainable Development*

The International Institute for Sustainable Development (IISD) is an independent think tank that has developed a number of information and guidance documents for range of industry sectors, including the infrastructure sector. The IISD recognizes that the development of infrastructure requires consideration of the impacts of the project on people and the planet. Sustainable infrastructure projects are projects that incorporate considerations for carbon and environmental footprints, fostering positive relationships local communities, stewardship of local ecosystems, and the financial viability of projects.

The approach that IISD uses for sustainable infrastructure is influenced by view that roads, buildings, energy and water infrastructure must be sustainable if society is going to meet the goals set out in the Paris Climate Agreement and the United Nations SDGs. IISD created the Sustainable Asset Valuation (SAVi) tool to enable better decision making, mitigate risks, generate returns, and optimize value for money across the lifecycle of an asset.

### *Institute for Sustainable Infrastructure (ISI)*

Institute for Sustainable Infrastructure (ISI) is a collection of organizations and individual professionals involved in the planning, design, construction, and maintenance of infrastructure. This nonprofit organization develops and maintains a sustainability rating system for all civil infrastructure through their main offering, Envision.

Envision is a resource for professionals involved in planning, designing, building, and maintaining civil infrastructure that helps practitioners meet the challenge of sustainable infrastructure. It is a framework and decision-making guide with industrywide sustainability metrics for all kinds of infrastructure projects. Envision helps users assess and measure the extent to which their project contributes to conditions of sustainability across the full range of social, economic, and environmental indicators.

# 3.4   Discipline Guidelines

Sustainability guidelines have also been developed by a number of technical or functional disciplines that address how sustainability can have an impact on the work of professionals in those disciplines. A number of international associations have developed sustainability guidance as well as numerous regional or country-specific guidelines that can be used by discipline professions to integrate sustainability into their work. We discuss a number of the main technical disciplines below, but we encourage you to look for local resources that can be used to support your department or apply to the region where the project is located.

## Engineering

The engineering profession supports society's objective for human and technological progress by the designing, inventing, building, and testing of structures, systems, machines, and materials. The engineering profession is now more conscious and involved in sustainability efforts, such as addressing climate change and social impacts.

Much of the world's infrastructure and facilities have been in place for many years with designs based on existing climate patterns. Now that we are feeling the effects of a changing climate, engineers need to revisit these standard designs to improve safety and protection for the employees and public who use them. Engineers must now be involved in addressing the impacts of the changing climate on infrastructure design, project development, and operations because it affects public safety and public interest. Engineers also have the opportunity to solve problems of a social nature, such as poverty or food security, by incorporating sustainability into decision making during project design.

A few of the associations that can be reviewed when developing major projects include;

- Engineers Against Poverty
- Engineers without Borders
- World Federation of Engineering Organizations (WFEO)

Each engineering department can review sustainability guidance that is available for their work and we discuss the integration of sustainability into project design and decision making in Chapter 10.

## Architecture

The architecture profession has the unique advantage of overseeing the design and construction of buildings while focusing on the structure's potential impact on the local social and natural environments – for example, incorporating systems to capture and recycle rainfall and utilizing the sun's energy with solar panels. The main goal for architects when integrating sustainability into their project designs is to create projects that have minimal harm to the local environment, while being visually appealing and fulfilling the structure's purpose. Many national or regional architecture associations have now addressed sustainable architecture by providing their members and the public with tools and resources on how to "build green."

## Construction

The construction industry has a significant role to play in ensuring that projects are developed sustainably. Planning a construction project to minimize water and energy usage, protect natural areas, and provide training and skills development to local people all contribute to sustainable development.

Construction associations are typically regional in focus. One example of an association that is addressing sustainability is the Canadian Construction Association (CCA). The CCA recognizes the importance of sustainability and encourages its 20,000 members to undertake initiatives that enable them to operate in an economically, socially, and environmentally sustainable manner. In 2016, the CCA commissioned "Corporate Social Responsibility in the Canadian Construction Sector: A Practical Guide to Corporate Social Responsibility (CSR)"[7] to help members understand the opportunities and benefits of CSR so the sector can actively contribute to improving the social, economic, and environmental health of Canadian communities.

The construction team can find additional resources from local construction associations, and we describe the tools and processes that can be used for integrating sustainability into construction in Chapter 12.

## Procurement and Supply Chain Management

The procurement and supply chain management profession can make significant impact on a nation's economy and help provide critical advantages for local businesses. By understanding that a project is part of a larger system, they can contribute to significant progress on social and environmental issues.

What a project buys, from whom, and how it uses the goods and services once purchased can have a significant influence on everything from performance and employee well-being to environmental impact, to positive relations with local communities. For this reason, the procurement and supply chain function of a project plays a key role in integrating sustainability. Procurement generally makes up a substantial part of the project budget and can have a significant influence on the overall sustainability of the project.

As listed above, ISO 20400, Sustainable Procurement, is a useful resource for projects wanting to integrate sustainability into their procurement processes. You will also find that various sectors and industries address sustainable procurement and have developed policy statements, guidelines, or tools to their memberships. We discuss integrating sustainability into procurement processes in more detail in Chapter 11.

## 3.5　Responsible Project Financing

Financial institutions and global finance organizations and lenders have recognized that environmental, social, and governance (ESG) factors are a significant risk for major projects. This has led to major projects being required to adopt standards for ESG management prior to being approved for project finance. Financial institutions, including banks, pension funds, and institutional investors, typically perform extensive due diligence on a project's ESG risk potential before lending money. It is becoming more common for these institutions to require regular third-party assurance as a condition for financing, to ensure that ESG commitments are being met and that project risks are being managed proactively.

A strong sustainability program is essential to addressing the concerns of financial institutions and demonstrating that the project is managing the ESG risks. It is very possible that a strong sustainability program will reduce the cost of borrowing money and improve overall project profitability due to having a lower risk profile and a larger potential pool of lenders. This is true for both industrial and government projects where financing could come from project-specific bonds, green bonds, or financing strategies like public-private partnerships. Sustainability teams should ensure that their programs and systems will meet the requirements of the responsible investing protocols to ensure that there are no issues with future project financing.

The international banking and investment community is structured to provide project advisory and financing services. Their primary goal is to protect their investments by having stringent screening programs to identify project and operational risks of their investments. Banks are active players in a broad range of sectors, including extractives, energy, forestry, telecom, industrial, infrastructure, petrochemical, and transportation projects. They have developed in-depth expertise in ESG risk assessments for a broad range of these and other industries, which are now regularly integrated into the financial risk assessment for potential investments.

### Principles for Responsible Investment

Supported by the United Nations, the Principles for Responsible Investment (PRI) is an independent organization that studies the investment implications of ESG factors. Signatories of the PRI can access these studies and utilize PRI findings by factoring them into their investment and ownership decisions. PRI signatories are typically asset owners such as pension funds, investment management companies, and financial service providers.

### Equator Principles

The Equator Principles (EPs) is a risk management framework that has been adopted by financial institutions to identify, assess, and manage the environmental and social risks in major projects. The EPs apply globally and to all industry sectors. Membership consists of almost 100 financial institutions, known as Equator Principles Financial Institutions (EPFIs), in over 30 countries. EPFIs commit to implementing the EPs in their internal environmental and social policies, procedures, and standards for financing major projects. They are also committed not to provide project financing or corporate loans to projects where the client is unable to or refuses to comply with the EPs.

The EPs requires members to adhere to 10 principles:[8]

Principle 1: Review and Categorization

Principle 2: Environmental and Social Assessment

Principle 3: Applicable Environmental and Social Standards

Principle 4: Environmental and Social Management System and Equator Principles Action Plan

Principle 5: Stakeholder Engagement

Principle 6: Grievance Mechanism

Principle 7: Independent Review

Principle 8: Covenants

Principle 9: Independent Monitoring and Reporting

Principle 10: Reporting and Transparency

## FIRST for Sustainability

A finance institution's level of exposure to environmental and social risks is directly related to their clients' projects and operations, including how their clients manage their environmental and social risks. Considering these risks in the transaction review process helps financial institutions to reduce their overall exposure to such risks. FIRST for Sustainability serves to engage, inform, and educate financial institutions about the benefits of environmental and social risk management. FIRST ("Financial Institutions: Resources, Solutions and Tools") provides guidance on how to implement an Environmental and Social Management system (ESMS), and execute social and environmental due diligence. FIRST for Sustainability is part of the services provided by the International Finance Corporation (IFC).

## Global Sustainable Investment Alliance

Global Sustainable Investment Alliance (GSIA) is a global collaboration of membership-based sustainable investment organizations whose mission is to maximize the visibility and impact of sustainable investment organizations at a global level. One of GSIA's primary goals is to integrate sustainability into financial systems and the investment chain. It is an investment approach that considers environmental, social, and governance (ESG) factors in portfolio selection and management.

# 3.6   Sustainable and Responsible Investing

Nowadays there are investment companies that focus solely on sustainability investment. And most financial institutions now offer investment products that consider a company's ESG performance. Investment research firms such as MSCI and RobecoSAM provide sustainability-focused indices, portfolio risk and performance analytics, and governance tools to institutional investors and hedge funds. Their offerings typically include in-house asset management, sustainability indices, corporate sustainability assessments, and customized portfolio benchmarking solutions.

The globally recognized Dow Jones Sustainability Index (DJSI) series, launched in 1999, is a set of indices that evaluates the sustainability performance of thousands of publicly traded companies. The DJSI is an analysis of company economic, environmental, and social performance data. It assesses issues such as transparency and corporate governance, strategies to mitigate climate change, risk management, and supply chain and labor practices. Companies that do not operate in a sustainable and ethical manner according to the DJSI are rejected from the list.

Project organizations should be aware of the sustainability requirements and responsible investing groups to understand how project sustainability can impact project financing, and the organization's stock price if the owner is a publicly traded company. For a smaller, private organization developing a project, it is prudent to be aware of sustainability expectations for larger organizations that may seek to acquire the project once it has been developed. Also, if the owner wants to sell the project after commissioning, then meeting the sustainability requirements of potential buyers can help to raise the value of the project.

# 3.7  Managing Standards and Guidelines

This chapter has provided an overview of the many available standards and guidelines that a project might need to follow or at least understand. The challenge is to capture the information from these documents that can be used as you develop the project. The information can be summarised in a simple tracking table or action log, as shown in Table 3.4.

The tracking table should include any standards or guidelines that the organization is a signatory to, has agreed to meet, or is required to meet for project approvals or financing. For example, if the organization is

Table 3.4   Sample standards and guidelines management tracking table.

| Selected Guideline | Principal/Element | Issue/Opportunity | Management |
| --- | --- | --- | --- |
| SDG | Decent work and economic growth | Develop Economic Development Plan with local community | Include in Community Agreement |
| SDG | Industry, Innovation, and Infrastructure | Incorporate innovation into procurement | Develop performance-based procurement strategy |
| UN Global Compact | Elimination of employment discrimination | Track direct and contractor employment data | Include in contracts; track in social monitoring program |
| UN Global Compact | Work against corruption | Ensure transparency in procurement process | Procurement plan |
| Equator Principles | Environmental and social assessment | Ensure full assessment is completed | Complete impact assessment |
| Equator Principles | Stakeholder engagement | Document engagement to demonstrate compliance | Engagement tracking system |

required to meet the Equator Principles in order to obtain project financing, then the 10 Equator Principles should all be given a specific management action to ensure that the required work has been completed and documented, and is available when required to meet project financing requirements.

## 3.8   Summary

Starting from international standards and guidelines for sustainability that span all sectors and industries, to those that are industry specific for major project development, you should now have a good overview of the existing support that projects can utilize to integrate sustainability. There are a large number of standards and guidelines; the ones presented in this chapter are just a few of the most popular ones. It is up to the project team to decide which are the most appropriate and will be most useful for their major project.

Application of these standards and guidelines for the development of major projects will be different from application for operating facilities, so consult with the issuing standards organization if required. They are usually ready and willing to assist their members or clients with interpretation and implementation of their standards and guidelines. Also consider consulting with industry peers for their experience and knowledge. Public expectations for sustainability performance by organizations is still evolving and so are the standards and guidelines, which is a good reason to stay connected with a sustainability network for your industry or technical discipline.

An understanding of the many standards and guidelines available and how they can support project development is important for the development of the project. Incorporating standards and guidelines into project planning and delivery can:

- Help to establish project sustainability goals and objectives (Chapter 6)
- Support the development of project key performance indicators (KPIs)
- Identify requirements that need to be included in the Commitment Action Log (Chapter 8)
- Provide guidance for project departments that are developing the Project Execution Plan (PEP) (Chapter 6)
- Support an understanding of what is important for the project (Chapter 4)

## Endnotes

1. The Sustainable Development Solutions Network (SDSN), "Getting Started with the Sustainable Development Goals: A Guide for Stakeholders," December 2014, accessed at https://sdg.guide/.
2. UN Global Compact, "Guide to Corporate Sustainability: Shaping a Sustainable Future" 2014, accessed September 20, 2018, at https://www.unglobalcompact.org/docs/publications/UN_Global_Compact_Guide_to_Corporate_Sustainability.pdf.
3. "IFC Sustainability Policies and Standards," accessed September 3, 2018, at https://www.ifc.org/wps/wcm/connect/Topics_Ext_Content/IFC_External_Corporate_Site/Sustainability-At-IFC.

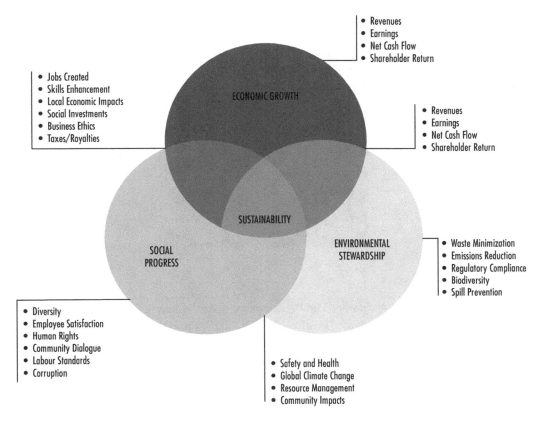

- Revenues
- Earnings
- Net Cash Flow
- Shareholder Return

ECONOMIC GROWTH

- Jobs Created
- Skills Enhancement
- Local Economic Impacts
- Social Investments
- Business Ethics
- Taxes/Royalties

- Revenues
- Earnings
- Net Cash Flow
- Shareholder Return

SUSTAINABILITY

SOCIAL
PROGRESS

ENVIRONMENTAL
STEWARDSHIP

- Waste Minimization
- Emissions Reduction
- Regulatory Compliance
- Biodiversity
- Spill Prevention

- Diversity
- Employee Satisfaction
- Human Rights
- Community Dialogue
- Labour Standards
- Corruption

- Safety and Health
- Global Climate Change
- Resource Management
- Community Impacts

Figure 4.1    Three Circles of Sustainability. Source: Adapted from McPhee and Peneranda (2013).

## 4.2   Mapping External Factors

Sustainability guidelines and standards (see previous chapter) are a good source of ideas to generate potential issues for your project. But there are other external factors that can have an impact on the project. One effective tool for assessing external factors is the PESTLe model, which looks at six external factors:

1. Political

2. Economic

3. Social

4. Technical

5. Legal

6. environmental (also called ecological)

The PESTLe model is based on an established business strategy model that focused on the first four factors and was known as PEST (or STEP) analysis. As a broader range of issues started to influence businesses

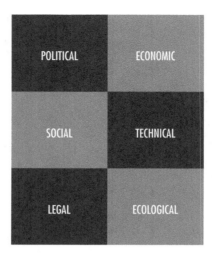

Figure 4.2    PESTLe Model.

and organizations, the model was expanded and there are now several different versions. We have focused on the PESTLe version, which can be adapted to other variations of the model, as described later in this chapter.

The PESTLe model provides the project team with the ability to explore more strategic issues that may not be part of their current thinking and identify emerging trends that could create problems for the project or future operations. The model can be shown in six boxes (see Figure 4.2), which is helpful for explaining and initial brainstorming of topics and factors that might be relevant to the project. This is a business strategy model, so the results will not be limited to just sustainability issues. It will also be useful for evaluating potential issues and opportunities for the project, future operations, and eventual closure or repurposing of the assets.

## PESTLe Factor Descriptions

A description of the six PESTLe factors for major projects is provided below and a table of project-related topics is included in the Appendix. Each project will have a unique set of factors and project teams should not be limited by the descriptions of the six factors. If you identify a trend or an issue that falls outside these descriptions, then you can expand the description or add a new factor to ensure that issues are being identified and managed.

### *Political*

Factors in the political environment primarily impact the project location but may also be associated with the organization's home country (if different), which could include new government initiatives or policy changes. Political factors that impact projects include tax and royalty policies, infrastructure investment, import tariffs, and carbon taxes. Governments also have a role to play in local infrastructure, healthcare, education, and skills development.

## Economic

Economic factors include macroeconomic factors like interest rates, exchange rates, and inflation as well as project specific factors such as commodity prices, access to financing, trends in socially responsible investing and green bonds, and trade agreements. Economic factors also include local economic issues like unemployment and the availability of skilled labor, infrastructure to support the movement of goods, local business associations, and local prices.

## Sociological

Sociological factors include global and regional trends in culture and how people live but should really focus on the local society for the project location. Local societies are a complex network of groups (as we discuss in Chapter 2) that will have different views of local social factors. Health and wellness, population growth, age distribution, education, gender roles, attitudes about work, safety, food security, traditional knowledge, language, culture, media, art, and music are just some examples of sociological factors. Project teams may not think that many of these should be part of delivering a major project but understanding the project's potential to negatively impact the local community is critical for understanding and managing project risks and ensuring that there is local support for the project.

## Technological

Technological change is happening at an ever-increasing rate, and project teams should monitor trends that can impact project design, construction, and operations, as well as local communities. Technological factors include a wide range of topics, such as:

- Innovation and technology incentives
- Automation and the industrial internet of things (IIoT)
- Electrification, renewable energy, and energy storage
- Electric and autonomous vehicles
- Internet connectivity and social media
- Environmental monitoring (satellites for methane and carbon dioxide emissions)
- Project design and delivery software tools

Recognizing emerging technologies provides project teams with an opportunity to optimize project delivery, reduce environmental impacts, reduce costs, and improve engagement with the local community.

## Legal

The key legal factors for projects are government approvals and permits to proceed with a project. Identifying regulatory trends early will help project teams manage potential future constraints on constructing or operating the project.

Other legal factors that could impact project delivery include workplace legislation like employment, health and safety, and employee data privacy requirements. Emerging requirements to reduce workplace harassment and bullying will also have an impact on project delivery, employee training, and contractor agreements. Additional factors are transparency and governance issues that may be driven by local legislation, international agreements, or regulations in the organization's home country. These might also apply to equipment suppliers and firms in the project supply chain.

### Environmental

Environmental factors include weather, climate change, natural disasters, and disease and pandemics that could impact project employees, local communities, or the supply chain. Environmental factors can also include the natural ecosystem services that would benefit the project or the local community such as access to fresh water, areas for waste disposal, impact of air and water emissions, and sources of renewable energy (i.e. wind, running water).

Emerging perceptions around environmental and ecological damage can influence project design and delivery. These issues are related to the use of plastics, choice of transportation mode (i.e. rail versus truck), disposal of toxic chemicals and heavy metals, and stakeholder expectations around closure and progressive restoration of areas impacted by the project.

## Using the PESTLe Model

There are a number of ways to develop the PESTLe model. But the best approaches involve bringing together a diverse group of participants in a workshop to develop a list of topics and explore how these topics could impact the project.

The first step in developing the PESTLe model is to list the trends and issues that could have an impact on the project for each of the six factors in the model. This would involve researching the project location and local trends to ensure that the external factors are relevant to the project site and represent the risks, challenges, and opportunities facing the project. It is also helpful to review the topics identified in the Three Circles of Sustainability diagram to ensure that they have also been captured in the analysis.

Once an external change or issue that could represent a risk or opportunity to the project has been identified, it is important to dig deeper. Rather than state high-level issues only, seek to understand and document how the issue creates specific risks or opportunities to the project.

### CASE STUDY: USING PESTLE TO MAP CLIMATE RISK

Our EPCM project was the construction of an industrial port facility on the eastern coast of North America. When we assembled a team to review potential strategic issues and assess external impacts to the project, we found that one of the biggest challenges was understanding the potential future impacts of climate change on the facility's development and its operation.

Our initial design drawings were from five years earlier but when we researched more recent storm data, it was clear that there had been an increase in hurricanes and storm events; a traditional 100-year storm had become a 20-year storm. Through the workshop we identified a number of specific risks caused by increased storm events, and this impacted our design and project planning work in the following ways:

- Increased rainfall required an increase in the facilities stormwater management capacity in order to ensure zero discharges during storm events.
- A higher probability of hurricane force winds required an updated design basis for structures including the conveyors, which can be damaged by the wind.
- Design for larger stockpiles was needed to account for the potential shipping delays in order to avoid production shutdowns due to storm events.
- A shift in construction planning was needed to avoid having a large number of cranes at the site during high risk times of year.
- It was necessary to ensure that contractors were aware of the increased risk so that emergency response plans could account for potential storm events and required emergency response.
- Discussions were held with the local community on an approach to cooperative emergency response plans that would benefit both the project and the local community in the event of a serious storm.

Table 4.1 is an example of how to develop the model and move from PESTLe factors to potential impacts and project-specific topics. After identifying risks and opportunities, the final step is to determine how the project team will manage these risk and opportunities.

Table 4.1   Example of mapping PESTLe factors to generate insights and opportunities.

| Element | Factor | Local Project Effect/Trend | Insights, Risks and Opportunities | Responsibility | Status |
|---|---|---|---|---|---|
| Political | Local elections | Change reduces project support | Impact to local permits | Government Affairs, Project Director | Monitor |
| Economic | Demographics | Youth employment | Partner with high school to train local workers | HR | Ongoing |
| Social | Internet | Lack of internet access | Share internet infrastructure with local community | Utilities design, Communications | Engage community |
| Technical | Electric vehicles | Increased electrical power required | Strain on local grid, Load balancing | Electrical design, Operations | Research required |
| Legal | New air quality regulation | Lower emissions standards | Study future impact, Design for new standard | Engineering | Ongoing |
| Environmental | Climate change | Severe storm events | Avoid construction during storm season | Scheduling, Construction | Move to Risk Register |

The output from the PESTLe model will also be used later in the book to build the project execution plan, develop risk management strategies, and improve project design and delivery. The project team can also use Table 4.1 to build an action log where each identified insight, risk, and opportunity is assigned a responsible person or department and then tracked to a resolution.

## 4.3 Value Chain Analysis

In this section, we move from a high-level external view of the project to a model that focuses on the activities that will be undertaken to deliver the project and how those activities can add value, decrease value, or introduce risks into the project. We have developed a new model called the Sustainable Activity Model,[2] which expands the traditional value chain concept to incorporate sustainability issues and show how they are integrated into all project activities and future operations activities. The Sustainable Activity Model helps to convert high-level sustainability vision statements into specific activities that can help to create a better project.

The Sustainable Activity Model (Figure 4.3) was originally developed for facility operations rather than the development of major projects. However, the approach works well to evaluate both the impacts of activities during project development as well as envisioning the impact of activities during operations that can be improved during design and project planning. By examining how project activities in each stage of a project's value chain can have an impact on both the traditional economic value and the social and reputational value, the project team can identify risks and opportunities that are not typically included in risk assessment or project planning. Management and mitigation plans can then be developed to address the identified issues.

Activities in the Sustainable Value Chain are divided into two main groups: Project Delivery Activities, which are part of producing the product, and Support Activities, which provide the foundation for delivery of the project activities.

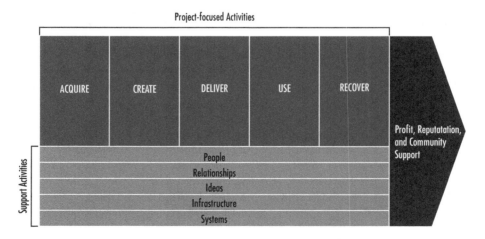

Figure 4.3   Sustainable Activity Model. Source: Adapted from McPhee (2014).

The model recognizes three key facts that can drive project strategy:

1. The value of a project is more than just the profit margin but includes reputation, brand value, and community support.
2. Sustainability can generate value by improving both internal and external engagement and collaboration.
3. The impact that a project has on the outside world needs to be included in project strategy and decision making.

## Understanding Value

Applying the Sustainable Activity Model to project decisions may encourage new ways of thinking about value, generate new value-creation activities, and enhance the organization's resilience against future changes as sustainability continues to evolve. Sustainable value is an expansion of the traditional view of value (typically limited to profit margin) to include the concepts of good will, reputation, brand value, and community support. For major projects, community support is critical to future success as banks and financing firms require responsible risk management under standards like the Equator Principles.

## Using the Model

Using the Sustainable Activity Model involves evaluating expected project activities within each element of the model and then exploring how the activities can work together to create additional value. The model helps project teams expand their focus to include impacts and opportunities external to the organization. The process includes:

1. Identifying activities that the project is currently planning and how these activities could have an impact on project profit and community support.
2. Evaluating how project activities can be changed or adapted to reduce negative impacts that can put the project at risk of a reduced profit margin or damaged reputation.
3. Creating new activities across the model that can improve performance and have a positive impact on the project's reputation.
4. Recognizing limitations of the project and identifying which activities will require cooperation with other organizations, local communities, or governments, to create enhanced value for everyone involved.

Some thoughts on how sustainability can be integrated into strategy for each element of the model are discussed in the following sections. As you read these sections, consider not just the ideas discussed here but also how to create additional value through new ways of thinking about your project activities and adapting to the challenges of sustainability.

The model output should not just be a list of activities and risks but also insights into the project and future operations. These can create opportunities for improved design and delivery of your project.

Table 4.2   Assessing activities with the sustainable activity model.

| Model Element | Activities | Risks, Insights and Opportunities |
|---|---|---|
| **Project Activities** | | |
| Acquire | | |
| Create | | |
| Deliver | | |
| Use | | |
| Recover | | |
| **Support Activities** | | |
| People | | |
| Relationships | | |
| Ideas | | |
| Infrastructure | | |
| System | | |

The model output can be collected in a table of activities along with the associated risks, opportunities, and insights, as shown in Table 4.2.

The model's elements are meant guide strategic thinking through the project activities, but they are not hard and fast rules. Activities may fit into more than one element, or you may think of an activity that does not fit well into any box. The important thing is to capture the activities somewhere and not worry too much about which element the activity is placed in.

## Project Activities

### *Acquire*

"Acquire" includes the activities to procure or extract the necessary raw materials, equipment, and supplies to run the project. This includes purchasing, supply chain management, interaction with local business, transportation of materials, and logistics. "Acquire" can also include the use of local natural resources like quarrying for sand and gravel, extracting fresh water for construction, and purchasing local food.

For remote project locations supplies need to be brought in to feed and clothe the workers and sustain daily life at the project site. Bringing materials, equipment, and supplies from outside of the local area to remote sites can impact the local economy, influence behaviors, and introduce invasive plants and animals.

### *Create*

"Create" essentially refers to the activities required to build the project, from design and construction to waste management and emissions. This includes activities to align construction methods with local skills and training programs, minimizing energy and water use, and looking at maximizing local construction opportunities such as "stick build" versus importing modular units with only final assembly completed onsite.

The choice of activities will impact employees and contractors in various and unique ways. Can construction activities include opportunities for on-the-job training and skills development? Do activities consider worker safety, repetitive strain injuries, and occupational hygiene?

Construction will also have an impact on the amount of waste produced by the project, such as air and water emissions including greenhouse gas emissions. The project team can look for opportunities to reduce waste and emissions by selecting and maintaining efficient construction equipment, working with suppliers to minimize packaging and implementing site-wide recycling, and waste management programs.

## Deliver

"Deliver" is the various activities to connect a project to the world around it, which for resource extraction and production facilities includes delivery of the product to the customer. This means sales and marketing, transport, and logistics, as examples. For power and infrastructure projects, "deliver" includes connections to existing infrastructure like power grids or local roads. For projects located in remote locations, the impacts of connecting a project to global markets can create challenges for the project. In many cases a linear service (i.e. road, train, or pipeline) is required to get the commodity to market. This can cause impacts such as connecting cultures and societies that were not previously connected. With improved transportation comes the movement of people, ideas, and the connection of marketplaces, providing opportunities for economic prosperity, improved education, and better health care. It can also introduce the risks of disease, drugs, weapons, human trafficking, invasive plants and animals, uncontrolled immigration, crime, and a dilution of local culture and language.

Project teams can influence whether the impact of connecting remote communities to the rest of the world is an overall positive or negative experience. Does the project choose to ignore potential local impacts, leaving impact management solely in the hands of the local government? Or do they pursue solutions and strategies to assist local communities to adapt to the pending changes?

## Use

"Use" includes activities that support the utilization of a product, facility, or infrastructure by customers. For infrastructure projects like highways and airports, support activities would include designing for the safety and security of the facility and evaluating how future operations will manage energy use, emissions, and changes in technology that could impact the infrastructure in the future. For example, how does the highway design account for trends toward electric and autonomous vehicles?

For resource and industrial facilities that sell a product, support activities include product stewardship issues around energy efficiency, toxicity, product safety, and recycling. Other activities relate to incorporating sustainability or social value into product branding. Diamond mining firms in northern Canada are an example of combining brand marketing in the natural resource industry, where conflict-free diamonds can generate higher value than other diamonds. The companies involved in mining these diamonds have embraced not only conflict-free mining operations but strict environmental and social policies as well. This helps to maintain their brand advantage. The diamonds are marked by a serial number that is microscopically laser-etched into the girdle of the diamond, scanned for identification, and provided with a Certificate of Authenticity under the Canadian Diamond Code of Conduct.

## Recover

"Recover" means activities that extract value from the end of a product's initial use. This includes recycling and reuse of materials during the project development, operations, customer use of the product, and the end of the project life. During project development, recovery activities include waste reduction, recycling, and reuse of construction infrastructure for operations or for use in the local community. Recovery activities also means progressive reclamation of areas damaged during construction that can be restored and revegetated once construction is completed.

To further improve value recovery, design, and project planning teams should look beyond the project development phase and consider what activities can support operations and plan for end-of-life. During operations, recovery activities might involve waste minimization, recycling, and water reuse that can be addressed during project design and planning. At the end of life, value recovery often brings in progressive reclamation to reduce financial bonding requirements and environmental cleanup costs.

## Support Activities

### People

"People" activities are related to hiring, employing, and developing project team members, from the traditional human resources functions of payroll and benefits to health and safety, skills development, and training. The focus of this activity should not be solely on the core project team or owner's organization but also include the people involved in the project from consulting firms and contractors. Although each of these groups may officially work for different organizations, they are all working on the project and project teams need to establish a minimum set of standards that apply to all project team members, such as minimum hourly pay or access to health care.

People activities are critical when the project is in a remote area or will be hiring a significant amount of labor from local communities. This means specific employee skills development or training programs to ensure that there is enough trained local labor available to work on the project. The activities may also include a focus on transferable skills that can be used by employees in the local community when project construction is completed. We discuss this in more detail in Chapter 11, "Procurement."

### Relationships

"Relationship" focuses on engaging with stakeholders and external networks including the local community, nongovernmental organizations (NGOs), industry associations, government, competitors, and educational institutions. These activities could include a wide range of engagement methods from in-person meeting to town halls to design workshops, as well as activities related to documenting and tracking the output from these meetings. Stakeholder engagement is discussed in more detail in Chapter 6.

### Ideas

"Ideas" focuses on both the formal and informal knowledge, and ideas about the project including everything from intellectual property to culture and traditional knowledge. Ideas, knowledge, and skills held throughout the entire project team can create value by creating cost savings, reducing environmental impacts, or improving communications with the local communities. Ideas are not limited to design teams but can come from any department or group within the project.

Activities that the project can pursue to improve value include activities related to:

- Internal and external R&D activities
- Sharing of best practices across industries or locations
- Improving learning across the organization
- Developing external networks to collect the best new ideas

For projects located in remote areas or where project teams are not from the same culture, a sharing of knowledge and culture can create value by building better understanding between groups and improving communication. Understanding local traditional knowledge can also assist project design teams in identifying the best location for facilities, access routes, and local weather events to create better project designs for the local environment.

## Infrastructure

"Infrastructure" refers to activities associated with construction and maintenance of the support infrastructure needed to construct the project and infrastructure required for operations, which could include roads, airports, power, water, landfills, maintenance buildings, and construction camps. These activities may be related to selecting the infrastructure location, deciding if it will be temporary or permanent, and determining whether it will be developed in cooperation with the local community or focused on the project alone.

It is key to remember that the focus of infrastructure activities is the structures needed to support the primary operations. For a highway project, for example, support infrastructure includes construction camps, a mobile asphalt plant, and maintenance yards for highway operations.

For projects in remote locations the majority of infrastructure may need to be developed for construction and maintained to support the operations. At a mine site, for example, infrastructure typically includes the basic utilities required for a small town: electricity, communications, drinking water, sewage treatment, and waste disposal. In some cases, for remote sites with fly-in fly-out workforces, infrastructure may include housing, shopping, recreational, and medical facilities to support the workforce.

The organization's activities to develop and maintain this infrastructure can have a large impact on the surrounding environment and society, and this presents both risks and opportunities that can create or destroy project value. Projects can choose whether they want their infrastructure to exist in isolation from the local community, in support of the local community, or integrated with the local community.

## Systems

"Systems" focuses on developing and supporting the systems and processes of a project such as legal, financial, quality, accounting, health and safety, and sustainability. For systems to create value, they need to be chosen to match the size and objectives of the project and implemented accordingly. Too many systems or the wrong systems are not only a waste of time but can direct focus toward the wrong things. Projects that have primarily financial and cost control systems will keep everyone focused on the financial performance of the project without enough focus on quality or maintaining good relationships with the local community. It is important to develop strong sustainability systems and metrics to help keep a balance between traditional cost and schedule focus and broader environmental and social issues that can help to create a better project.

## Model Output

Once the team has reviewed the project activities and potential risks and opportunities, the output is collected into a table of risks, insights, and opportunities (see Tables 4.3a and 4.3b). The output can be used either as

Table 4.3a    Sustainable activity model: sample list of project-focused activities.

| Model Element | Activities | Risks, Insights and Opportunities |
|---|---|---|
| **Project Activities** | | |
| Acquire | Supply chain | |
| | Raw materials | |
| | Resource extraction | |
| | Support local small businesses | |
| | Procurement policies | |
| | Water supply | |
| Create | Production efficiency | |
| | Worker training | |
| | Waste management | |
| | Air and water emissions | |
| | Greenhouse gas emissions | |
| | Occupational hygiene | |
| Deliver | Logistics | |
| | Energy use in transport | |
| | Connections to markets | |
| | Transport issues | |
| | Invasive species | |
| Support | Security | |
| | Safety in Design | |
| | Design for Environment | |
| | Responsible Care | |
| | Product quality | |
| | Responsible supplier | |
| | Product toxicity | |
| Recover | Separate | |
| | Recycle | |
| | Manage | |
| | Product stewardship | |
| | Recycle opportunities | |
| | Progressive Reclamation | |

Table 4.3b   Sustainable activity model: sample list of support activities.

| Model Element | Activities | Risks, Insights and Opportunities |
|---|---|---|
| **Support Activities** | | |
| People | Health and safety | |
| | Training | |
| | Employee development programs | |
| | Business/financial training | |
| | Access to health care | |
| Relationships | Community | |
| | NGOs | |
| | Gov't, shareholders, PR | |
| | Health in the community | |
| | Neighboring property impacts | |
| | Social auditing | |
| | Community agreements | |
| Ideas | R&D | |
| | Culture | |
| | Best practices | |
| | Traditional knowledge | |
| Infrastructure | Location | |
| | Integration | |
| | Security | |
| | Power | |
| | Water | |
| | Waste management | |
| | Roads, Ports, etc. | |
| | Shared infrastructure with local community | |
| System | Finance | |
| | Governance | |
| | Legal | |
| | Quality | |
| | IT | |
| | Sustainability systems | |

an action log, like the output from the PESTLe model, or as a list that can be referred back to later in the project. This will help the team assess risks, review opportunities, and look for innovative new ideas that can create a better project and generate additional value for the owners.

# 4.4   Focus on Materiality

The next step in building an understanding of the important sustainability topics is to rank the issues, opportunities, and ideas according to their representation of the largest potential positive and negative impacts

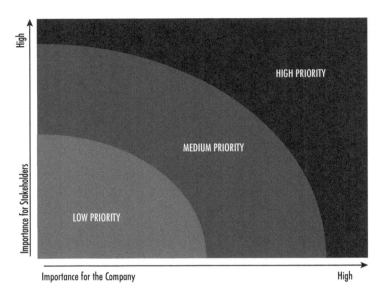

Figure 4.4    GRI Materiality Principle.

to the project. One well-established method of ranking and focusing sustainability topics is the materiality principle (see Figure 4.4) that was introduced by the Global Reporting Initiatives (GRI) in their guidelines, used to develop annual sustainability reports.[3] The Materiality Principle in the G4 version of the GRI Guidelines states:

> The report should cover Aspects that reflect the organization's significant economic, environmental and social impacts; or substantively influence the assessments and decisions of stakeholders.[4]

One of the advantages of the materiality mapping process is that it allows the project team to focus attention on the largest or potential impacts of the project. We often have a bias toward the types of sustainability issues that are most prevalent in the media (carbon footprinting, water) or those issues where someone on the project team has a particular interest or expertise. Using a model that maps all of the issues, challenges, and activities, allows the team to identify all possible opportunities to create value and manage risks, and to focus on the material issues that will require the most attention.

## Who Are Stakeholders?

In a broad sense, stakeholders include the local community, local businesses, financial investors and shareholders, project employees, and people outside of the local community like NGOs, unions, and country residents of the project site. But taking this broad approach to stakeholders can distort the materiality process and can create a false sense of alignment on topics. For instance, an investor is a project stakeholder, but investors have many of the same financial and economic concerns as the organization, so incorporating their concerns in the materiality mapping can create a false perception that there is alignment between the project organization and their stakeholders.

For project development, there is a higher value in focusing materiality on the local community and local regulators who will be approving the project. Other stakeholders can have an impact and shouldn't necessarily be ignored, but their priorities should not override local concerns. We will discuss more about stakeholder analysis and engagement in Chapter 6.

## Materiality Assessment

Materiality assessment takes a structured approach to evaluating the topics that have been identified throughout this chapter using the steps outlined below. A sample materiality table is shown in Table 4.4, along with a materiality map, shown in Figure 4.5.

1. Take the list of topics, activities, and issues from the previous models and extract the main topics that have been identified.
2. Evaluate on a scale of 1 to 10, how these topics rank in importance for the project and the organization.
3. Evaluate on a scale of 1 to 10 how these topics rank for stakeholders, especially local stakeholders, based on engagement and surveys.
4. Calculate an approximate 'impact' by multiplying the two rankings.
5. Map the results.
6. Do a reality check by reflecting if it makes sense.

Table 4.4    Sample of sustainability topics and materiality ranking.

| Topic/Issue | Organization | Stakeholders | Impact |
|---|---|---|---|
| Use of plastic | 2 | 2 | 4 |
| Endangered species | 4 | 5 | 20 |
| Waste management | 3 | 6 | 18 |
| Employee safety | 9 | 8 | 72 |
| Local suppliers | 5 | 9 | 45 |
| Air quality | 5 | 7 | 35 |
| Local employment | 7 | 9 | 63 |
| Sustainability ranking | 7 | 2 | 14 |
| Renewable energy | 6 | 5 | 30 |
| Organic food | 1 | 1 | 1 |
| Energy efficiency | 9 | 5 | 45 |
| Responsible investment | 8 | 3 | 24 |
| Community health | 3 | 8 | 24 |
| Internet access | 6 | 4 | 24 |
| Fresh water | 8 | 7 | 56 |
| Skills development | 6 | 6 | 36 |
| Local hunting | 1 | 7 | 7 |
| Climate change | 6 | 8 | 48 |
| Recycling | 2 | 4 | 8 |
| Progressive closure | 2 | 5 | 10 |

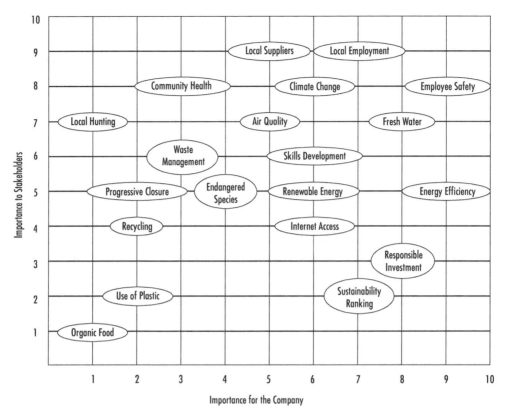

Figure 4.5    Sustainability Materiality Mapping.

A template excel spreadsheet to help build this model is available on the book website at www.IntegratingSustainability.com.

## 4.5  Summary

The strategy tools described here help the project identify, explore, and understand the wide range of issues that must be managed in order to focus on key issues for the project and be strategic in integrating them into the project. This structure also helps to support other parts of project delivery, including:

- Project goals and objectives
- Risk management
- Project and contractor key performance indicators (KPIs)
- Design work shops
- Areas for innovation

- Opportunities to improve and maintain positive relationships with local communities
- Improving the environment
- Creating benefits for the local community

Admittedly, a project team might experience resistance to employing these models because they are additional studies and an additional workload, perceived as making the project more expensive. It is important to remember that part of this exercise is to do the upfront planning in order to avoid the risk of rework later in the project. The output should include not just what the project team should start doing, but also what tasks they should stop doing or at least spend less time on. To borrow a title from a Forbes business blog:

If Sustainability Costs You More, You're Doing It Wrong[5]

# Endnotes

1. McPhee, W., and Peneranda, R., "Managing External Risks on EPCM Projects," EPCM for Mining, Energy and Infrastructure Projects Conference, Toronto, July 2013.
2. McPhee, W., "A New Sustainability Model: Engaging the Entire Firm," *J. Business Strategy* 35, no. 2 (April 2014).
3. Global Reporting Initiative, "Defining What Matters: Do Companies and Investors Agree on What Is Material?" 2016, accessed October 28, 2018, at https://www.globalreporting.org/resourcelibrary/GRI-DefiningMateriality2016.pdf.
4. GRI, G4 Sustainability Reporting Guidelines, Implementation Manual, 2013, p. 11.
5. Crespin, Richard, "If Sustainability Costs You More, You're Doing It Wrong," *Forbes*, CSR Blog, August 2013, accessed November 3, 2018, at https://www.forbes.com/sites/csr/2012/08/13/if-sustainability-costs-you-more-youre-doing-it-wrong/#36a8460128d9.

# CHAPTER 5

# Project Management

One of the fundamental principles of project management is that early planning and establishing structure is critical to project success. The classic project management influence diagram (see Figure 5.1) shows the how early investment in project management allows the project team to influence the outcome of the project. Making changes later in the project ends up costing more than if they are addressed early in the project. The same concept is very true of sustainability management and the integration of sustainability into project development. Investing the time upfront to ensure that sustainability integration provides project teams the ability to influence success and manage better projects.

Traditional project management views sustainability as a separate topic often relegated to another department or external consultant. This traditional approach misses out on the opportunity to control sustainability issues. Not having control over the management of sustainability can increase project risk or result in significant delays and rework because teams must respond to constraints or issues raised by regulators or local communities as the project progresses.

Furthermore, it is far worse is to wait for major issues like a significant construction delay or a lawsuit to attempt to fix sustainability issues. There are numerous examples of projects being shutdown mid-construction or requiring rework because of issues that could have been avoided if they were identified earlier in the process and managed in a proactive manner.

Integrating sustainability into project management requires looking at all the tools being used and making sure that sustainability is fully integrated into the structure and details of the management systems. This is not a difficult process but will require the support of everyone in the project team.

In this chapter we will address integrating sustainability into the main project management tools, including:

- Project Steering Committee
- Project Charter
- Organizational Structure

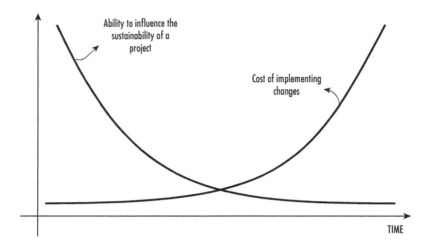

Figure 5.1    Ability to influence project sustainability.

- Project Schedule
- Project Execution Plan
- Communications Plan
- Change Management

In subsequent chapters, we will focus on specific tools that can support integrating sustainability into project management, including:

- Stakeholder Engagement Tools (Chapter 6)
- Risk Management (Chapter 7)
- Sustainability Management Tools (Chapter 8)

## 5.1    Sustainability Steering Committee

One of the first and most important sustainability management tasks is to create a Sustainability Steering Committee to provide the project team with direction and create a central point for discussion and decision making around sustainability topics. The committee can be the voice of the project owner to ensure that short-term, project-delivery thinking is balanced with longer-term sustainability thinking.

Responsibilities of the Sustainability Steering Committee might include:

- Provide direction and strategy for the project.
- Provide a platform for open discussion among the project team leadership.

- Review and communicate major risks and opportunities.
- Develop key messaging for external communications.
- Guide the project's response to critical issues and emergencies.
- Make decisions on key issues to resolve conflict in the project team.
- Provide direction for commitments, sustainability metrics and reporting.
- Track performance against sustainability plans and targets.

Membership of the Sustainability Steering Committee should include key decision makers as well as the project leaders who are involved in sustainability issues or will need to manage the impact from the project's decisions and actions. Membership should include:

- Owner Representative(s)/Board Member(s)
- Project Director
- Head of Finance
- Legal
- Sustainability
- Engineering
- Procurement
- Construction
- Human Resources
- Operations
- Communications

The committee will be expected to provide direction and strategy for the project, which includes the integration of sustainability into the project charter and development of the sustainability policy. The sustainability policy will need to be reviewed and updated periodically to reflect the evolution of the project and input from the local community and other stakeholders.

The committee will also act as a forum for information sharing across disciplines and to ensure a balanced response to project issues. By providing a platform for open discussion among project leadership, the committee can help to manage key issues, ensure proactive dispute resolution, and encourage project leadership to look for innovative solutions, rather than viewing sustainability as win-lose proposition.

As we will discuss more in Chapter 7 on Risk Management, sustainability issues can be a major source of project risk and opportunity. The Sustainability Steering Committee has a role to play in reviewing project risks and prioritizing risk management plans to effectively mitigate potential impacts. The committee should also take a lead role in looking at opportunities for project improvements that not only reduce risk but also create better projects.

Communicating a clear and consistent project message that reflects the sustainability policy and project goals and objectives is critical to achieving and maintaining a clear vision of the project for both internal and external audiences. The committee should be involved in developing and approving key messaging for the project.

The collection of senior leaders on the Sustainability Steering Committee creates an ideal group to deal with and manage critical issues and emergencies, such as media issues and community protests. By having a mix of owner representatives, project leadership, legal, and sustainability groups in the same room, the project can provide a measured and well thought out response to issues if necessary.

In many cases, sustainability objectives align with overall project objectives. However, it would be naïve to suggest that there will not be times when sustainability objectives are not aligned with project goals. This typically happens when short-term project decision making collides into long-term sustainability thinking. The Sustainability Steering Committee can act as a mediator to discuss issues and find creative solutions and, if necessary, make decisions regarding key issues to resolve these conflicts.

The committee can lead the development of sustainability key performance indicators (KPIs) that can be integrated into the KPIs for the overall project. Each member of the committee will have responsibility for ensuring that relevant information from their discipline, regarding commitments, constraints, alternatives, and opportunities for example, is provided to the committee and is being properly considered.

The committee will also perform regular performance reviews against sustainability KPIs and make recommendations to adjust the programs to reflect changing conditions, new information, and project evolution from design to construction to operations.

## 5.2  Project Charter

A well-developed project charter provides everyone on the project team with a shared understanding of the project's foundation. It provides basic information related to what will be built, project objectives, and how everyone will work together to achieve the project goals. Establishing a clear charter provides the project owner with the ability to define the project to the project team and the project stakeholders. Once approved, the project charter provides a baseline for the team and can be regularly referred to in order to keep the project on mission, support change management, and guide decision making.

Integrating sustainability into the project charter requires considering each element of the charter and then evaluating how the organization's objectives, sustainability challenges, and local community interests can be included to help create clear objectives and a vision for the project. The structure and contents of project charters varies across industries and organizations but Table 5.1 lists some of the typical topics that they address. It also lists some details that have traditionally been included and some sustainability topics that are often included in modern projects.

The project charter should be created during early project development (i.e. prefeasibility) but will need to be updated as the project moves through design, development, and construction to ensure that it continues to capture the project's main objectives and challenges.

Table 5.1    Integrating sustainability into the project charter.

| Charter Element | Traditional Topics | Sustainability Topics |
| --- | --- | --- |
| Project Statement of Work | • Design and construct a facility to produce _____ | • While minimizing environmental impacts and supporting the local community |
| Business Case | • Return on investment (ROI)<br>• Internal rate of return (IRR) | • Good will and brand value |
| High-Level Budget | • Capital cost for project | • Total cost of ownership<br>• Costs to support local community |
| Agreements | • Project contracts<br>• Procurement<br>• Sales/off-take agreements | • Community agreements<br>• Commitments |
| Standards and Regulations | • Engineering standards<br>• Environmental regulations | • Sustainable design standards<br>• GHG and water reporting goals |
| Key Risks and Opportunities | • Financial risks<br>• Schedule risks<br>• Safety risks | • Environmental and social risks<br>• Community development opportunities |
| Key Stakeholders | • Shareholders<br>• Suppliers<br>• Government Regulators | • Local community<br>• NGOs |

# 5.3   Sustainability Policy

A sustainability policy is an important document that provides a standard set of guidelines for the entire team to follow through all stages of the project. Policies will often address a wide range of topics that support the project's sustainability and contribute to the sustainable development of the local community in areas such as health, safety, and environmental management, and sincere engagement with the local community.

The policy should apply to all project employees, including consultants, contractors, and suppliers. Everyone will be expected to demonstrate their personal commitment to the project sustainability goals through their decisions and actions. To ensure that everyone understands and remembers the policy, it should be included in employee contracts and procurement contracts, posted on bulletin boards, used in management system documents, and incorporated into employee performance metrics.

The sustainability policy can also be used for external communication, put on the organization or project social media sites, and included with regulatory filings.

Most sustainability policies can be somewhat aspirational and set a high goal for the project and this can create problems later in project development. If these high standards are not met, stakeholders may push back that you are not meeting your stated policy objectives or commitments. In order to ensure that the policy is achievable, it is important to get full support for the policy from the Sustainability Steering Committee and the project owner.

Sustainability policies may also need to reflect or reference other policies that the organization already has. For example, the organization may have a health and safety policy that focuses on the health of the organization's employees. When that policy is incorporated into the sustainability policy, the focus may need to be expanded to include not just employees but also the health and safety of the local community that may be impacted by project activities like transportation and construction.

Like other organizational policy documents, the sustainability policy should be concise and should reflect the values of the organization and the project. If the project is being completed by an organization that has other projects or other operations, then the policy can be created by adapting existing policy documents to fit the specific conditions and issues identified for the current project (see Chapter 4).

If the organization has been formed for the purpose of developing the project, then the sustainability policy may need to be developed from scratch. There are numerous examples of Sustainability Policies available from other organizations in your industry, which can be borrowed and modified to suit the current project. But it is important to update these policies to reflect new and emerging approaches to sustainability, local issues, and project-specific issues. Some of the topics frequently included in sustainability policies are shown in Table 5.2.

Table 5.2    Sustainability policy topics.

| Topic | Focus |
| --- | --- |
| Health and Safety | • Health and safety of employees, contractors, and neighbors<br>• Safety culture with safe behavior and training programs |
| Environment | • Stewardship of natural resources by minimizing environmental footprint<br>• Reducing waste<br>• Using energy, water and other raw materials efficiently |
| Compliance | • Follow all applicable legal requirements and government policies<br>• Achieve industry best practices |
| Human Rights | • Respect for local culture, customs, interests, and rights of communities<br>• Support vulnerable or previously disadvantaged groups |
| Engagement | • Engage with local communities through meaningful, transparent, and respectful communication<br>• Work collaboratively to identify and mitigate project impacts |
| Community | • Respond to the concerns of local communities in a timely manner<br>• Provide regular updates to project information<br>• Honor commitments made with the local community<br>• Contribute to the social, cultural, and economic development of the local community |
| Workplace | • Create an inclusive, respectful work place that is free from harassment and violence<br>• Support a diverse workforce and provide an environment where people are with respect and can realize their full potential |
| Governance | • Project will operate with fairness and transparency in our dealings and contracts<br>• Measure, review, and communicate on project progress |

## 5.4   Project Goals

In traditional project management, key project goals focused exclusively on cost, schedule, and quality. As projects have evolved over time, project teams have added safety to these traditional goals. As requirements for project sustainability continue to grow, teams must also incorporate a broader set of goals related to social responsibility, eco-efficiency, and community development.

Establishing goals and metrics for sustainability can be challenging because they aren't always easy to reduce to simple, measurable metrics or key performance indictors (KPIs). But project teams shouldn't ignore this process simply because it is difficult. The development of goals and metrics for sustainability can be essential for success in a modern project and they help to create better projects for both owners and the local community.

The process to understand and identify the most significant project sustainability topics was described in Chapter 4, and the topics identified through a materiality assessment can provide a starting point for developing project sustainability goals. The process involves taking the top-ranked topics identified in the materiality assessment and provide a metric to track and monitor each of the top-ranked topics. A sample of topics (taken from Table 4.6) and related metrics is shown in Table 5.3. The specific topics and metrics will be dependent on the specific challenges of each project. The Global Reporting Initiative, which was discussed in Chapter 3, is a good source of possible metrics to use.

Table 5.3   Sample sustainability metrics.

| # | Topic/Issue | Impact | Metric |
|---|---|---|---|
| 1 | Local Employment | 63 | • Percent of local labor by labor category |
| 2 | Fresh Water | 56 | • Volume of water used for construction (m3/week) |
|   |   |   | • Volume of treated water returned to the environment (m3/week) |
| 3 | Climate Change | 48 | • GHG emissions for transportation (tCo2/100,000 km) |
|   |   |   | • GHG emissions for construction (tCO2/$ capital cost) |
|   |   |   | • GHG per unit of production for operations |
| 4 | Local Suppliers | 45 | • Value or percentage of local supply |
| 5 | Energy Efficiency | 45 | • Energy (kWh) per unit of production for operations |
| 6 | Skills Development | 36 | • Total hours of training for local employees |
| 7 | Air Quality | 35 | • Particulate matter and contamination levels at the boundary of the project |
| 8 | Renewable Energy | 30 | • Percentage of energy from renewable sources for operations |
| 9 | Responsible Investment | 24 | • Meet requirements of the Equator Principle |
| 10 | Community Health | 24 | • Percentage of local population with access to medical care |
| 11 | Internet Access | 24 | • Percent of local population with internet access |

# 5.5 Structuring the Project Organization

There is no standard organizational structure for a major project that has emerged as the best way to integrate sustainability. Each project team will include many different organizations (owner's team, consultants, contractors, and suppliers) and each will have their own structure that fits with their organization, and the role that each group plays on the project. The organizational structure will also change dramatically as the project evolves from a few people during early feasibility studies to hundreds of team members during construction.

In an ideal future world where sustainability has been fully integrated into the delivery of major projects, there may not be a need for specific sustainability roles within the project team. But while project teams are still developing the skills and experience required to integrate sustainability, there continues to be a need for specific sustainability-related roles involving:

- Organization and management of sustainability topics
- Coordination and collaboration between departments, groups, and organizations
- Oversight of risks and opportunities
- Sustainability communication both internally and externally
- Training and education of project teams

Integrated sustainability teams should report to both the project director, who is responsible for delivering every part of the project including sustainability, and the owner or Sustainability Steering Committee. Reporting to the Sustainability Steering Committee provides the necessary support if there is conflict between the project's traditional objectives of on-time and on-budget delivery, and the sustainability objectives of minimizing the environmental footprint and maintaining a positive and strong relationship with local communities. A simplified organizational chart is shown in Figure 5.2.

Incorporating sustainability into the project structure can be challenging but it is better than having a Sustainability Team completely separate from the rest of the project team, especially if that team is a separate consulting organization. This can create significant communication issues and reduces the opportunity for collaboration and innovative solutions that can help create better projects.

The organizational structure should also reflect the responsibilities of the Sustainability Team, which can range from a small core team focused on the high-level sustainability program or a large team that manages the many departments supporting the delivery of sustainability activities. With a focused approach, the Sustainability Team will act as an oversight and support group that is responsible for sustainability policy, management systems, commitment tracking, and auditing.

If the Sustainability Team is given a broader mandate, then they would be responsible for oversight and support, and manage many project activities directly related to ensuring sustainability goals and objectives are achieved. These activities could include permits and approvals, environmental management, health and safety, stakeholder engagement, government relations, and communications.

The structure and responsibilities will also change over time, with the Sustainability Team being responsible for a broad range of activities in the early stages of the project (when the team is small), then evolving to an oversight role as responsibilities shift and the team grows. For example, during early site work (surveying

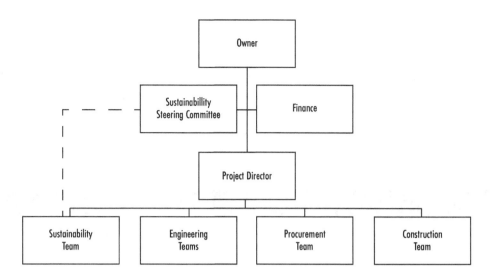

Figure 5.2    Simple project organization chart.

or geotechnical drilling), health and safety management may fall under the sustainability team, but when the project moves into full-scale construction the construction manager may be better placed to manage health and safety issues.

## 5.6    Project Execution Plan

A core document for planning the development of major projects is the Project Execution Plan (PEP), which describes how the team will deliver the project. Each group or department completes a section describing how they will deliver their piece of the project and the project management team brings it all together into a comprehensive plan.

Typically, sustainability issues will be covered in a PEP by adding separate sections for environmental management, permitting, and stakeholder engagement. But this approach is superficial, with sustainability being an add-on to the side of the project. It does not facilitate full integration of sustainability issues into the PEP, nor into project planning.

A more comprehensive approach that ensures that sustainability risks and opportunities are managed by the entire project team involves incorporating sustainability into every section of the PEP. Each department will need to assess how sustainability could impact on their scope of work and what tools and processes they should use to manage sustainability. There is a temptation to add this discussion at the end of each section, but a better approach is to add the sustainability discussion at the beginning of each section so that it can help to guide development of each department's execution plan for. For most departments, sustainability should be added right after an introductory section, outlining the key issues, metrics, methods, and processes that will be used by the department. An sample outline that could be used for each section of the PEP is provided in the tip box but should be modified to fit the specific needs and challenges of each project and each department.

Each department or group that is developing a section of the PEP should spend some time understanding the project issues, challenges, and opportunities that were identified in the previous sections of the book (Chapters 3 and 4). It is important for each group to assess how these issues apply to their work and how they can improve their portion of the project by creating innovative solutions or following sustainability standards and guidelines that apply to their discipline. As we discussed in Chapter 1, sustainability is a team sport and it is important for everyone on the project team to consider how their activities can have a positive impact and help create a better project.

## TIP: ADDING SUSTAINABILITY TO THE PROJECT EXECUTION PLAN

Each department's section of the Project Execution Plan should include a section on sustainability. If we assume that any department's section (indicated by Chapter X) starts with a section on objectives, the next section should be on sustainability integration. A general outline of the sustainability section for each department might look like this:

### X.2 Sustainability Integration for [Department Name here]

X.2.1 Stakeholders
- What groups (internal and external) will be impacted? How?
- What will we do to manage impacts?

X.2.2 Issues, Risks, and Opportunities
- Identify key risks, issues, and opportunities from project resources and our own experience.
- How will these be managed?
- Who is responsible for managing the outcome?

X.2.3 Standards and Guidelines
- How do the project selected sustainability standards and guidelines impact our work?
- Are there other guidelines for our work that we should be considering (i.e. industry, discipline guidelines)?

X.2.4 Integration into the Project Plan
- How do we integrate sustainability into our section of the project plan?
- How do we set design standards and make decisions?
- What information do we need to do our work?

The PEP also must address how sustainability fits into other parts of project management and execution that are described in this chapter and in subsequent chapters, including:

- Stakeholder Engagement Plan (Chapter 6)
- Risk Management (Chapter 7)

## Tracking and Auditing

The Project Communications Plan should include protocols for tracking and auditing project communications to ensure that the correct people are preparing, delivering, and signing off on project messaging documents and procedures. The tracking and auditing section should describe roles and responsibilities for approving key messaging and documentation, how external documents will be tracked and managed, and how communication events will be documented and tracked by the project team. As well, coordination between the many departments that will be communicating with external stakeholders (corporate, legal, finance, procurement, construction, etc.) needs to be managed at the level of the Project Execution Plan.

## Complaints and Escalation

One area of communications that can pose the largest risk to the project is how complaints are managed. Prompt and polite response to a complaint or inquiry can help to build good will with the public by clearly demonstrating respect for the concerns of the local community. The complaints procedure should include easy ways for the public to contact the project team that is appropriate for the communication capabilities of the local community, and include time commitments for a response to the complaint or request. The complaints procedure may also need to align with the human resources department and the employee complaints process because employees may also be members of the local community. It should include processes for escalating complaints that are considered more serious, or where the local community has expressed safety concerns. If necessary, the complaint may need to be escalated to become an emergency response. More on complaints management in Chapter 6, "Stakeholder Engagement."

## Emergency Response

Communication is also critical during an emergency or a critical incident. Projects must respond to emergencies directly related to construction or facility operations but may also be expected to support the local community in the event of a natural disaster or local crisis. In many cases in developing or remote regions, the project emergency response equipment, training, and personnel is superior to the local capabilities. So project teams should be prepared to respond to both project and community emergencies. The crisis communications in the Project Communication Plan should be integrated with communication in the project's Emergency Response Plan, which discussed in more detail in Chapter 12.

# 5.9   Change Management

The Project Execution Plan should include processes for change management that address how a change in one part of the project can impact other parts of the project. The procedures should help avoid unintended consequences where positive impacts from a change are overshadowed by negative impacts that were not expected. This is particularly true for changes that create sustainability issues where government regulations or community agreements can limit the changes that can be made or slow down the implementation of the changes. For instance, if a design change implemented to reduce capital costs results in an unexpected environmental emission that is not covered by project permits or approvals, it could create a schedule delay while permit applications are updated and government sign-off is achieved.

To reduce the risk of unexpected impacts, change management procedures should include a review of engineering design or procurement changes to ensure that there are no impacts on permits, the environment, or the local community. If the project uses a change management sign-off procedure, then the Sustainability Manager should be included in the process to ensure that these issues are addressed.

Project changes can also be initiated by sustainability topics in several ways:

- Community design workshops might create opportunities for design changes that can improve the overall project.
- Community complaints or audit findings might generate a requirement to change project procedures to avoid environmental damage or reduce community concerns.
- Ongoing evolution of industry best practices from projects could create opportunities for project improvements.
- New information regarding environmental conditions, changing climate, or the local communities could create a need for project changes.

Once initiated, these sustainability-driven changes should follow the project change management procedures to ensure that there are no unexpected impacts on the project feasibility or performance.

## 5.10   Project Team Roles and Responsibilities

Project Execution Plans will often include a Roles and Responsibilities section to clarify which departments are responsible for which areas of the project, and how members of the management team will mutually support each other. Sustainability affects every project department and each of these departments can impact external stakeholders and impact the project's success. Therefore, it is important to include appropriate sustainability topics in each department's list of responsibilities.

The Sustainability Team will be responsible for ensuring that project teams and subcontractors understand the project commitments and the expectations for dealing with stakeholders including the public, regulators, and indigenous communities through orientation and training programs.

The roles and responsibilities for key project team members are described in Table 5.4. This same approach can be taken to include sustainability issues in the responsibilities of other managers on the project team including Health and Safety, Human Resources, Legal, and Communications.

Table 5.4   Roles and sustainability responsibilities.

| Role | Responsibilities |
|---|---|
| Owner | <ul><li>Provide guidance and direction for the sustainability charter, goals, and policy</li><li>Convene and chair the sustainability steering committee</li></ul> |
| Project Director | <ul><li>Ensure the implementation of the sustainability plan through all phases of the project</li><li>Guide and direct the sustainability program from feasibility to operations</li><li>Ensure that sustainability is integrated into project planning and execution plans</li><li>Manage sustainability commitments, risks, and opportunities</li><li>Build a project culture that supports inclusion, diversity, and open communication</li><li>Support building good will and local community support for the project</li><li>Support the transition of the sustainability program to operations at the end of the project</li></ul> |
| Chief Financial Officer | <ul><li>Ensure that budgets are in place to support the requirements of the sustainability program</li><li>Coordinate with project leadership to ensure that project plans meet the requirements for project financing (Equator Principles, Green Bonds, etc.)</li><li>Provide guidance on total cost of ownership for the project versus lowest capital cost</li></ul> |
| Engineering Manager | <ul><li>Responsible for delivery of the sustainability program for the engineering team</li><li>Ensure that change management procedures include a sustainability review</li><li>Ensure that project commitments are incorporated into the project design</li><li>Support the use of Safety in Design, Design for Environment (DfE), Life Cycle Analysis (LCA), and other procedures to improve the overall design of the project</li><li>Support the development of drawings, documents, and media required for public meetings, permits and approvals, and project communications</li></ul> |
| Procurement Manager | <ul><li>Establish procurement procedures that are transparent, fair, and equitable</li><li>Support building good will and local community support through local procurement and employment</li><li>Ensure that all contractors and suppliers meet environmental and social requirements established for the project</li><li>Ensure the logistics plans improve road safety and minimize environmental impacts</li></ul> |
| Construction Manager | <ul><li>Be responsible for environmental plans and systems during construction</li><li>Ensure employees and contractors are trained in and follow employee code of conduct requirements</li><li>Support building good will and local community support for the project</li><li>Work to minimize the project footprint, waste generation, and emissions</li><li>Ensure worker health and safety on the project site and the safety of the local community</li></ul> |
| Sustainability Manager | <ul><li>Be responsible for the development and implementation of the sustainability plan throughout the project</li><li>Support building good will and local community support for the project</li><li>Ensure sustainability training is completed for all team members</li><li>Support the project director with managing commitments, risks, and opportunities</li><li>Track and report on sustainability metrics including audit and compliance reviews</li><li>Monitor environmental requirements on the construction site</li><li>Coordinate communications with the local community</li></ul> |

## 5.11  Summary

Integrating sustainability into project management activities as early as possible is critical to the success of major project. This helps ensure that sustainability issues and challenges are identified and managed along with the rest of the project. Taking the time to ensure that sustainability becomes a fundamental part of project management allows project teams the ability to influence success and manage better projects. If sustainability is left out of project management activities then the project team has no control over critical issues that can impact project success.

The following chapters dig deeper into the details of project management around stakeholder engagement, risk management, and sustainability management. The book then moves into the details of project delivery, with a focus on integrating sustainability into design, procurement, and construction.

# CHAPTER 6

# Stakeholder Engagement

Too many major projects fail to meet their scheduled milestones due to community opposition. The success of a major project is directly related to the level of support from local communities at any given time during the life of the project. Therefore, the integration of stakeholder engagement strategies into a major project is critical to achieving success.

The primary goal of stakeholder engagement is to achieve mutual understanding and trust between the organization and the stakeholders in order to achieve a comfortable, if not strong, relationship of coexistence and mutual success. Thus, it is critical to have a stakeholder engagement strategy that outlines who, how, when, and for what purpose your project team must engage with key stakeholders. Dialogue that results in a project design and delivery approach that is mutually acceptable to all stakeholders (with the understanding that, as with any relationship, there will be compromises) is more likely to be successful, with less exposure to uncertainty and risk.

Stakeholder engagement may be the primary strategy in reducing the project's exposure to social risk. But also note that engaging stakeholders can also enhance the project beyond expectation. Strong community support enhances the project and the organization's reputation. Even for a major project that is considered to be contentious, maintaining a sincere stakeholder engagement strategy will help to assure local communities that the project team listens and is making a sincere effort to create mutually beneficial solutions. Strong, positive relationships with local communities are very important. They support the project to help secure government approvals and financial investment. These relationships can also be collaborative, furthering the success of environmental impact mitigation plans, monitoring, or even design, which can be reduce overall project costs.

Throughout the life of the project you should have an ongoing objective of earning trust and maintaining strong relationships with individuals who represent the key stakeholder groups. The strategy should include regular check-ins with these individuals to understand their current perceptions, identify any new concerns, or exchange updates on project progress and news regarding their stakeholder group. Simply put, ongoing stakeholder engagement is about maintaining a relationship that is mutually respectful and mutually beneficial.

Engagement can take many different forms, such as public meetings, working groups, and individual meetings. They can be formal presentations or information brochures, or they can be as informal as home visits. However, the chosen engagement methods should be appropriate for the local cultural context. This chapter provides you with guidance on how to identify and engage key stakeholders and set the project team up for enjoying strong stakeholder relationships.

# 6.1   Reasons to Engage

Stakeholder engagement is the primary strategy for minimizing the project's exposure to social risks that are present when relationships with local communities are not well-established or confrontational.

## Build Good Relationships

Stakeholder engagement efforts help build good relationships with local communities. It helps the project team learn about the hopes and fears of the various community members, especially in regard to the project. Stakeholders have the ability to influence the success or failure of a project, whether by impacting the permitting process or building up the project's reputation as a "good corporate citizen."

## Transitions

The project will need engagement plans that help to manage transitions between project phases. Transitions can be quite impactful to local communities. For example, project ramp up from scoping to construction is particularly dramatic. There is usually a sharp increase in employees, construction activity, traffic, dust, noise, and other impacts. The reverse is true for transition from construction to operations where there could be job losses and a decrease in the local economy. Preparing key stakeholders for scheduled project transitions is central to avoiding unnecessary concerns or managing the project's impacts on the local community.

## Unplanned Changes

New issues will arise during project delivery that can impact stakeholders, such as a project delay or a change in project ownership. The project team should engage with key stakeholders as soon as possible to ensure that the information the stakeholders are receiving is credible and accurate. Second- and third-hand sources can distort the actual situation and create mistrust and uncertainty among stakeholders. Provide as much information as possible and share what you know, and also what you do not know. If the project has been halted but you are uncertain when it will be restarted, say so and then commit to finding out and sharing updates with the stakeholders as you receive them.

## Supporting Scoping Studies

Stakeholder engagement is important for specific scoping studies, such as part of the impact assessment, relocation planning, community needs and capacity studies, or economic development planning. The intention of such engagement exercises is to learn as much as possible from local communities in order to develop a good social and environmental plan, relocation plan, or local employment and procurement plans. Be clear with local communities on the purpose of each specific engagement and ensure that they understand why you need to talk with them.

### TIP: BE CAREFUL OF ENGAGEMENT FATIGUE

One thing the project team needs to be careful of is to avoid "engagement fatigue." It is good have a thorough stakeholder engagement strategy but not so much that your stakeholders get tired or, even worse, exhausted from your engagement efforts. Be thoughtful and considerate in your approach by ensuring to engage the appropriate stakeholders who are relevant to the objective and topic you need to discuss. Wherever possible, combine topics into one stakeholder meeting if the attendees are relevant to both topics. Also bear in mind that requesting a meeting with local communities, in particular, means that you are asking for their time, which is unpaid. Meetings should be focused and efficient and stakeholders should feel that they are being heard, that their time is valuable, and that their opinions are respected and appreciated.

## 6.2    Identifying Stakeholders

In practical terms, a stakeholder is any individual or group who has a vested interest in the project. Some of the many types of stakeholders are listed in Table 6.1. Three items should be understood when identifying the project stakeholders:

1. Who is likely to be impacted by the project? Do they live in or near the project site? Do they work in or visit communities or natural areas in the area around the project?

2. Who is an "influencer"? Is this person well-respected in their community and do they have the ability and power to influence other people? Influence can be formal, such as a government representative, or informal, such as a well-respected village elder, or a local celebrity with a strong social media following.

3. Who has a vested interest in the project? Who wants to see it succeed or fail, and why? Think about what people might have to lose or gain by your project's success or failure.

One key tool in identifying stakeholders is the project description that provides an understanding of the project scope, location, and footprint. Stakeholders should be identified not just for the primary project site but for other areas that could be impacted by the project, including stakeholders along logistics routes or linear infrastructure such as rail lines, roads, or power corridors.

Another resource for identifying project stakeholders is the impact assessment (IA) that identifies the area of influence (AOI), which is characterized by the extent of project impacts. Communities that are

Table 6.1    Possible types of stakeholder groups.

| Organization/Corporate | Government | Community/Society |
|---|---|---|
| Employees | Regulators | Local communities |
| Contractors | Legislators | Local media (radio, TV) |
| Suppliers | Local government | Non-government organizations (NGOs) |
| Shareholders and investors | Environmental department | Civil society organizations |
| Unions | Economic development | Advocacy groups |
| Customers | Health agencies | Cultural associations |
| Consumers | Education | Hunting and fishing clubs |
| Financing companies | | Labor and trade associations |
| Other local projects | | Youth groups |
| Industry associations | | Faith-based organizations |

located within the AOI are often referred to as communities of influence (COIs). Through the process of an IA, a comprehensive understanding is developed about the level and types of impacts that the project will have on the COIs, other stakeholders, and the environment and socioeconomic situation in the AOI. Examples of these impacts include dust, noise and community safety risks caused by an increase in project-related traffic, ground vibration from blasting, or an increase in the local population due to job seekers migrating from other regions and settling into local communities, which can put stress on local infrastructure.

## TIP: COMMUNITIES ARE NOT "HOMOGENOUS"

For projects with multiple locations or a linear infrastructure, local opinion can vary significantly from community to community. As well, communities are not homogenous, so public opinion of the project can vary significantly even within one community. Young people who see the project as a chance to get a well-paying job might support the project. On the other hand, senior residents might focus more on the potential disruption and thus disagree with the project. Assessing whether groups within the community will support the project will often result from their perception of the risk-reward balance. As you develop the stakeholder engagement plan, it can help to identify whether individuals will perceive the project to have a positive or negative overall impact on themselves and their community.

Stakeholders who live and work within the area of influence can be identified by reviewing:

- Who owns the land?
- Is it the land indigenous or tribal land?
- Are there farmers, hunters, or cottagers that live on the land?
- Are there schools, hospitals, or clinics?

- Is there a local radio or newspaper?
- Are there other companies or industries operating in the area of influence?

  It is also important to find out how land in the area of influence is used:

- How do people use the area, including indigenous peoples, women, youth, and elders?
- Are there graveyards and sacred sites?
- Are there people who use roads, rivers, or other access ways through the AOI?
- Are there communal areas for gathering, such as festival grounds and golf courses?
- Is the area used for agriculture, harvesting, hunting, or fishing?

## TIP: MANAGING CONSULTANTS

The process of many scoping studies includes the development of an impact assessment (IA) that is usually developed by an external team of experts including biologists, sociologists, hydrologists, and archaeologists. These consultants operate from the project site for long periods of time. From the perspective of local communities, they are often seen as members of the project team. This means that whatever they do or say will reflect on the project and the organization. And once the field work is complete, the consultants return to their office or home country, and the project team remains at the site, continuing relationship building with local communities.

We recommend that the project team maintain an active engagement during the scoping activities, especially when the consultants are working within the local communities and environment. The team should ensure that the consultants are respecting local customs, being respectful, and that whatever they do contributes to positive community relations on your behalf.

The project team should facilitate introductions to local community members and clearly explain that the consultants are working with the project for a set amount of time to do a study on the project's behalf. Request their permission for the consultants to conduct interviews, hold public consultations, and access local areas to study the environment. Ensure that anyone who has concerns or questions should know that they can come directly to the project team for more information or to raise a complaint.

Tell local community members that the purpose of the IA is to study the local communities and local environment, and to make recommendations on the possible impacts the project may have. Explain how the IA process fits into the project objectives and will help make the project a success. And ask for their support, because any proper social and environmental IA will include key stakeholder interviews, public consultations, focus groups, and access to the local land and water.

Consultants should have zero authority to make promises on behalf of the project. It is a good idea to include this information as part of site orientation for the consultants. Site orientation should also include key points about the local communities and cultural norms. It just takes one unaware, uninformed external consultant to inadvertently offend, insult, or disrespect a community member, whether during workhours or on a weekend while casually exploring the local area. Remember that external consultants typically work on a project for a limited amount of time, but it is the project team who will be left to repair community trust that has been broken.

## Local Community Groups

Major projects have many and diverse stakeholder groups, from employees and shareholders to media and government. These stakeholders can all impact the project's success or failure. However, from the perspective of integrating sustainability into project delivery, local communities are the primary stakeholder group. For all the reasons we have discussed throughout this book and particularly in this chapter, it is critical to understand and respect the communities closest to your project site, and to earn their trust and respect.

As a starting point, Table 6.2 shows a collection of community elements as well as the groups and institutions that may be impacted by project development. By no means is this a complete list of community groups. We intend it as an overview of the types of groups that a project team might engage with. Stakeholder planning and strategy should consider each of these elements and evaluate the potential opportunities for consultation and collaboration.

Table 6.2   Local community groups.

| Community Element | Groups and Organizations |
| --- | --- |
| Cultural | Indigenous communities |
| | Education/schools |
| | Religious groups |
| | Social clubs |
| | Sports teams |
| | Family/community groups |
| | Communication/media |
| Health | Hospitals |
| | Trained practitioners |
| | Health education |
| | Safe food/water supply |
| | Sanitation |
| | Safe environment |
| | Physical safety |
| Economic | Marketplace |
| | Financial systems/banks |
| | Property rights |
| | Infrastructure |
| | Transportation systems |
| Legal | Police |
| | Judiciary/courts |
| | Jails/punishment |
| Political | Local government |
| | Country government |
| | Military |
| | Status organizations |
| | Tribal/caste systems |

When seeking to understand the communities in your project's area of influence, do not assume that they are amorphous groups by overly simplifying or generalizing characteristics, attitudes, histories, or experiences. Communities are an informal assembly of individuals and there is no easy way to define "they" or "them." Each community is a complex, interlinked, overlapping network of people and groups. For instance, a local community member could be a project employee, union member, local city councilor, coach of a youth sports team, and be an avid hiker on the local trails, or fish local rivers for their family's primary food source. Each one of these roles could have a conflicting view of the project.

## Indigenous Engagement

Communities that self-identify as indigenous have ancient ties to a specific land, territory, and natural resource, whose culture is handed down through generations, and who have experienced marginalization, subjugation, or discrimination, are characterized as indigenous peoples. And according to the United Nations Declaration on the Rights of Indigenous Peoples, they have a right to self-determination. Embedded within this universal right to self-determination is the standard for Free, Prior, and Informed Consent (FPIC).

FPIC is a principle that states, "All peoples have the right to self-determination" and that "all peoples have the right to freely pursue their economic, social and cultural development."[1]

In the context of major project development, a stakeholder engagement program must be cognizant of the rights of indigenous peoples by honoring their right to pursue economic, social, and cultural development, and to self-determination. When the project causes impact to an indigenous community, the project team should follow the principles of FPIC from the start of the project. The FPIC process is inclusive for indigenous communities to participate in decision making regarding projects that have an impact on their communities and lands.

FPIC is not unlike engagement strategies that are used for all local communities. However, FPIC is a specific program that pertains to indigenous peoples that empowers them to negotiate the conditions under which the project will be designed, implemented, monitored, and evaluated. These negotiations will often be documented in a Community Agreement or an Impact and Benefit Agreement. More on this later in the chapter.

Develop engagement strategies for indigenous communities that respect language and customs, cultural differences between the project organization and the community, and how they perceive the land, their relationship with the land, and how they currently use and have used the land over generations. A strong indigenous engagement program incorporates respect for the indigenous community's value and use of time, as well as the communications and decision-making processes within the community. Strong and positive engagement with indigenous peoples contributes to project success and community success.

# 6.3   Understanding Project Stakeholders

A number of tools can be used to understand project stakeholders, a few of which are discussed below. It is important to remember that understanding stakeholders is not achieved by completing forms, rather by engaging and talking to stakeholders. The intent is to provide a template that can support the conversation with stakeholders and to document what has been learned in order to share learnings and understanding within the project team.

## Stakeholder Summaries

It is helpful to create a stakeholder summary document that succinctly summaries the characteristics of each community and community group or individual, the potential impacts they may experience from the project, and their concerns. It also helps to note things like preferred language and form of consultation. (A sample Stakeholder Summary template is provided in Appendix B.) The stakeholder summaries can be helpful in assessing risks and should be reviewed regularly, particularly the stakeholders who are likely to be impacted by the project. The summaries can also be reviewed in advance of a meeting to remind yourself of their concerns or expectations. They are extremely useful for sites that operate on rotational schedules where roles are usually shared, and during times of transition to a new stage of the project development.

## Stakeholder Mapping

A stakeholder map is often used to visually lay out where a stakeholder is positioned in terms of the level of interest they may have in the project, and the level of influence they could have on the project's outcome. There is no one right way to develop a stakeholder map but one traditional version is shown in Figure 6.1.

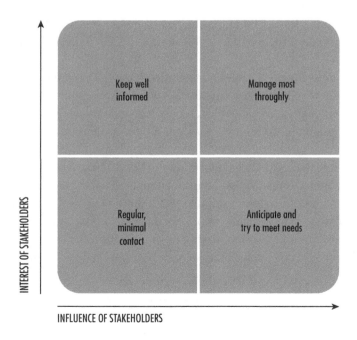

Figure 6.1    Stakeholder mapping.

## Site Tours

It is extremely effective to host tours of the project site for key stakeholders. Site tours demonstrate a willingness to be transparent and build credibility and trust with stakeholders. And they help stakeholders to better understand the project and what to expect when the construction starts.

The project team can host an "open invitation" open house, where anyone can drop by for a tour on a designated day. Or open houses can be arranged for specific stakeholder groups, such as schools and training institutions, women-led businesses, indigenous elders and leaders, city planners and city officials, or job seekers.

## 6.5   Documenting Engagement

It is important to document key stakeholder engagements throughout the project life in order to effectively track engagement and commitments, provide records for other project team members, and have documentation if required for legal purposes. It is important to establish what forms of engagement need to be documented in a formal system, which engagements can have less formal documentation (like notes from a telephone call), and what engagements can be left undocumented. In the early days of project development, it is easy to document and manage engagements as there will be only a few team members and limited engagement. But as the project develops it will become increasingly more complex to document engagement, especially, for example, during construction.

Documenting engagement events generally include recording issues raised and by whom, especially recording any commitments that were made to stakeholders on behalf of the project. Notes or minutes should be taken during meetings or immediately after an engagement session. For formal meetings, like working groups, the meeting minutes should be reviewed and accepted by all participants. For informal meetings, record the general conversation and any commitments or concerns that were raised. To help facilitate good documentation, develop a project template for stakeholder meeting minutes and one for recording less-formal conversations.

Documenting engagement can be done using informal methods like an engagement log in a word processor. Some projects use stakeholder management software of some kind to document stakeholders and log engagements. Tracking engagement with stakeholder software can be especially useful for projects that engage with many different communities, such as linear infrastructure projects where there is a large number of stakeholders and a large variety of issues. These programs are limited by the number of users, so as projects move from development to construction, the team may need to use a separate tracking system for procurement activities with local suppliers, local employment, community complaints, and human resources for local employees.

## 6.6   Communicating

Another aspect of stakeholder engagement is project communications, but it is important not to mistake communications processes for active stakeholder engagement and dialogue. The tools used to communicate can support your engagement efforts but are not methodologies for true engagement. Communications tools are listed below.

## Project Website

A website with project information, contact information, a community hotline, and an email inquiry account is a must for communications with stakeholders. A project website provides stakeholders with 24-hour access to project information and is a good place to share project reference materials (project designs, maps, and impact assessment documents), schedule of open houses, project announcements (employment opportunities, request for proposals and invitations to bid), and how to file a complaint or grievance (see Chapter 8).

## Social Media

Social media can be effective and efficient in maintaining contact with some stakeholders. Social media such as Twitter, Facebook, or LinkedIn are only as effective as you are at using them. Social media is efficient for quickly transmitting information but not as effective as personal contact, which is key to building trusting relationships. It is hard to have an effective dialogue with stakeholders over a public media forum.

Your project should have standards of engagement that pertain to social media. Only certain project team members should have authority to communicate on these media, usually the communications team or a team member with experience in communications. Managing the size of the team that posts on social media can ensure that messages are aligned with project messaging and communications standards, and that accurate information is distributed. An external communications company or specialist may be required for projects that are complex or that might be perceived as contentious when it comes to environmental and social impacts.

The project should still have a policy for all project workers about the use of social media related to the project and their work. Team members should understand that they cannot share confidential information, publicly complain about their employer, or slander project stakeholders.

## Newsletters and Brochures

Newsletters and brochures can be used to supplement the project website and can be an important source of information for stakeholders who are not internet connected or do not typically check websites or social media. They can be distributed via local libraries or community centers or delivered door to door, depending on local needs. Newsletters should be provided in the local languages to ensure that the project information is accessible to all community members.

## Traditional Media

Traditional media like radio, TV, and newspapers still have an important role to play in communications with the local community. This is especially true in developing economies where local media outlets are the key method for transmitting information and engaging stakeholders.

## Access Number and Email Address

A project contact phone number and email for the project should be established as another method for individuals to request further information or raise any concerns or complaints about the project.

## Site Signage

Site signage at the entrance to construction sites should be provided to warn people about potential safety risks and construction activities, for example. The signage should also be placed at any location where the local community could encounter construction activities (walking or cycling trails, hunting routes, etc.).

# 6.7  The Stakeholder Engagement Plan (SEP)

A stakeholder engagement plan (SEP) is the project's strategy for stakeholder engagement and is a key part of the project execution plan. When executed, adhered to, and monitored regularly, an SEP will help to create an environment where the external stakeholders are supportive of the project and the project team. When engagement efforts are transparent, sincere, and proactive, an organization can build and maintain strong relationships with its key stakeholders. Sincere stakeholder engagement includes follow-through on commitments, responding in a timely manner, being realistic in what your organization can do, and being honest about what the organization cannot do.

Your project team will need a strategy for stakeholder engagement, so all team members understand the engagement process, the organization's expectations, and everyone's roles and responsibilities. The SEP is the overarching document that is used to tell employees what is expected of them regarding engaging stakeholders. It should be developed using a consultative approach that includes team members responsible for local community relations, functional leads, and project management. The SEP should be designed so that it is considerate of stakeholder needs of how and when they would like to be engaged. (As discussed earlier, we recommend asking communities how they wish to be engaged.) After all, for the plan to be effective and successful, it must be informed by appropriate consultative process.

The project team is ready to develop a plan for stakeholder engagement once the following tasks have been completed:

1. Agreed on the focus and objectives for stakeholder engagement
2. Agreed on the key messaging for broad, overarching statements on behalf of the project
3. Identified and understood project and corporate policies for sustainable development, stakeholder engagement, and any other relevant policies
4. Identified and understood the various national requirements and voluntary standards or guidelines that the project must adhere to when engaging stakeholders
5. Have a defined project footprint and the potential environmental and social impact area of your project through an impact assessment

6. Assembled a list of stakeholders who may be impacted by your project and who can influence the project, and developed a stakeholder map

7. Have consulted these stakeholders to understand how they want to be engaged, how often, and their preferred method of engagement

As with any project plan, an SEP should be supported by an appropriate schedule, budget, and human resources. It should be reviewed and updated for applicability and effectiveness on a regular basis and especially when there is a change in the project status or the project transitions to a new stage of development.

The SEP should provide clear directions on how to record stakeholder meetings, where to file them, and how to flag issues or concerns for follow-up. It should also include directions on how to capture commitments made to the stakeholders, and how to manage and track each commitment. The SEP should also include processes for stakeholders to easily provide input, feedback, or complaints on project activities. And it must include an expected response time for all stakeholder inquiries and level of engagement depending on the type of feedback, inquiry, or complaint. The SEP should outline the various ways for stakeholders to be engaged, including a website with project information and contact information, a community hotline, email inquiry account, community meetings, cultural events, and so forth. A sample table of contents for a Stakeholder Engagement Plan can be found in Appendix C.

## Scheduling

Incorporating stakeholder engagement tasks into the overall project schedule is important so that sufficient time is set aside for design workshops, for example, to develop high-level design strategies with the local community and town hall meetings to present design information. The project schedule should also reflect time for procurement teams to meet with the local business community to discuss contract opportunities and to engage with potential local employees to discuss job opportunities.

As the project moves into construction, the schedule needs to include time required to inform local communities of upcoming project activities to avoid project delays or blockades due to lack of information or understanding. The most efficient projects are managed so that project activities are prefaced by adequate stakeholder engagement resulting in far fewer delays. Project activities that will be disruptive or may impact the local community (arrival of additional employees; traffic disruptions; dust, noise, and other nuisances) or have a high environmental or social impact would obviously need to be accompanied by high engagement with the relevant stakeholders.

## Monitoring

It is challenging to actually "measure" the effectiveness of your stakeholder engagement plan. The number of engagements may indicate how much time and resources are invested in engaging local communities, but it is not truly reflective of their efficacy, or the strength of the project's relationships with them. There are some indicators that can be tracked to shed some light on how stakeholder relationships are evolving. Examples include monitoring the number of complaints that the project receives or tracking the number of calls into the toll-free line (positive calls, negative calls, and general inquiries).

The most effective method for measuring the strength of your stakeholder relationships is to repeat the perception survey on a regular basis. These studies are well worth the time and investment to understand as much as possible about the concerns that the local community has and how they feel about the project. Findings give a strong indication of the level of community support that the project may or may not have.

## 6.8    Community Agreements

A growing number of major projects are using community agreements (sometimes referred to as Impact and Benefit Agreements), which document the outcomes of stakeholder engagement. In some cases, a formal agreement with a local community is integral to building trust and a long-term relationship by detailing how the project will share benefits and mitigate or manage environmental and social impacts, among other commitments. A community agreement can be anything from a memorandum of understanding to a legal agreement in which specific project benefits are listed and agreed upon.

Community agreements often include a commitment for the project to support local contractors and businesses, implement indigenous agreements, agreements on how and when to engage, tracking and reporting of engagement, cultural awareness training, and opportunities for local capacity building.

There is a strategic value to defining expectations in a written document so that there is a clear understanding of what benefits the project and organization will share with and distribute to local communities. Written community agreements help reduce misunderstandings between the project, the local government, and the local community, and can also significantly reduce the chances of "scope creep," which can often happen when communities request additional concessions from the project in order to maintain their support for the project.

## 6.9    Additional Tools

There are a few key tools that should be implemented on all major projects to support good relationships with local communities, including managing complaints and tracking commitments. These are fleshed out in more detail in Chapter 8, "Sustainability Management Tools." For now, we have provided brief descriptions to give a quick idea of how they fit into the overall stakeholder engagement strategy.

### Managing Community Complaints

Throughout the life of a project, the project will receive complaints from the local communities about impacts, nuisance activities, or general concerns caused by the project activities or workers. Local communities are typically the first to experience tangible impacts from project activities, and any complaints or concerns that they raise should be documented, addressed, and managed to avoid further issues.

### Tracking Project Commitments

It is inevitable that, in order to get a major project off the ground, commitments to local communities will be made at various levels. These commitments are based on sharing the economic benefits of the project, such as employment, and implementing environmental programs to manage impacts. Commitments may be made during project approvals through impact assessment processes, at town hall meetings, or through negotiating community agreements.

Fulfilling commitments and demonstrating fulfillment is critical to project success. Unfulfilled commitments break trust and can destroy the project's social capital. Every major project should have a commitments management plan that identifies accountabilities for making and fulfilling stakeholder commitments.

## 6.10   Summary

A strong stakeholder engagement strategy for local communities that is properly resourced, monitored regularly, and adapted to changing conditions or issues will significantly help reduce a project's exposure to social risk. In this chapter, we have covered the basics of stakeholder identification, tools for engagement, and tips for understanding local communities.

The understanding of stakeholder concerns and expectations provides a foundation for integrating sustainability into the delivery of major projects. This information should be used to identify project risks, establish sustainability management systems, and prepare for the high impact activities associated with procurement and construction. As the book continues, we will provide addition tools and approaches to maintain ongoing stakeholder engagement and structured follow-through on project commitments made during stakeholder engagement.

## Endnote

1. Food and Agriculture Organization of the United Nations, "Free Prior and Informed Consent: An Indigenous Peoples' Right and a Good Practice for Local Communities: Manual for Project Practitioners," 2016, accessed March 9, 2019, at http://www.fao.org/3/a-i6190e.pdf.

# CHAPTER 7

# Managing Risk
# and Opportunity

Integrating sustainability topics into project risk management is critical to effective risk management. One thing that makes sustainability risks more complex to manage than traditional project technical risks is that they often involve external factors that lie outside the project's direct control and require collaboration across departments. This does not mean that sustainability risks cannot be understood, managed, and mitigated. It simply means that project teams must pay close attention to risk management processes and procedures to ensure they are capturing the right risks, honestly assessing the impacts, and developing proactive management plans.

Effective risk management is becoming more important to:

- De-risk projects to support project financing and insurance as more major projects run into development and construction issues
- Manage the rapidly changing impact of social media and connectivity that makes anyone with a cell phone a potential investigative reporter and allows any community to assess how your organization has acted on other projects around the world
- Managing the potential physical, political, and financial impacts of a changing climate
- Understanding the impacts of social changes from demographics of an aging population to migration and pandemics

The benefit of a good risk program is that the project runs more smoothly, and the project team can focus on the challenges of creating a better project rather than running from one crisis to the next. Taking the time to complete a risk register and risk mitigation plans as early as possible in the project, and committing the effort required to monitor and update the plans regularly through project development are keys for project success.

The risk management process can be used to identify opportunities that could improve the project by reducing environmental impacts or support the local community. These can even reduce the total cost of ownership and create better projects.

The risk management process includes:

- Setting the stage to evaluate risks by reviewing project information, goals, and objectives
- Describing what success looks like
- Understanding the level of impact and likelihood that are important to the project
- Identifying and assessing risks in a workshop that brings a wide range of project team members together
- Developing risk management plans that identify the risk management measures available, who will be responsible for the management, and how often the risk will be reviewed and reassessed

This chapter describes some of the standard approaches to risk and opportunity management. Your organization may use a different approach, but the changes and adaptations that can integrate sustainability into the risk management process that are explored here are still relevant.

## 7.1 Risk Workshops

One of the most common approaches to developing risk management plans for a major project is to hold a series of risk workshops that bring together key project team members for a focused discussion to review key project risks, identify their severity, and develop risk management plans.

### Getting the Right People at the Table

Risk workshops leverage the wisdom of crowds: the collected knowledge, experience, and insights of the project team. In order to have the most successful risk workshop you need to ensure that there is a diverse collection of wisdom in the room. Doing a risk workshop with a team of civil engineers, for example, helps to identify risk associated with structures and roadways but probably does not help address risks associated with greenhouse gas emissions, workforce training, or project impacts on the local community. Some key members of the project team who should be invited include:

- Owner's representative
- Engineering design teams
- Procurement
- Construction
- Operations
- Sustainability

- Finance
- Environmental management
- Community relations
- Government relations
- Human resources
- Health and safety

The risk team can be augmented by external development partners and contractors on the project, who can provide further insights into local issues and challenges. This might include the impact assessment (IA) consultant who is supporting the project approvals process, or a local contractor who is employing local workers and executing skills development programs.

Also consider using a skilled risk facilitator who can organize the workshop and guide the discussion. An external facilitator can ensure that information is provide ahead of time, risks are properly documented, each group is given time to present and discuss risks, and everything is documented for future management and tracking of project risks. Part of a good facilitator's job is to make sure that everyone is given the same opportunity to contribute. Risk workshops can easily become focused on a particular type of risk. At the end of the workshop you could end up with a large number of small risks associated with one topic and not enough risks in other areas. It is more efficient to identify a set of risks and set a follow-up session (such as a hazard assessment session for design safety risks) as the risk management action to allow the broader session to continue.

## Be Prepared

Project risk workshops can often take several days to complete. While this is an important investment in good project management, maximizing the efficiency of these workshops helps the team to focus on the managing key risks rather than spending time reviewing background material. This is especially true for sustainability risks that tend to be project-location specific. Many project team members may not have a clear and full understanding of local conditions and challenges. In order to improve the efficiency of the risk session, the host or facilitator can provide supporting documentation for the risk team to review before the session. Some documents that could support the risk workshop include:

- Project Execution Plan (Chapter 5)
- Project Charter (Chapter 5)
- Output from PESTLe and Sustainability Activity Model tools (Chapter 4)
- Community concerns collected from stakeholder engagement (Chapter 6)
- Organization policies and goals (including the Sustainability Policy) (Chapter 5)
- Community agreements
- Summaries of the Impact Assessment or major project approval submissions

Depending on the stage of the project and the team's experience with the project location, there may be a need to execute additional research to support the risk workshop. For example, if the project is in a country that the project team has not worked in before, then researching the political, economic, and cultural aspects of the host country before the risk workshop will help to identify and assess local risks. Some possible sources of information include:

- Global Risk Reports
- Country resources
- National and regional newspapers
- Social media
- Local consultants or community relations teams

This research can be used to prepare or update a Project Risk Checklist that is provided to the team prior to the workshop. Advance preparation would help stimulate discussion on country and local risks that the team may not have previous experience with.

## Setting the Stage

The first step in a risk workshop is to set the stage by establishing a baseline of understanding for the entire risk team. This includes reviewing the core background information for the project such as the project charter, to ensure that there is agreement on the overall project goals. If integrating sustainability into major projects is a new concept for your team, then taking time early in the risk workshop to review the sustainability goals can help to create a focus on environmental and social risks and avoid debates about the purpose of sustainability throughout the workshop.

Setting the stage should also involve defining what success looks like by turning high-level project goals into more concrete objectives. For example, the high-level goal of delivering the project on-budget could be defined by including the current target budget. The statements defining what success looks like should be captured and agreed to by the team before continuing with the risk workshop and can provide a reference point for the team to help resolve debate or focus discussion.

The next step before discussing specific risks is to establish definitions for the impact and likelihood of specific risks. The potential severity of a risk is defined as potential damage that a risk could create (impact) times the probability that the risk could occur in the defined time frame (likelihood). As per the following equation:

$$\textbf{Risk severity} = \textbf{Impact} \times \textbf{Likelihood}$$

## Likelihood

The risk team should evaluate a scoring system for the likelihood portion of the risk occurrence that establishes a range of outcomes from a rare occurrence to something that is almost certain to occur. An example of a range of risk likelihoods is shown in Table 7.1.

Table 7.1   Risk likelihood definitions.

| Score | Likelihood | Definition |
|---|---|---|
| 5 | Almost Certain | Already occurring or certain to occur |
| 4 | Likely | >25% |
| 3 | Moderate | 5–25% |
| 2 | Unlikely | Low probability <5% |
| 1 | Rare | <1% |

When assessing risks, one way to define the likelihood is to look at other projects in the region, organization, or industry to see if the risk has occurred in other projects and how often it has occurred. For example, if the project is located in a region where safety statistics have typically been poor, then the likelihood of a safety risk would be ranked higher than it might be in other regions. This doesn't mean that safety risks are accepted by the project but, by raising the likelihood and severity of the risk, the team can increase efforts to manage safety risks in order to meet project goals.

## Impacts

The next step is to create a range of potential impacts for risks. Since there are a number of different types of impacts to a project, the impact needs to be assessed in terms of traditional project risks (like financial and schedule) as well as for other potential impacts (like people and safety, environmental, and reputation/community support). Each project is different, and the team will need to define impacts that are specific to the project goals and objectives. An example of risk impact definitions is shown in Table 7.2.

Table 7.2   Example of risk impact definitions.

| Score | Impact | Financial | Schedule | People/Safety | Environmental | Reputation/Community Support |
|---|---|---|---|---|---|---|
| 5 | Catastrophic | >$10 million | >6-month delay | Serious injury Large layoffs Unionization | Large-scale spill Habitat damage Enforcement action | Lawsuits Loss of approvals Protests |
| 4 | Major | $3–$10 million | 3- to 6-month delay | Lost time Injury Staff quit Layoffs | Permit delays Wildlife deaths | Negative global press, Work stoppages |
| 3 | Moderate | $1–$3 million | 1- to 3-month delay | Medical attention Staff unhappy High absenteeism | Regulatory fine Multiple small spills | Negative local press |
| 2 | Minor | $300k–$1 million | 1-week to 1-month delay | Minor injury Formal complaints | Regulatory warning | Formal complaints |
| 1 | Insignificant | < $300k | <1week | Complaints | Small spill | Complaints |

## Assessing Nonfinancial Risks

Nonfinancial risk impacts can create a lot of debate during risk workshops. So it is important to spend time up front to understand how to balance the financial and nonfinancial impacts and establish definitions that everyone can accept prior to digging into the risk evaluation.

One way to connect financial and nonfinancial risks is to correlate the nonfinancial impacts back to financial impacts. In some cases, the correlation will be direct. In other cases, the financial impact may need to be calculated by estimating the financial impact of another type of risk impact. For example, a large fuel spill could create a direct financial impact from cleanup costs, plus the indirect cost of a one-week schedule delay during construction. The financial impact would be calculated from expected standby rates for equipment and labor. Do not get too concerned about the accuracy of the correlations as no risk estimates are accurate, but a correlation can help to align the risk impact definitions.

Some techniques to correlate nonfinancial impacts and financial impacts include:

- Health and safety incidents have costs for lost time, investigation, and corrective actions.
- Risks associated with employee morale can be assessed by looking at turnover rates, absenteeism, and the cost to hire and train new employees or contractor workers.
- Lack of skilled employees can be assessed as the cost of construction delays or accidents.
- Engineering design problems can be assessed by the cost of rework,
- Environmental impacts like spills can be assessed by the cost for spills and potential fines that might be applied.
- Loss of community support can lead to delays in approvals, which has a direct impact on the project schedule and on the project's net present value (NPV).

Working with finance and procurement to understand the potential cost of schedule delays at each stage of the project can provide a good basis for the project team to assess project risks, especially related risks related to sustainability, which may seem "soft" to a highly technical project team.

This approach is not foolproof and should be reality checked so that the correlations do not become too focused on the financials. For example, the financial impact of fatality onsite during construction can be calculated and applied as a financial rating in the risk impact table but should not be used to reduce the impact to anything less than catastrophic.

## 7.2   Project Risk Register

Once the stage has been set and everyone is ready to discuss the project risks, the risk workshop can continue with the development of the risk register. The risk register is used to document possible risk events, document the potential severity of risks based on current project plans, identify risk management plans that can reduce risks, and then document the revised project risks with the management plans in place. A well-structured risk register will also identify who is responsible for ensuring that risk management is in

- Monitored – to evaluate if a risk is increasing or decreasing in impact or likelihood over time as the project develops.

- Controlled – to reduce potential impacts or likelihoods.

- Mitigated - by changing activities or designs to minimize or eliminate a risk.

- Transferred – to another party to reduce the project's risk.

Integrating sustainability into project delivery is a fundamental part of good risk management. Both the likelihood and the impact of many risks can be mitigated with strong community support. Communities are far less likely to protest, delay approvals, file lawsuits, or blockade construction sites if they believe that the company is operating with good intentions, is listening to concerns, and is working with the community to manage issues and concerns.

## Environmental Risk Management

Managing environmental risks on a project can range from improving project design to reduce emissions to spill response during construction. Some environmental damage is unavoidable in developing major projects as most projects involve impacts like disturbing land and transporting materials to and from the project site. The goal of risk management is to understand which environmental risks could have an impact on the success of the project.

Monitoring environmental risks includes establishing an effective environmental management system (see Chapter 10) that provides the project team with metrics on the performance of the project. It also allows the team to respond to risk events and increase risk management procedures if there is an increase in the environmental events.

Environmental risks can be controlled by moving project facilities away from local communities to reduce noise or pollution concerns or by installing pollution control equipment to reduce emissions. Mitigating environmental risks might be achieved by changing activities or designs to completely eliminate impacts. This could be changing chemical processes to use nontoxic, green chemistry or by replacing diesel power generation with renewable energy to reduce emissions.

Environmental risks can also be transferred to another party to reduce the risk that the project is required to manage. This could include:

- Buying pollution liability insurance
- Transferring the responsibility for environmental management to contractors
- Purchasing new technology with performance contracts to reduce project risks for renewable energy or water treatment systems where suppliers have more expertise than the project team

## Social Risk Management

Mitigating sustainability risks related to stakeholders and the local community can be more complex and challenging. There may not be technical solutions and you cannot buy insurance to protect against a loss of public support for the project. Managing social risks requires that the project team develop strategies and tools to establish clear communication, build trust, and support the local community.

Social risks can be accepted by the project team, but acceptance should not be the default option for social risks. The level of acceptance should be a strategic decision by the owner or project leadership that is based on the project charter and goals. Evaluation should encompass the level of social risk the project is prepared to accept, the level of impact it could have on the project schedule, the organization's reputation, and the long-term impact to operations that can be tolerated.

If the impacts of social risks are not well understood (especially in the project's early phases), then the best approach to risk management is to monitor the risks to see how the project messaging and the stakeholder engagement activities are being received by the local community, as discussed in Chapter 6. If the risk of a negative reaction from the community starts to increase, then the risk management approach can be elevated, and a more active approach can be taken.

A Sustainability Management System (see Chapter 8) can be used to manage social risks by ensuring that commitments made by the project team are understood and followed through by the project team. This can include developing a community agreement that clearly defines the potential impacts from the project and the benefits that the project will have for the community. It is difficult to transfer social risk away from the project and it is probably not a good idea to try. The project team can make sure that contractors and suppliers understand and share the risk by incorporating commitments and expectations for dealing with the local community into the procurement contracts (see Chapter 11).

Transferring social risk to another party through an insurance policy is not an option but you can think about a good sustainability management program as an insurance cost. How much would a project owner pay if they could buy insurance for events that damaged the project's community support? Would investors or financing firms require projects to have a "social insurance" policy if it was available? The answer is, of course they would. Building strong relationships and trust with the local community is the equivalent of buying insurance. It does not mean that there will be no damages from an event that impacts relationships with local communities, but that the damages will be lower. Similar to insurance policies that have deductibles, the sustainability program will not eliminate costs but can reduce the risk of large payouts and help to restore community support following an event. And like regular insurance that has a policy limit or aggregate limit of liability, the sustainability program does not provide endless protection against damages from poor performance or negligence.

## Risk Management Action Plans

Risk is not managed simply by drafting a plan. Risks are managed by modifying activities, designs, behaviors, and processes in order to mitigate the risk. Each of the key mitigations will need to be documented, with a focus on:

- Who will "own" the mitigation?
- When will the mitigation be implemented?
- How often will status of the risk be monitored?

| Risk ID | Risk Event | Current Risk | | | Risk Management Plans | Risk Owner |
|---|---|---|---|---|---|---|
| | | Likelihood | Impact | Severity | | |
| 5 | | 5 | 5 | | | |
| 4 | | 4 | 4 | | | |
| 9 | | 3 | 5 | | | |
| 3 | | 3 | 3 | | | |
| 8 | | 4 | 2 | | | |
| 10 | | 2 | 4 | | | |
| 7 | | 5 | 1 | | | |
| 2 | | 2 | 2 | | | |
| 6 | | 1 | 3 | | | |
| 1 | | 1 | 1 | | | |

Figure 7.3    Risk register with planned risk management.

The risk management plans should be discussed during the risk workshop and documented in the risk register, as shown in Figure 7.3.

## Evaluating Residual Risk

The next step in the process is to reassess the identified risks, assuming a reasonable and practical implementation of the proposed risk management measures. This step follows the same process that was used to evaluate the initial risk score. Each risk is reassessed for the likelihood and impact. Then the severity is calculated to establish whether the risk is low, medium, high, or extreme, as shown in Figure 7.4. If there are still risks identified as high or extreme following risk management, then the project team will need to look for new risk management options that can reduce these risks or ensure that the project team is focused on monitoring and controlling these risks.

| Risk ID | Risk Event | Current Risk | | | Risk Management Plans | Risk Owner | Residual Risk | | |
|---|---|---|---|---|---|---|---|---|---|
| | | Likelihood | Impact | Severity | | | Likelihood | Impact | Severity |
| 5 | | 5 | 5 | 25 | | | 3 | 5 | 12 |
| 4 | | 4 | 4 | 16 | | | 2 | 4 | 8 |
| 9 | | 3 | 5 | 15 | | | 2 | 5 | 10 |
| 3 | | 3 | 3 | 9 | | | 3 | 2 | 6 |
| 8 | | 4 | 2 | 8 | | | 4 | 2 | 8 |
| 10 | | 2 | 4 | 8 | | | 2 | 4 | 8 |
| 7 | | 5 | 1 | 5 | | | 3 | 1 | 3 |
| 2 | | 2 | 2 | 4 | | | 1 | 2 | 2 |
| 6 | | 1 | 3 | 3 | | | 1 | 3 | 3 |
| 1 | | 1 | 1 | 1 | | | 1 | 1 | 1 |

Figure 7.4    Risk register with residual risk severity.

Risk management measures can rarely make risks go away entirely, so do not be overly optimistic about management plans. For example, you might indicate that a good environmental management plan will mitigate the risk of a major spill event. However, if your organization has only had limited success getting employees and contractors to follow environmental management plans in the past, then it cannot be assumed that your next environmental management plan will be any more successful and that spills will be eliminated.

## 7.4  Opportunity Management

Effectively managing risks is a fundamental part of good project management. It can reduce costs, avoid schedule delays, and allow projects to run more smoothly. But integrating sustainability into project management also requires identifying and implementing opportunities to reduce impacts, share economic benefits with local community, and deliver better projects.

Identifying opportunities can take place throughout the project delivery process but early identification of opportunities can ensure that the maximum benefit is achieved. Opportunities identified through the project sustainability strategy process (discussed in Chapter 4) can be used to pre-populate the opportunity register. Engaging with the local community (see the stakeholder engagement process in Chapter 6) may also provide ideas for project improvement, ideas influenced or drawn from traditional or indigenous knowledge, and intimate understandings of the local environment and landscape.

The opportunity register can be completed at the same time as the risk register. However, sometimes the focus on negative outcomes can put everyone in a mood of seeing primarily the project's pitfalls and less likely to find the opportunities. If the project is using a separate opportunity workshop, make sure that any ideas or opportunities to improve the project that are raised during the risk review process are captured and documented in the opportunity register.

Developing an opportunity register follows the same process as developing a risk register. The same tools that were used during the risk workshop can be used in an opportunity workshop. Conducting a pre-mortem can also be applied to identify opportunities. Consider these questions:

- The project was completed on time and under budget. What went well?
- We just won a major sustainability award for delivering the best project. What did we do to create success?
- The town council just gave the project director the keys to the city. How did we earn and maintain the community's support and respect?

Often, when assessing a particular project risk, the team will realize that mitigation might also create an opportunity for something positive from the project, in addition to reducing the risk. As an example, a risk that the local community could become angry with the project for not fulfilling promises to hire local people could be mitigated by job training programs to develop basic job skills in the local community. That risk mitigation could be taken a step further to create an opportunity to develop local skills by creating a local apprenticeship training program that would reduce project costs by developing highly skilled local employees that reduces construction costs and creates a skilled workforce for future operations.

Opportunities can also be identified early in the project lifecycle. During the design stage, engineering and architecture teams should be challenged to develop innovative solutions for reduced environmental impact, energy efficiency, and safe project delivery (discussed in Chapter 10). During procurement, bid documents and meetings should encourage contractors and suppliers to provide innovative options and solutions to improve logistics, reduce impacts, promote the local workforce, and leverage responsible supply chains (discussed in Chapter 11). All of these opportunities should be documented and tracked in an opportunity register.

## Opportunity Impacts

The definitions used for risk likelihood can also be used for the likelihood of an opportunity being successful, but the definitions of impact need to be adjusted to reflect the positive impacts that could occur. Some examples of opportunity impact definitions are listed in Table 7.3. Note that your project team can develop their own definitions based on the specific project goals and objectives.

## Opportunity Capture Plans

An Opportunity Capture Plan can be used to track and manage the potential opportunities in the same way that a Risk Management Plan is used. The plan should outline the process used to collect opportunities, define who will be responsible, and shape the schedule to investigate opportunities and execute selected opportunities. Investigation opportunities might involve the use of design workshops (potentially with the local community), options analysis and trade-off studies, and engagement with contractors and suppliers to see if potential opportunities are possible. Exploring and evaluating opportunities could also involve collaborating with research institutions, developing relationships with other projects in the local area, or developing innovation challenges to get input from project employees (see Chapter 10, "Design").

Table 7.3  Example of opportunity impact definitions.

| Score | Impact | Financial Savings | Schedule Improvement | Environmental | Reputation/ Community Support |
|---|---|---|---|---|---|
| 5 | Huge | >$10 million | >6 months saved | Net-zero for energy and water use | Global awards |
| 4 | Major | $3–$10 million | 3 to 6 months saved | Carbon-neutral | Positive press |
| 3 | Moderate | $1–$3 million | 1 to 3 months saved | Green Chemistry Standards | Local recognition |
| 2 | Minor | $300k–$1 million | 1 week to 1 month saved | Reduced emissions or waste | Positive community Feedback |
| 1 | Insignificant | <300,000 | <1 week | Improved air quality | Positive employee feedback |

| Opportunity ID | Opportunity | Opportunity Capture Plan | Opportunity Owner | Opportunity Score | | |
|---|---|---|---|---|---|---|
| | | | | Likelihood | Impact | Severity |
| 5 | | | | 1 | 2 | 2 |
| 4 | | | | 2 | 3 | 6 |
| 9 | | | | 3 | 4 | 12 |
| 3 | | | | 4 | 5 | 20 |
| 8 | | | | 1 | 3 | 3 |
| 10 | | | | 5 | 1 | 5 |
| 7 | | | | 4 | 2 | 8 |
| 2 | | | | 3 | 5 | 15 |
| 6 | | | | 2 | 4 | 8 |
| 1 | | | | 4 | 4 | 16 |

Figure 7.5    Opportunity register.

## Opportunity Register

The opportunity register looks just like a risk register except that there is often no need to assess the impact of the opportunity under current management practices since opportunities tend to be new activities or new execution plans that don't have a current approach. An example of an opportunity register is shown in Figure 7.5.

## Opportunity Mapping

Similar to risk mapping, opportunities can be ranked by calculating the potential for a positive outcome (Outcome = Likelihood x Impact) and mapping the opportunities in a table (see Figure 7.6), or by calculating the potential outcome and ranking the opportunities from high outcome to low outcome.

| Opportunity | | | | | | |
|---|---|---|---|---|---|---|
| Huge | Major | Moderate | Minor | Insignificant | | |
| 5 | 4 | 3 | 2 | 1 | | |
| 25 | 20 | 15 | 10 | 5 | Almost Certain | 5 |
| 20 | 16 | 12 | 8 | 4 | Likely | 4 |
| 15 | 12 | 9 | 6 | 3 | Moderate | 3 |
| 10 | 8 | 6 | 4 | 2 | Unlikely | 2 |
| 5 | 4 | 3 | 2 | 1 | Rare | 1 |

Figure 7.6    Opportunity mapping.

Once the outcomes have been mapped and ranked, the project team can focus on the opportunities with the highest potential outcome score and spend less time on opportunities that may have a lower potential outcome. This doesn't mean that the opportunities with a low outcome should be ignored, but they may not have a high enough payback to justify a full trade-off study or research project.

## 7.5   Summary

As we have discussed, integrating sustainability into a good risk management program doesn't require a lot of changes to the standard risk processes. What is required is to ensure that an effective risk management program is fully implemented and that steps are taken to ensure that sustainability risks are fully included and discussed. Steps include:

- Ensuring that knowledgeable people from various areas of sustainability are invited to the risk planning meetings and workshops
- Using structured tools like PESTLe analysis to explore a broad range of external risks
- Recognizing project goals related to community support and environmental impacts
- Scheduling meetings and workshops to ensure that there is time to discuss all risk topics, including sustainability topics
- Looking at opportunities not just to reduce risks, but to also create a better project
- Ensuring that there is effective follow-up on risk and opportunity management plans that include sustainability topics

Transitions between project phases or major changes in the project execution plan can introduce new risks or increase the severity of known risks. The risk and opportunity management strategies and plans will need to be updated as new risks are identified and as the project moves from design and procurement to construction and commissioning.

Sustainability risks are also changing rapidly. A project team may need to adapt quickly to changes in community and stakeholder expectations, increasing regulations, and evolving sustainability goals around climate change, water management, energy efficiency, and contributing to local employment.

# CHAPTER 8

# Sustainability Management Tools

By this point in the book you have should a good understanding of what sustainability means to your project team and its importance to the overall success of your major project. Chapter 5 provided a framework for integrating sustainability into project management, including a project charter and sustainability policy, plus how to embed sustainability into the project's execution plan, schedule, and change management processes. In this chapter, we provide high-level guidance on the critical tools required for integrating and managing sustainability on major projects. This includes developing a sustainability framework, management systems, mechanisms for managing project commitments and complaints from local communities, and sustainability monitoring programs.

One intention for sustainability management tools is to help us identify and take advantage of any opportunities to make sustainability part of the project's core and embed the application of sustainability principles into the project team's decision making. Note that, like standard project management tools, it is not possible to directly transplant sustainability management tools from a template or from one project to another. As we have discussed, all projects and stakeholders are different and so each tool must be customized to suit the project, the organization, and the stakeholders. Therefore, we provide guidance and samples of tools that can be tailored to the needs of your project and stakeholders.

## 8.1  Sustainability Integration Framework

A project's sustainability integration framework document provides team members with the overall approach, strategy, and resources that will be used to achieve the project's sustainability objectives. It is applied throughout the life of the project in order to embed the consideration of sustainability within planning, design, procurement, and construction. As with all project planning documents, the framework is a living document and should be updated periodically to reflect evolving project issues such as changing geopolitical situations, policy mandates, and best practices. The framework establishes a clear understanding of the project, as guided by the sustainability policy and project charter (see Chapter 5), among all project stakeholders, including the organization, contractors, and local communities.

A sustainability integration framework provides the project team with:

- Clear guidance on integrating sustainability into the project development, without being overly prescriptive
- An umbrella approach for all project activities so that teams can see the connection between their work and the overall project goals
- Understanding of project objectives and priorities for integrating sustainability into the project, communicated through a framework
- Access to effective coordination between project disciplines and across project phases

## TIP: BUILDING FROM SUSTAINABILITY OBJECTIVES

A sustainability integration framework should clearly articulate the project's sustainability objectives (as discussed in Chapter 5). For example:

- The project must promote sound environmental and social practices.
- The project encourages transparency and accountability.
- The project will contribute to positive community development impacts.
- The project will address challenging issues that are important to sustainable projects, including climate change, supply-chain management, and human rights.

Statements such as these allow for the flexibility a project team needs to maximize opportunities to integrate sustainability.

The structure of such a framework depends largely on project type, size, complexity, and the external factors in which you are building a major project. You might need to provide more directions and requirements for the different project departments to do particular tasks (or stop doing certain tasks).

A fairly common way of setting up a prescriptive framework is to organize your project's sustainability integration tasks by three key project areas:

1. Project delivery
2. Environmental management
3. Social responsibility

Table 8.1  Sustainability integration framework sample deliverables.

| Project Delivery | Key Deliverables |
|---|---|
| Project delivery that provides a high-level approach to sustainability management by establishing clear objectives, tracking of key project commitments, and support for design, procurement, and construction activities. | • Commitment log<br>• Opportunity register<br>• Procurement support for requests for proposals and bid evaluations<br>• Engineering support for design teams and change management<br>• Construction support to construction team |
| **Environmental Management** | **Key Deliverables** |
| Environmental management provides detailed management strategies for regulatory and permit requirements and includes the plans and procedures to deliver the project with a minimum impact on the environment. The environmental management system (EMS) will include environmental monitoring and reporting on specific construction activities. | • Environmental protection plan and supporting plans and procedures<br>• EMS documentation<br>• Environmental sampling program<br>• Data management and reporting program<br>• Permit register and permit support<br>• Environmental monitors for construction<br>• Auditing of construction program<br>• Worker training and orientation materials |
| **Social Responsibility** | **Key Deliverables** |
| Social responsibility will map and track project stakeholders, manage and track project commitments, as well as establish plans for effective stakeholder engagement, economic development, community liaison, and complaint management. | • Community agreement<br>• Data collection, monitoring, and reporting<br>• Communications plan<br>• Project website and regular updates<br>• Stakeholder engagement support<br>• Community liaison during construction<br>• Complaints management |

See Table 8.1 for the type of deliverables that might be included in the three areas of the sustainability integration framework.

## 8.2  Management Systems

A management system is a systematic approach put in place by the project management team to establish plans and procedures, track performance, and mitigate, minimize, and manage various risks to the project success. An effective management system will provide detailed processes to fulfill the sustainability integration framework and is a key component of any project. The subject, scope, and complexity will vary according to the issues identified as material to the project and its stakeholders (see Chapter 4).

As we discussed earlier, sustainability is a team sport. It incorporates all project functions, from environment to construction, to human resources and health and safety. For a project management system to be truly integrated with sustainability, every project function must go through a systematic and thoughtful process to optimize for sustainable development and mitigate related risks. An environmental management system (EMS), for example, would include the environment, safety, and construction departments developing a series of detailed plans and procedures to support the delivery of the project, including waste management, water management, emergency response, and spills response.

As another example, members of the construction team, who are developing the construction management plan (CMP), will need to work with the environment, procurement, and human resources departments to understand the project's construction strategy, and explore opportunities to build sustainability goals into the plan. For example, the blasting schedule or construction of access roads might be reviewed for environmental impact and possible community impacts, such as managing traffic near schools.

We warn against developing a management system for sustainability that stands separate from the rest of the projects management plans and procedures. This could contribute to a disconnection of sustainability from the main project and reinforce the "silo" approach traditionally seen on major projects and make it more difficult to integrate sustainability into the project.

## Typical Management System Structure

For a management system to be successful, effective, and efficient, it must be based on a formal structure of defined elements. Management systems for major projects include plans for achieving goals and establishing guidelines for measuring the impact of these objectives. Table 8.2 shows the common elements that are typically included in a management.

Table 8.2   Common management system elements.

| Element | Mechanism of demonstration |
| --- | --- |
| Management is involved and committed to sustainability. | Policy statement |
| Management approves the performance in terms of expectations, requirements, and/or thresholds, which must be met and verified at a specific level of performance. | Performance standards that meet the expectations of the framework |
| A plan or program specifies how the project team will achieve the performance standards. | Execution plan |
| Further support to the management plan could encompass background information, tools, or templates that would be used to execute the management plan. | Guidelines (optional, although recommended) |
| Key performance indicators (KPIs) track progress and measure achievements, and how, when, to whom this data must be reported. | Monitoring, evaluation, and reporting plan |

## 8.3　Managing Commitments

As projects are being developed, the organization and the project team will make promises or commitments to stakeholders that are considered necessary to secure the regulatory approvals and community support required to build the project. Commitments are often activities the project will complete to minimize negative impacts, such as developing and following environmental management plans. Or they can be related to creating positive benefits for the local community, such as providing skills development training.

Commitments can come from a number of different sources connected to both the owner and the project team. Some sources of commitments include:

- The organization's stated goals and objectives on their website, sustainability report, or promotional materials

- The organization's promises to meet an industry standard or reporting program like the carbon disclosure program (CDP)

- Promises made to the local community at a town hall meeting, working group, or other meeting

- Impact assessments (IA) that include specific commitments related to mitigating project impacts

- Community agreements that have been reached through detailed and strategic discussions between the project team and local communities

- Requirements required by regulatory approvals

### TIP: SO WHAT IS A COMMITMENT?

A commitment is typically a high-level, long-term promise, rather than an item on a to-do list. For example, making a public statement (verbal or printed) that your project will hire a certain percentage of the total labor force from the local communities is a formal project commitment. Promising to reply to an individual request for information about job training – while it might support the larger commitment – is considered a task.

Another distinction is that activities required to meet detailed requirements under a regulatory permit are not typically documented and tracked as commitments. The commitment would be to maintain the required regulatory permits for the project, and the details would be managed in a permit register and environmental management system (EMS).

One issue that the project team needs to be aware of is that a commitment can be made outside of a formal process by someone making a spontaneous statement. This can happen when a project representative makes a public commitment on behalf of the project during a public meeting, a media interview, or in a conversation with a stakeholder. The project may think that commitments are only made by formal documents, but the local community will often consider verbal promises to be formal commitments.

Every project must have a policy for who can make commitments on its behalf when interacting with stakeholders, which is typically the project leadership. The remaining project team needs to be fully aware that they do not have the authority to make promises, and they must be equipped with a scripted response to help them say no. Many people in the best of circumstances find it hard to say no to a member of the local community, and do not realize the harm that can be caused by saying yes with zero follow-up. Regardless how big or small the offhand promise may be, eventually empty promises made by any person associated with your project will erode stakeholder confidence and reduce community support for the project.

---

### TIP: EVERY TEAM MEMBER IS A "PROJECT AMBASSADOR"

Every project employee and contractor represents your project, and whatever they say publicly about the project or its host communities, they are saying on behalf of your project. So making statements such as "Lots of jobs are coming, of course you'll get one!" or criticizing nearby communities and culture, such as "Man, the local food here really sucks!" will be detrimental to your project's reputation, and ultimately to your relationship with local communities.

Be clear and direct with project employees and contractors – communicate broadly and frequently that such behavior will not be tolerated. Keep it front of mind and help ingrain it in your project's culture through onboard training, cross-cultural training, and included into sustainability shares or morning toolbox meetings.

---

## Commitment Strategy

Many project commitments get made as a result of standard industry or regional requirements but often commitments are the result of working with the local community to resolve a local issue, or find ways of creating shared value between the project and the local community. From a strategic perspective, the project team should ensure that commitments will help create a successful project, which is directly dependent on the relationship with local community. In other words, commitments should support both the project and its stakeholders. Benefits that are purely for the benefit of the community alone would be considered philanthropy and not true sustainable development.

As we discussed in Chapter 6, stakeholder engagement and managing relationships with local communities continues over the life of the facility. Commitments will also extend beyond the project development to include operations, closure, and decommissioning. When developing commitments that go beyond project development, it is important to look for opportunities that create benefits for the operations as well as for the local community. For example, commitments that contribute to building municipal infrastructure or supporting local education programs will not only enhance the relationship between the project and the local community, they will also support future operations and help the community thrive.

In addition to being aligned with the local communities, commitments should:

- Be aligned with the project and organization's objectives, core values, and sustainability goals
- Not create a negative impact for another community or stakeholder
- Be ethical and not lead the project and organization into corrupt business practices

Projects need to get better at making and fulfilling clear, realistic, and productive commitments. Projects can get into trouble when they make promises to stakeholders that are unrealistic or have not been approved by project leadership. One option is to have the sustainability steering committee act as the commitment approving authority. The committee as a broad cross-section of leaders from different departments that can assess commitments to ensure that there are no unintended consequences to a commitment. For example, the construction manager could review commitments to flag any commitments that might create unrealistic barriers to the planned construction activities and schedule. Getting commitment buy-in from the project leadership through the committee can also reduce the potential for management pushback later in the project when the commitment might have a bigger impact than expected.

The best way to do this it to have a commitments management plan that:

1. Identifies who on the project team is accountable for making and keeping commitments

2. Clarifies what types of commitments can and cannot be promised and how they can benefit the project and/or the stakeholder

3. Establishes parameters for a commitment register to log and track commitments, and a procedure for managing the register

4. Includes a plan for communicating progress on meeting commitments with relevant stakeholders during the delivery stage

## Managing Commitments through Project Delivery

Managing commitments is a critical piece to managing risks for every major project. And although it is not a new concept, we are surprised at how often project commitments are not managed, and sometimes not even identified. In many cases, the growth of the project team and the changeover in staff as the project moves from feasibility and approvals to procurement and construction can result in commitments being lost. A well-managed commitment action log can help to ensure that commitments are not forgotten.

Sustainability issues cross over between departments. However, every commitment must be assigned to one department or individual to lead it. If the commitment requires involvement of other groups then it is the responsible department's job to engage with the other groups and ensure there is clear communication so that the task can be completed and the commitment managed. If your organization uses RACI charts (responsible, accountable, consulted, informed), then the commitment register can be modified to incorporate the RACI approach.

A major project should have one point of contact who leads the entire commitments management plan. This person can coordinate between project departments that are executing the commitments and track the progress of all commitments. The benefits of coordination between project departments can often go beyond the goal of fulfilling commitments. Cross-collaboration between departments can lead to identification of additional opportunities and innovative solutions to implement additional sustainability initiatives.

## 8.4   Developing a Commitments Action Log

A commitment action log is a comprehensive list of all promises the project has made. As discussed earlier, these are promises made in project documentation or public statements, including the environmental and social impact assessment, stakeholder consultation meeting minutes, and community agreements. The action log is a "living" list, meaning that it should be reviewed and updated regularly to reflect the current status of the project's progress in fulfilling its commitments.

A log of commitments is created in order to:

- Identify critical path issues and possible impacts on engineering design and construction plans from social commitments.

- Ensure that all commitments are properly incorporated into project design and execution.

- Demonstrate your project's fulfillment of the community benefits agreements.

Building a commitment action log takes time upfront in the project schedule to document and organize project commitments that have been made to stakeholders. But early project planning saves time and avoids rework later in the project. Managing commitments is like any other task management program in project management. Each task needs a clear objective or requirement, responsibility, deadlines, and status tracking to make sure everything is on schedule.

# Steps to Build a Commitment Action Log

## Step 1: Assemble Documentation

The first step in creating a commitment action log is to collect all project documentation that may contain commitment statements. A list of possible documentation includes:

- Social and environmental impact assessment
- Environmental impact statement
- Town hall and community meeting presentations and minutes
- Working group meeting minutes
- Community agreements (legal and otherwise)
- Media releases or media statements
- Media or public interviews with project/organization representatives/spokespeople
- Organization sustainability reports and annual reports
- Organization or project website
- Other public documentation, statements, or correspondence

## Step 2: Identify Commitments

The next step is to carefully review each document for statements in the form of promises and flag the commitments that the project or the organization has made. Some examples of language that you might see that represents a commitment include:

- "The project will implement noise and dust reduction measures in compliance with local environmental regulations."
- "A project complaint mechanism will be implemented prior to the start of construction. It will be culturally appropriate and include an anonymous hotline."
- "The project will maintain regular communications with local government."

## Step 3: Assemble a Master Action Log

The next step is to assemble all commitment statements into a spreadsheet or commitment software. The commitment action log should have three main sections that include a section that describes the commitment, a section that describes how the commitment will interact with the project, and a commitment management section. Each project is different and each project team will need different information in their commitment action log. A list of possible columns is provided below, and a simplified version of a commitment log is provided in Figure 8.1.

| | Commitment Information | | | Project Information | | | Commitment Management | | |
|---|---|---|---|---|---|---|---|---|---|
| | Name | Description | Stakeholders | Department | Impact | Risk | Owner | Plan | Status |
| 1 | | | | | | | | | |
| 2 | | | | | | | | | |
| 3 | | | | | | | | | |
| 4 | | | | | | | | | |
| 5 | | | | | | | | | |
| 6 | | | | | | | | | |
| 7 | | | | | | | | | |
| 8 | | | | | | | | | |
| 9 | | | | | | | | | |
| 10 | | | | | | | | | |
| 11 | | | | | | | | | |
| 12 | | | | | | | | | |

Figure 8.1    Simplified commitment action log.

- Commitment Information
  - Commitment number
  - Commitment title
  - Commitment description
  - Source of commitment (Reference to document, event, or another source)
  - Date commitment made
  - Stakeholders (who was the commitment made to)
  - Target date to fulfill the commitment (if applicable)
  - Category (used to sort commitments; see box below)
- Project Information
  - Location that commitment applies to
  - Department(s) impacted
  - Work breakdown structure (WBS)
  - Impact on the project
- Commitment Management Information
  - Owner or responsible party (We recommend listing roles rather than specific names to manage changes in team personnel.)

- Management plan (used to manage the commitment such as an environmental management plan or economic development plan)

- Status (open, completed, in-progress, at-risk)

- Percentage complete

- Fulfillment (indicate how the commitment was fulfilled)

- Corrective action

- General comments

## TIP: SAMPLE COMMITMENT CATEGORIES

Adding a sustainability category to the commitment register can help the team sort the commitments and look for opportunities to manage similar commitments by combining the management approach. A starting list of categories can be drawn from the list of topics identified in Chapter 4, and a sample list is provided here.

- Economic:
  - Local employment
  - Skills development
  - Human resources
  - Health and safety
  - Security
- Social:
  - Community relations
  - Resettlement and land acquisition
  - Education
  - Traffic
  - Community safety
- Environmental:
  - Air quality
  - Water quality
  - Waste
  - Waste water
  - Monitoring
  - Energy efficiency
  - GHG emissions

### Step 4: Manage Commitments

Tracking the fulfilment of project commitments is critical because it keeps the project on top of stakeholder expectations and helps to anticipate and plan for project delivery. The commitment action log should be monitored regularly, depending on the risk level of your project, demands from stakeholders, and the types of commitments that have been made. Progress should be reviewed with each responsible department and with the project team as a whole and at least monthly.

There should also be a formal, high-level review of the commitment action log with project leadership and the sustainability steering committee to officially close out fulfilled commitments, ensure remaining commitments are on track, add any new commitments, and develop corrective actions for commitments that are not on track to be met. The high-level reporting should be rolled up to project leadership and the sustainability steering committee at least quarterly to ensure priority is being placed on meeting commitments and to create an environment of accountability and awareness.

We have found that the relationships between how well a project team manages its commitments is directly related the strength of its relationship with the local communities. When the project team does not prioritize commitments management, the lack of follow-up and communication can cause mistrust from local communities to rise and create strained community relations and loss of community support for the project.

### TIP: A WORD ABOUT USING SOFTWARE

Most management and tracking requirements (like the commitment action log) can be supported by software tools. There are many tools on the market, including software programs, cloud-based databases, or basic spreadsheets. The choice is up to you. We do not endorse any one software tool, but we do recommend understanding that each tool is only as valuable as the users are adept at using the tool. Each user must have a high comfort level with the program so that the tool is used as often as needed and to its maximum potential, making it as valuable to the project as possible. Otherwise such tools can simply bog the project down in unnecessary problems. For any tool, including a simple spreadsheet, rollout and training are key to getting buy-in from the project team members who will be relying on it.

## 8.5   Managing Complaints

Each project should have a complaint mechanism (also called a grievance mechanism) to receive and process community concerns about issues pertaining to the project, and to facilitate resolution of the complaints. Complaints can be related to anything environmental and social, as well as project scheduling or construction activities. A project-level complaint mechanism is a process for receiving, evaluating, and addressing project-related concerns from affected communities.

There are several critical reasons for installing a complaint mechanism on your project as early as possible:

- To proactively address community complaints, thereby preventing escalation to legal action against the organization
- To serve as an early warning sign of significant or recurring issues that might signal a systemic problem
- To ensure that the project is responding to complaints that are only within the project-affected area and are directly related to the project or employee activities
- To ensure that all complaints from stakeholders are dealt with appropriately, with corrective actions being implemented where possible, and the complainant is informed of the outcome in a timely manner
- To inform and involve project management so that decisive action can be taken
- To provide project leadership with an early warning of potential legal actions and/or negative publicity toward the organization

## Managing Complaints through Project Delivery

How a project manages complaints from local communities is critical to building trust and credibility, thereby preserving and strengthening local community support for the project. It is important to establish a community complaint mechanism as early as possible in the project. Waiting for construction (or even preconstruction) phase, when the number and severity of complaints tends to be the highest, is too late. By starting early, your project team can take the opportunity to carefully design a complaint mechanism that is effective, using the time to revise and improve the system, before construction begins. And, as you will see further on, engaging local stakeholders in the process of building a community complaint mechanism will help to further build a strong relationship with the local communities.

Typically, the complaint mechanism is owned and managed by the project's community relations or social responsibility department. Complaints, like commitments, however, very often cross over between project departments. Generally, the most active departments in resolving complaints during project delivery are construction, environmental, and stakeholder engagement.

Overall management of the complaint mechanism should be assigned to the role of a sustainability manager, social responsibility manager, or similar function. Many projects will have a community relations officer (CRO) who receives the complaint, follows up with the complainant, and engages the relevant project team members to identify and implement a resolution. The CRO coordinates between the relevant project departments, ensures their participation for resolution, and makes certain that the complainant is kept informed of progress. They should have clearly defined objectives and assigned responsibilities for response time and regular reporting to project leadership. The CRO will identify the team members required for addressing and resolving complaints, manage the complaint register, engage or consult with relevant project departments, secure external support when specialist information is needed, track progress of complaints, and forward feedback to the complainants.

The number and type of complaints are good indicators of how a project may be performing and the perception of the project in the local community. The CRO should keep track of open and closed commitments and the type of commitments, and provide regular reports to project management. These weekly or monthly complaint reports are reliable for identifying early warning signs for the project team to watch for and prevent larger issues from occurring.

Complaints must be monitored regularly to ensure that local stakeholders are being heard and responded to in a timely and effective fashion. Monitoring is also required to ensure that the design and implementation of the complaint mechanism responds to the stakeholder's needs effectively, thereby reducing project risk. Monitoring helps identify common or recurring issues, issues that require structural solutions or policy change, and it enables the project to capture lessons learned. Monitoring measures can be as simple as tracking the number of complaints received, resolved, or those requiring third-party input.

## Complaint Mechanism

Exploring and installing appropriate methods for managing complaints is critical to any project management. A complaint mechanism is proactive, responsive, and transparent and will therefore reduce exposure to litigation and related risks and help maintain strong relationships with local stakeholders.

The project should clearly state, as often as necessary, that local community members are encouraged to share concerns freely, with the understanding that no retribution will be exacted for participation. The project should always strive to provide fair and equitable resolutions for any damage caused by the project, employees, or contractors performing project-related activities. Some project-related complaints will seek recourse and/or compensation for damages (such as to property damage) caused by the project. It is important to establish an unbiased system for assessing damage and establishing fair structures for compensation as early as possible. For example:

> For verifiable damage to personal property caused by project-related activities, the project/organization's first effort will be to effect prompt repair or replacement of the damaged property. If this is not possible, then the project/organization will provide alternate reasonable, in-kind compensation. Monetary compensation will be a last consideration.

## Worker Grievance

A project should always consider having a separate grievance mechanism for receiving and managing issues from its workers and contractors. Workplace grievances are handled by industrial relations or the human resources department and are focused on issues related to employment. Examples include unsafe working conditions, workplace bullying, and compensation issues.

## Resettlement and Land Acquisition

If your project involves the resettlement of people and communities in order to acquire land for the project, a separate complaint mechanism should be established to deal with concerns related specifically to the resettlement process to serve the key stakeholders involved. This would include people to be relocated, the leadership and government administrations, impacted businesses, land owners, land users (i.e. farmers who use the land for agriculture or animal grazing), and host communities. Resettlement and land acquisition in and of itself can be a highly politically and emotionally charged process that is challenging for any of the stakeholders affected. It involves financial compensation or in-kind compensation (i.e. housing, land, plants/trees, and others). Resettlement can impact culturally sensitive sites, sacred sites, and communal sites. It can reveal and highlight historic attachments to the land that may be generations old. And since the resettlement program is integrated into the overall project execution schedule, these complaints need to be prioritized, addressed, and resolved swiftly and with much care and empathy as possible, so has to minimize impact on project execution and the local communities involved.

## Indigenous Peoples

If applicable to your project, we highly recommend creating a complaint mechanism that is dedicated to the needs and concerns of indigenous peoples, one that is culturally sensitive and accessible so that it respects language and customs, recognizes the role of elders, is gender sensitive, and is respectful of the indigenous community's relationship with the natural environment. It may formally include elders and other indigenous community leaders in the process or reporting and resolving of a complaint.

## 8.6   Developing a Complaint Mechanism

There are three primary areas to look for guidance and requirements in building your project's complaint mechanism:

- The organization's relevant policies
- Industry standards
- National regulatory requirements

   In addition to these resources, the following international guidelines and industry standards may useful to you in developing your project's complaint mechanism:

- IFC Performance Standard 1: Social and Environmental Assessment and Management Systems[1]
- IFC Performance Standard 5: Land Acquisition and Involuntary Resettlement

- Equator Principles: Principle 6, Complaint Mechanism[2]

- Free Prior and Informed Consent: An indigenous peoples' right and a good practice for local communities – Manual for Project Practitioners[3]

- ISO: ISO/DSO 26000 for Corporate Social Responsibility; Complaint Mechanism Section 7.6.3[4]

- EBRD European Bank for Reconstruction and Development; Guidance Note for Complaint Management[5]

Beyond these formal guidance notes on developing a project complaint mechanism, we have assembled additional tips in order to make your mechanism effective.

## Make It Appropriate

The process for developing a complaint mechanism should incorporate consultations with representatives from local communities to understand local customs around communication, and specifically for resolving issues and disputes. This information should then be designed into the complaint mechanism so that it is culturally appropriate and therefore more effective. This is particularly important in societies that have distinct segregation of roles and responsibilities, gender imbalances, hierarchical leadership, and where indigenous peoples reside (see above).

## Make It Accessible

Information about the complaint mechanism must be easily and readily available to local communities and other key stakeholders. It is important that the mechanism is straightforward and easy for community members to access with no difficulty and zero cost, meaning that communities should face no obstacle using the mechanism. It should be easily understood, written in non-jargon and in local languages. The complaint mechanism should also be transparent, meaning that all stakeholders should be able know (or easily find out) how to report a concern or file a complaint, and fully understand the process for how and who will address their complaint.

Posters, pamphlets, and a website should be developed that clearly detail the different ways an individual with a concern can contact the project team, including in-person, or by telephone, email, or website. The complaint mechanism should provide a variety of ways to make a complaint that are adapted to the local culture. This can further help people to overcome such barriers as language, literacy, awareness, gender-relation issues, distance, or fear of retribution or reprisal.

A complaint mechanism should consider local norms on gender relations of the cultural region in which your project is being developed. Understand whether women have equal rights and agency to voice their own opinions and concerns. Must she be accompanied by a husband, father, or brother when speaking to outsiders? Are women potentially at risk of retribution from their own communities for filing a complaint, and how can you design confidentiality into your complaint mechanism to address this concern?

## Predictability

The complaint mechanism should be predictable by providing a clear timeframe for each stage, and clarity on the types of processes and outcomes that can and cannot be offered, at all phases of the mechanism – meaning the first time a complaint is received, the follow-up, the resolution, and the next steps if a resolution is not possible.

## Scale

The project's complaint mechanism should reflect the scale of the project, the severity of the adverse social impacts that were identified in the project's impact assessment, and the likely frequency and/or seriousness of potential complaints. Also consider whether local communities have confidence in the national legal system, and the extent of any historic negative legacies or lack of trust in companies or industries similar to yours. For example, mining, nuclear, and hydro industries often have negative reputations that can influence the level of trust that the community has in the project and their expectations for the complaint mechanism.

## Boundaries

Your project team should not attempt to receive or resolve any complaint that is outside of the project-affected area. Rather, your mechanism should include a list of the appropriate local authorities that the complainant can contact to address such issues.

## Engage Specialists When Needed

Your team should not presume be the leading authority on all topics. Rather, the team should seek to engage specialists from project partners, local institutions, or non-government organizations, when required.

## Types of Complaints

Complaint mechanisms should be flexible. Rather than prescribe a specific procedure for each particular type of complaint, it is helpful to establish a "menu" of possible options appropriate for different types of complaints. Project team members, organization personnel, and community members then have action guides when a dispute arises. See Table 8.3.

## Addressing Complaints

Developing resolution options, preparing a response, and closing out complaints are critical components to the complaint mechanism. Responses should be prompt, culturally appropriate, and documented, and confidentiality should be honored. Stakeholders should be kept informed of how their complaint is being managed and its resolution throughout the process.

Table 8.3   Types of complaints for major projects.

| Type of Complaint | Examples |
|---|---|
| Relatively minor and one-time problems | • Organization equipment causes damage to an individual's property<br>• One-time disagreement between contractor and a local employee over working conditions |
| Relatively minor but repetitive problems | • Noise and dust complaints during construction<br>• Destruction of landscape<br>• Project traffic blocks the local access roads |
| Major claim, significant adverse impact on a larger group or several groups | • During construction, organization uses some land beyond the initial agreement with a community for temporary land use<br>• Misconduct of foreign workers |
| Major claim, significant adverse impact on a larger group or several groups | • Employment opportunities do not meet expectation of local communities (no clarity regarding employment policies)<br>• Significant water contamination (less fishing, unclean water) or water shortage<br>• Violence against women due to shifting power roles in communities |
| Major allegations regarding policy or procedure | • Allegations of systematically inadequate land compensation<br>• Communities not provided with disclosure of project information and fear, uncertainty, or rumors leading to civil unrest and violence |

If a claim is not accepted (because the complaint is outside the project boundaries, for example) and no further action will be taken, be diplomatic in response and provide evidence as to why the complaint is not accepted.

If a claim is accepted by the project, a preliminary response of acceptance should be provided within a reasonably short period of time and should propose next steps and actions to be taken for resolution. This is the time where the project team would consult internally for resolution, engage appropriate department representatives, carry out individual or group meetings with complainants, or engage external specialists to help clearly define the issue and find a resolution.

When a resolution is found (and when it is not), a response must be given to the complainant and documented. If the complainant is satisfied, then be sure to document their agreement. Where a complainant may not be satisfied with proposed resolution or outcome of proposed corrective action, further steps are required and will depend on severity of the issue, the level of complainant dissatisfaction, and the project's organizational structure.

Complaints are "closed" only when an agreement with the complainant has been reached. If the issue was resolved to the satisfaction of the complainant, get a confirmation on file, along with case documentation.

## 8.7   Monitoring Sustainability Performance

Major projects need a comprehensive, long-term program to monitor their sustainability performance. The monitoring program should connect the project from baseline, scoping, and impact assessment stages through construction and operations and to end-of-life stages. A good sustainability monitoring program will ensure that information is not lost between the project stages and that the organization can demonstrate that they are taking the concerns of the local community and local government seriously.

It is important to establish the project sustainability monitoring program as early as possible in the project, ideally during the baseline assessment and feasibility phases. The monitoring program should identify the issues that are of concern to the project and its stakeholders. This means consulting with local community and governments and seeking their input on project metrics and monitoring plans. It is an ideal opportunity to establish formal working groups that include diverse stakeholder participation, such as local community members, nongovernment organizations, technical specialists, and members of a variety of other community or cultural groups. Engagement for monitoring sustainability performance demonstrates to the local communities that the project and the organization is taking the long-term social and environmental impacts seriously. It demonstrates transparency, which helps build credibility and stronger relationships.

As part of the impact assessment process, a set of parameters is established for baseline studies that is aligned with government approvals. But they do not always address all concerns raised by the local communities. This is especially true for monitoring the detailed impact of construction that can have short-term but serious impacts on the local community (such as traffic disruptions, increased crime, increased cost of food and rent, and strain on healthcare facilities). Establishing a broader range of baseline parameters and an early start to monitoring additional impacts allows the team to measure and understand baseline conditions before construction activities began. Then complaints can be better managed with facts rather than through community perceptions.

Looking beyond the traditional baseline monitoring and using community engagement and consultation can improve the social monitoring program and ensure that right data is being collected. The monitoring program can incorporate requirements from the commitment register, including approvals, permits, and community agreements. Key social areas to track could include levels of employment, levels of education and skills training, and community impacts (traffic, crime levels, etc.).

Environmental monitoring plans are typically established for the main areas of potential impact (water, land, wildlife, air, etc.). Plans should also capture baseline and long-term potential impacts from project development and operations that have been raised by the local community during consultation and project development. Identifying and tracking the "hot-button" issues for the community can help build trust and avoid potential future issues.

Before project construction starts, ensure that there is an early baseline for all metrics and establish plans to monitor throughout the project lifecycle. The plans should define the frequency of monitoring, which might change as the project develops, especially during construction. The project should also include the monitoring of potential changes to the local environment from external impacts like other projects, local development, and climate change so that the project does not carry the blame for impacts that were caused by other factors or stakeholders.

## 8.8   Summary

Through this chapter, we have provided a very high-level overview of what we believe are the top management tools for integrating and managing sustainability into a major project. The sustainability integration framework provides the overall approach, strategy, and resources to achieve sustainability objectives on the project. Management systems that have been integrated into project delivery will be more effective at sustainability integration than a standalone "sustainability management system." Managing commitments and a protocol for receiving and processing complaints is important to earning and maintaining local community support for the project. And finally, monitoring the overall sustainability performance of your project is critical to measuring success and identifying early warning signs of when you are not meeting sustainability performance targets.

The sustainability management tools help to support the delivery of major projects, including providing organized and comprehensive information for:

- Engineering design and decision making
- Procurement strategies and bid specifications
- Construction planning

Sustainability is an evolving field. So the tools described in this chapter will need to be adapted to fit the unique challenges of each major project and to reflect new project management tools, organizational changes, and societal expectations.

## Endnotes

1. "IFC Performance Standards" accessed February 10, 2019, from https://www.ifc.org/wps/wcm/connect/Topics_Ext_Content/IFC_External_Corporate_Site/Sustainability-At-IFC/Policies-Standards/Performance-Standards.
2. "The Equator Principles, accessed February 10, 2019, from https://equator-principles.com/.
3. "Free Prior and Informed Consent: An Indigenous Peoples' Right and a Good Practice for Local Communities," accessed February 10, 2019, from http://www.fao.org/3/a-i6190e.pdf.
4. "DIN ISO 26000 Guidance on Social Responsibility (ISO 26000:2010)," accessed February 10, 2019, from https://www.en-standard.eu/din-iso-26000-guidance-on-ocial-responsibility-iso-260s00-2010/.
5. "Grievance Management Guidance Note: EBRD Requirements," accessed February 10, 2019, from https://www.ebrd.com/downloads/research/guides/grievance.pdf.

## Permitting Plan

A permitting plan should be used with your permit register to support the permit applications process. It should detail the process for identifying, tracking, and completing regulatory permits. Your permit register will help ensure that permitting occurs in a timely and orderly fashion and that no permit applications "fall through the cracks" or result in project delays. The permitting plan will also ensure that the change management process is followed and any change in engineering design or construction plans will require a regulatory review process to identify any permit changes required due to the change.

## Beyond Regulatory Compliance

Most regulations are designed for projects to meet minimum environmental, social, or economic requirements and may not be sufficient to satisfy the local community or project commitments. Permit applications should be aligned with the organization's internal policies and the project's commitments to ensure that there is zero disconnect between the permit documents and other public documents.

# 9.3   Summary

Project approvals and permits is a significant phase in the life of a major project and can pose considerable risk to the project schedule. Getting the project approvals and permits in place should not be seen as the end goal for the project, but rather as a starting point for the management of permits and maintaining the overall legal compliance of the project. The project sustainability planning should be carried through into the engagement with the local community and the approvals process.

Approvals and permits provide valuable information for the project team. Permit requirements must be integrated into detailed design and included in procurement documents so that construction contractors are aware of the permit requirements before their work starts. The systems and tools required to track environmental performance and compliance with permits is outlined in more detail in Chapter 12, "Construction Management."

# CHAPTER 10

# Design

Integrating sustainability into design activities is a fundamental part of developing more sustainable projects. Sustainability can and should be included in every stage of the design, from early concept and feasibility studies to detailed design activities. Sustainable design should also be considered by every design and engineering discipline, not just the environmental engineering or infrastructure departments where the impacts are more evident. Every department can look at their contribution to the project's environmental footprint, impacts along the supply chain, how designs can be adapted to support local employment and local supply, and how operations will impact the local community.

There are a number of initiatives and tools that the project design team can use to consider design alternatives and improve the sustainability of the project, including:

- Design basis document to capture sustainability goals and assumptions
- Design for the environment (DfE) and sustainable design
- Design for closure and progressive reclamation
- Safety in design
- Lifecycle analysis
- Options analysis and alternatives analysis to optimize water and energy use, waste management, carbon footprint, or community impacts
- Sustainable decision-making tools to evaluate trade-offs between technical, social, environmental, and financial performance
- Innovation processes to reduce impacts and create benefits across the project

Integrating sustainability into project design is an emerging concept. Design teams can benefit from training on the concepts and processes used to design more efficient and resilient projects. Training can include a session with each group discipline to discuss sustainability goals, objectives, and commitments. These workshops can also help explore new opportunities that can be incorporated into the engineering design and tracked in the opportunity register.

Training sessions can also include instruction on some of the well-established programs that help to support sustainability in the design process, such as Design for Environment (DfE), Safety in Design (SiD), and Life-cycle analysis (LCA).

Sustainability is creating more complex business and technical environments for major projects. If your project team is going to meet the challenge of this new reality, then they will need to adapt and find new ways of collaborating to solve problems. We are usually more comfortable solving problems that we have seen before but with the rapid changes occurring in the world, we are faced with new problems that do not have proven solutions.

When the project team faces a challenge that encompasses more than one technical discipline or where a technical problem overlaps with a social or environmental challenge, there is a need for collaboration with multidisciplinary teams that can bring a broad range of experience and expertise to the problem. These are not just technical specialists but could include business, sustainability and social experts, academics, suppliers, and community members.

One of the benefits of an integrated sustainability program is that groups within the project team are connected and can share knowledge and ideas to combine all of the individual skills and experience in the project team to solve more complex problems. With complexity as the new reality, project teams need to find new ways of working together, across geographies and technical specialties, to meet this challenge and build better projects.

This chapter provides the reader with an overview of integrating sustainability into design documents like the design basis, how to get community input through design workshops, and incorporating innovation. The chapter also provides a review of decision-making tools and how adding sustainability factors to decisions can improve outcomes. The chapter ends with a discussion of how project design needs to take account of issues related climate change and the growing requirement to reduce greenhouse gases (GHGs).

# 10.1  Design Basis

One of the key documents used to define design objectives and establish base assumptions for all design teams is the design basis document. Although this is typically a very technical document, it is important to incorporate sustainability information into the design basis to reflect local conditions, regulatory constraints, and project commitments. It is important to avoid using a template from the last project without a detailed analysis to confirm that the assumptions in the design basis still hold. Development of the project execution plan (PEP) includes a discussion of the sustainability issues for each department (see Chapter 5), which is a good source of information and topics that need to be covered in the design basis.

The design basis will typically include assumptions about the local climate and weather conditions that could have an impact on construction or operations. Given the reality of climate change, the design basis should cover not just the historical weather conditions, but potential future weather conditions and how the weather might change over the life of the project. Construction design might not change significantly from current conditions, but climate projections indicate that projects in most regions of the world will face significant changes in storm events, precipitation, and temperature over the life of the project. If there is debate among the project team regarding the extent of climate change that is expected to occur, then it is reasonable to use a range of estimates based on available climate modeling to capture uncertainty and variability. Then create engineering designs that provide acceptable safety factors or provide the project with the ability to adapt to changing conditions over time.

Another local condition to consider in the design basis is the potential range for the cost of carbon and the cost of water based on the best available information. Even if the region where the project is based does not have a carbon pricing program in place yet, there is still potential for impact by future local carbon pricing structures or international programs. Including a range of potential pricing options can allow design teams to perform sensitivity analysis on key decisions to evaluate the impact of future pricing and select the design option that provides the best total cost of ownership across the range of potential carbon prices.

Some locations are also looking at putting more realistic prices on the use of water. So, if the project is expected to use large quantities of water, then applying possible water pricing scenarios can help improve decision making and design development. This could mean evaluating extreme cases where water is not available, and the facility needs to be a zero-water discharge facility.

The design basis should also include any regulatory constraints that will limit designs or the logistics of getting components to the site. For example, a reference to the permit register (Chapter 9) or to key regulatory documents that each discipline needs to be aware of.

The design basis might also reflect design constraints that the project has committed to through the approvals process, during consultation, or in a community agreement. If you have developed a robust and easy-to-use commitment register (Chapter 8), then the design basis should reference the commitment register and require design teams to check their design work against the register. If the commitment register is not well developed or has limited access, then the design basis must include the key design commitments that the design teams will need to incorporate into their work.

The design basis should be a fairly static document that provides consistent information to the design team as the project evolves from concept to detailed design. Note that the document may still need to be updated during the project to reflect new information, ongoing input from the local community, and changes in the commitments made by the project team.

## 10.2 Selecting a Location

One of the first main decisions that must be made in project development is the location of the project. This includes the main facility and all the supporting infrastructure required to manage the construction and operate the facility. For natural resource projects, location of the main facility is constrained by the location of the resource. For public infrastructure projects, location is based on where the people are located. For both situations, there are still many details that need to be resolved, such as the route of the access roads or the location of maintenance facilities.

Typically, project location decisions are focused on operational requirements and economic analysis, but project teams also need to consider sustainability issues around environmental and social impacts, and interactions with the local community. The strategy for choosing locations should consider:

- Minimizing footprint to reduce environmental and social impact
- Evaluating options for choosing a brownfield site for redevelopment rather than using a greenfield site
- Locating the facility in a high unemployment area where the project can have a positive economic benefit, access to employees, and opportunities to build community support
- Avoiding high-risk areas like sensitive environmental locations with unique ecosystems or endangered species
- Leveraging local knowledge to help refine locations for facilities and infrastructure
- Understanding areas where the community is likely to have a not-in-my-backyard (NIMBY) reaction

## Stranded Assets

Another key issue to look at is what the location will be like at the end of the project or the end-of-life of the facility to ensure that the project will still be viable in the future. Facilities that are no longer economically viable due to changing climate, access to natural resource, or social changes are considered stranded assets. Some examples include:

- Operations in semi-arid regions that run out of water for production as rainfall patterns change
- Coastal facilities that could flood with rising sea level and larger storm events
- Infrastructure designed for old weather patterns that are no longer economical as storm events become more severe, more frequent, and disrupt operations
- Cold climate resource projects that have limited access because winter roads no longer freeze

When evaluating locations for project facilities and supporting infrastructure, project teams need to assess how a changing climate may impact the project in the future and include these potential changes in the location selection to minimize the risk that these assets will become stranded and devalued in the future.

## Integrated Infrastructure

Selecting locations and development strategies for project infrastructure must also consider how the project infrastructure fits with the existing infrastructure used by the local community, or with infrastructure that could be developed to improve conditions within the local community. Infrastructure that would support local development includes water and waste water treatment, electrical power, roads, waste management facilities, and communications (especially internet access). This is especially true for many natural resource projects that are being developed at remote locations where the infrastructure for the facility needs to be developed and maintained to support the operations.

Table 10.1  Integrated infrastructure strategies.

| Infrastructure Strategy | Description |
| --- | --- |
| Isolation | Fenced compound structures have no exchange of services/infrastructure. |
| Support | Infrastructure is built larger than necessary and excess power or water is sold to the local community to generate additional revenue for the operations. |
| Purchase | Power or water is purchased from local utilities to help support the local economy. |
| Integrated | Shared/coordinated infrastructure is developed in partnership with the local community. |

The project's infrastructure strategy can have a large impact on the surrounding environment and local communities, which presents both risks and opportunities for the project. The infrastructure strategy can range from an isolationist approach (the project infrastructure is not connected to the local community) to a fully integrated approach. A range of infrastructure strategies is outlined in Table 10.1.

When evaluating supporting infrastructure options, assess the use of partnerships with the local community and the local government to manage shared infrastructure. As discussed in Chapter 2, this could be managed through the use of public-private partnerships (P3s) or people-public-private partnerships (P4s) for all of the parties to share in the investment for the infrastructure (roads, power, or water) and then recover the investment from user fees or tolls.

Using a shared infrastructure strategy can also have a benefit for closure planning. Shared infrastructure can be sold or deeded to local governments or communities at the end of the project life, which can decrease closure bonding or asset retirement obligations (see Chapter 14).

## Resettlement/Land Acquisition

In some cases, a major project will require the acquisition of land or buildings and the resettlement of people to construct the main facility or supporting infrastructure. This can happen where a community is located above a natural resource or where linear infrastructure needs to pass through a community. The legal complexity of resettlement and land acquisition makes it difficult to discuss in general terms, as each country and region will have its own laws and customs. But project teams should keep in mind several key things to support the overall sustainability of the project:

- Minimizing the amount of land required by minimizing the project footprint and carefully selecting infrastructure routes can help to reduce the impact of the project.

- Negotiating land acquisition with the government is legally required, but even more important is open and transparent discussions with the local community on land acquisition and resettlement process.

- Discussions with the community and the impacted individuals should include one-on-one and group workshops to make the resettlement process as positive as possible.

- Evaluate ways to support the people being resettled, which could include preferred employment or small business contracts.

Table 10.2   Advantages and disadvantages of locating on a brownfield site.

|  | Greenfield Development | Brownfield Development |
|---|---|---|
| **Advantages** | • No preexisting community relationships<br>• No contamination<br>• No demolition required | • Existing relationships with the community<br>• Opportunity for land restoration<br>• Access to a skilled workforce<br>• Existing infrastructure (roads, power) |
| **Disadvantages** | • New community relationships<br>• Project will damage the environment<br>• No existing Infrastructure | • Poor relations with community<br>• Contaminated land<br>• Unknown hazards<br>• Outdated, damaged infrastructure |

## Greenfield versus Brownfield Locations

Another option that should be considered for the location of a project is whether to construct on a greenfield site or a brownfield site. Greenfield sites are locations where there has been no development and the environment is undisturbed. Brownfield sites are locations that have been developed and the environment has experienced some level of environmental damage.

Developing a new project on a greenfield site has a lot of advantages as there are no legacy issues that must be managed, and the local community is less likely to have preexisting negative attitudes toward the project. The downside is that the project will damage natural land or land that is used for agriculture.

Developing on brownfield sites is often avoided because a new project generally does not seek to manage cleanups, such as old spills and broken infrastructure. But there are also many advantages to working on brownfield sites, such as functioning infrastructure (access roads, water supply, landfill). They may need repairs but are already constructed. There may be a local workforce that is already trained and, sometimes, government incentives to redevelop the region. The advantages and disadvantages of developing a new project on both brownfield and greenfield locations is summarized in Table 10.2.

# 10.3   Community Design Workshops

Community design workshops or design charettes are often used in the design of community infrastructure like parks and revitalized community planning. At the workshop, members of the local community and project team members get together to discuss the project goals, challenges, and design solutions. The same approach is also valuable in the design of any major project where the project impacts the local community. This could include access roads, impacts to local water bodies, or opportunities to create shared infrastructure.

A community design workshop is unlike a traditional public meeting where the team describes the project design to the community and the community shares opinions or asks questions. Rather, a community design workshop is a collaborative process that leverages local knowledge and wisdom to provide design alternatives that could potentially improve the initial project designs.

Hosting a community design workshop (or multiple workshops) helps to build trust in the community by demonstrating that the team is open to input from the community, values their local and traditional knowledge, and is listening to their concerns about the impact of the project on their community. Helping to identify alternatives and develop solutions for the project builds support for the project among the participants in the workshop.

The workshop also brings together people from different parts of the local community. They can help build relationships that might not already exist and provide a framework for future engagement with the community. Workshops usually involve community leaders, local government and policy makers, community-based organizations, and interested community members.

## Who Should Be Involved?

The success of a community design workshop will depend in part on who attends the workshop. In small communities, you can invite the entire community but in larger communities having everyone attend can result in too many people to be constructive. Some teams focus on local representatives who are involved in planning or local government. But it is important to get input and build support from a broad range of the local community. Some groups that should be invited (adapted from National Charrette Institute[1]) include:

1. Decision makers like include regulators, departmental managers, or local elected officials
2. Groups that are historically left out of the public process, including indigenous communities, youth groups, and women's groups
3. Individuals directly affected by the project, especially people whose property or business is affected and those living or working within the project area
4. Individuals who may provide valuable information for the project and project area, including members of the local indigenous community, academics, or experts in the local area
5. Stakeholders who have the power to promote the project, including local business association or chamber of commerce
6. Stakeholders who have the power to block the project

## Workshop Process

The process for a community design workshop will vary depending on the type of major project, the location, and the degree of impact on the local community. For public infrastructure projects like highways and public transit projects, community workshops could form a core part of the development of the project and require numerous multiday workshops to get the required level of engagement and input to the design. For resource or industrial projects in a remote area, there may be a need for frequent and elaborate public engagement, but there are still numerous benefits to engaging the nearest communities, especially for linear infrastructure, including roads, rail lines, ports, and utilities (water and electrical).

The design workshop should always begin with introductions to the project team, an outline of the project, and the format of the workshop. Depending on whether the local community has been involved in design workshops, it may be necessary to start training on the process of a design workshop, expectations of the participants, rules of engagement, and how the information will be captured and used by the project team.

The workshop can then move to an update from the project team on project details and specific challenges that will be addressed in the workshop. This can include any challenges that the team is currently facing and how they would like the community's help with the design.

The next stage is to engage the workshop attendees in generating new ideas that can be used to solve design challenges or support options analysis. For infrastructure projects, having maps or 3-D models of the project area can be helpful. Attendees can point out areas that are important to the community or locations where the project could be built. Ideas can be captured on Post-it Notes or drawn directly onto project maps. A project team member should take comprehensive notes and record ideas as the workshop progresses.

Depending on the level of engagement required by the project team, the idea generation stage may be useful without any detailed follow-up. But it is often useful for the attendees to review one another's ideas and work through the pros and cons of the design ideas. This can help to identify ideas that have broad support and do not create conflict between different groups in the community. It can also allow the design team to engage in more detailed conversations with attendees on why they are suggesting certain alternatives, and to explain why certain ideas may not be possible due to design limitations or regulatory constraints.

Following the workshop, the design team should prepare a report on the ideas collected, how they are going to be integrated into the design, and where additional work is required to develop the ideas. The report should consider the capabilities of the local community and their preferred method of communication. It is often effective to meet with the community to present the report and explain how the ideas have been used. The updated maps and diagrams that were used during the workshop can be presented to clearly demonstrate the value of the ideas. This not only shows that the project respects the input of the local community, but it also builds trust and helps to maintain the community support throughout the project development.

## CASE STUDY: COMMUNITY WORKSHOP SOLVES INFRASTRUCTURE PROBLEM

Our project had been put on hold. The local community was mostly supportive of the new mine development except that our rail line that would be used to transport diesel fuel into the site and transport ore out of the site passed right alongside a local community, and also along a lake that was both their source of drinking water and a popular fishing spot. After numerous unsuccessful meetings with the town council and local regulators, we held a workshop with the local community to discuss the challenges of building a rail line and the requirements to move material into and out of the site.

Although our focus was on improving the design of the original route that had been selected by the rail design team, the community members kept suggesting that there was an alternative route outside of town that avoided their water supply lake. We had maps of the area and the community members were able to draw the suggested route. After the workshop, the rail design team agreed to investigate the suggested route, but they said that there was little chance it would work based on their aerial surveys of the area. To their surprise, when they walked the proposed route with local community members, they discovered that it was not only viable but would provide a shorter route to the site.

Within weeks, the project was back on track (pun intended), the local community removed their objections to the project approvals, and the new route was not only viable but ended up being 40% cheaper than the original route. Integrating sustainability and engaging the local community helped create a better solution for the project. If only we had held the design workshop earlier in the design process.

## 10.4   Innovation

Projects are facing increasing levels of public scrutiny and are being held to a higher standard for managing environmental impacts and co-creating economic benefits with local communities. Meeting these challenges requires project teams to find new, innovative solutions instead of using the same design and processes that have been used historically on projects. Innovation can occur anywhere across the project team, but the focus of innovation will often occur during the design process, where the project team is making decisions about where to build the facility, what processes and equipment will be used, and how the project will be built.

### Opportunity Register

As discussed in Chapter 7, "Managing Risk and Opportunity," integrating sustainability into project design can include identifying and implementing opportunities to reduce impacts, improve the local community, and deliver better projects. Throughout the project development process opportunities can be included in the opportunity register and used to drive innovation in project design. These opportunities should be included in an opportunity capture plan that documents how each opportunity will be managed, who will be responsible, and the schedule to investigate opportunities and execute on selected opportunities.

### Innovation Targets

One way to drive innovative solutions is to establish innovation targets that every project department can work toward. This helps to engage everyone on the project team in generating ideas to improve the project. There are often many small ways to improve a project and these shouldn't be discouraged, but the focus of innovation should be on material or significant changes to the original design. The project can establish a set of innovative targets that can be used to track impacts to demonstrate savings and improvements to senior management, and communicate innovative solutions to owners, regulators, and the local community. Examples of innovation targets include:

- Cost savings in $ of capital cost, $/unit operating costs, or $ of total cost of ownership
- Local job creation in person-years during construction or full-time equivalents (FTEs) during operations

- Local contracting increased by either $ procured locally or as a percentage of $ Local/$ Total
- Environmental impact in $tCO_2$/unit produced, or $tCO_2$ during construction
- Schedule improvement in days saved

## Innovation Competitions

Another approach to generate innovative solutions to project challenges is to develop innovation competitions that address key risks or opportunities identified during project development. Innovation competitions can be focused on internal teams where the project team including consultants and suppliers are challenged to solve problems. Innovation competitions can also be expanded to include external resources like industry researchers, universities and colleges, and the local community.

## Change Management

Developing innovative solutions can create positive benefits for the project but can also create unintended negative consequences. It is important to include change management procedures (see Chapter 5) in the innovation process to evaluate the potential impact of innovation on other project areas.

# 10.5 Decision Making

For every project, decisions must be made to prioritize actions, choose locations, select technologies, choose suppliers, and procure equipment, material, and services. This means that integrating sustainability into project design requires integrating sustainability into decision-making tools and processes.

The organization may have set ambitious sustainability goals, but when sustainability concepts move from high-level organizational strategy down to the reality of project design and construction, they must evolve to reflect the practical requirements of project development and operations. It doesn't matter how green or sustainable a design is, it still needs to work.

The tools described below can support design teams and project leadership to make the tough decisions needed to balance financial and operational goals with environmental and social responsibilities. This section will discuss several design tools, including:

- Trade-off studies
- Multi-criteria design analysis
- Lifecycle assessment
- Environmental economics

## Trade-off Studies

Trade-off studies or alternatives analysis is the starting point for most technical decision-making processes. They involve researching and completing preliminary design work on a number of possible options for design

| Sustainability Aspect | Aspect Weighting | Selection Factor | Weighting | Scoring (from 1 to 5) | | |
|---|---|---|---|---|---|---|
| | | | | Option One | Option Two | Option Three |
| Operational | 20% | Proven Technology | 2 | 5 | 4 | 2 |
| | | Safety | 5 | 4 | 2 | 5 |
| | | Construction Schedule | 4 | 2 | 3 | 4 |
| | | Reliability | 3 | 3 | 2 | 3 |
| | | Easy to Service | 1 | 1 | 0 | 5 |
| SCORE | | | | 64% | 48% | 79% |
| Economic | 30% | Capital Cost | 5 | 2 | 3 | 4 |
| | | Operating Cost | 3 | 3 | 2 | 4 |
| | | Project Risk | 4 | 4 | 3 | 2 |
| | | Payment Terms | 2 | 2 | 2 | 4 |
| | | Currency Exchange Rate Risk | 1 | 2 | 4 | 2 |
| SCORE | | | | 55% | 55% | 67% |
| Environmental | 20% | Carbon Footprint | 3 | 1 | 2 | 4 |
| | | Emissions | 5 | 1 | 3 | 4 |
| | | Water Use | 2 | 3 | 2 | 4 |
| | | Risk of Spills | 4 | 1 | 3 | 5 |
| | | Wildlife Interactions | 1 | 3 | 3 | 3 |
| SCORE | | | | 28% | 53% | 84% |
| Social | 30% | Local Employment | 5 | 3 | 2 | 4 |
| | | Noise and Dust | 4 | 1 | 3 | 5 |
| | | Youth Employment | 2 | 3 | 3 | 3 |
| | | Traffic Disruotion | 3 | 3 | 1 | 4 |
| | | Responsible Supply Chain | 1 | 1 | 3 | 5 |
| SCORE | | | | 47% | 45% | 84% |
| OPTION WEIGHTED SCORE | | | | 49% | 50% | 78% |

Figure 10.1   Multi-criteria decision analysis example.

to transport materials by rail or truck can be supported by calculating the carbon footprint of both options to understand the potential carbon reduction of transporting materials by rail.

Developing the project's carbon and water footprint can not only help decision making but can support reporting to groups like the Carbon Disclosure Project, calculating the impact of future carbon taxes, and, in the case of natural resource or production facility, providing input data to LCA analysis being completed by the organization's customers.

Performing a full LCA for many project decisions is often not necessary so the design team should select an approach that meets the level of accuracy that is required for the decision. A streamlined approach is

Table 10.5  Lifecycle screening.

| Lifecycle Component | Impacts | Opportunities | What can you change? |
| --- | --- | --- | --- |
| Materials and Supplies | | | |
| Transportation | | | |
| Construction | | | |
| Operation | | | |
| End of Life (Disposal/Recycle) | | | |

often sufficient to provide an indication of how to compare the design options. The first step in a streamlined approach is to choose the key factor that will be used for the LCA depending on the expected impacts of the design. Indicators that can be used for an LCA include area of land disturbed, resource consumption, energy use, water use, carbon emissions, or waste production. For example, a decision to select an energy system would look at energy use or carbon emissions but a decision about construction methods might look at area of land disturbed.

The next step is to screen the decision options to see where impacts are created along the lifecycle. This is also an opportunity to look for innovative solutions to find ways of changing the details of the design option to reduce the largest impacts. For example, if food supply for the construction activities has a high impact from transportation of materials to the job site, then there may be opportunities to look at local supply to reduce the largest impact. This analysis can be captured in a summary table, as shown in Table 10.5.

Once you have identified the key impacts for each of the design options, the next step is to calculate the footprint of each of the options. Comparing the area of disturbed land can be fairly straightforward but calculating carbon footprints should be done using accepted methods so that the results can be used for future reporting, if required.

Like all decision tools, LCA has issues that need to be reviewed before making a design decision based on the output of the assessment. Some key issues include:

1. A focus on one environmental aspect like carbon footprint without looking at other impacts that may be important

2. Analysis to reduce impacts on a global level (carbon footprint) that might create higher local environmental impacts

3. Decisions that are based primarily on the environmental aspects that ignore or deemphasize the social impacts to the local community

4. Failure to include impacts that are harder to quantify and therefore difficult to include in the calculations

## Environmental Economics

Another approach that is similar to lifecycle assessment is environmental economics, which uses a financial analysis of a wide range of project impacts to evaluate design options. This provides an alternative decision approach to LCA in cases where there are competing decision factors that might include economic benefits of the project versus environmental damage versus both positive and negative social impacts.

Environmental economics is well developed for public infrastructure projects where it considers the choices that people make and the costs and benefits of design options. For example, the design of a public park would consider the benefits of people enjoying the facilities and the surrounding nature by predicting the number of visitors, time spent in the park and the financial value of that time.

The process can also be applied to other types of projects where the facilities will have an impact on the local community or on the environment. The process allows the design team to meet both project economic and sustainability goals by weighing the costs and benefits of design alternatives.

## *Economic Analysis*

The basis of comparison in environmental economics analysis is purely economic so everything needs to be converted into a financial impact. There are a number of ways of doing this, depending on whether the impact is financial (profits, jobs, taxes), environmental (loss of habitat and ecosystem services), or social (life expectancy, social cohesion). The social impacts can be the most difficult to convert into financial values, but economists use a variety of methods, including actuarial calculations, surveys, and values inferred from similar activities. Some examples to demonstrate the types of calculations that can be used to convert environmental and social impacts into financial values include:

- Carbon emissions can be calculated by local carbon tax rates or preferably by the global social cost of carbon.

- Water use can be calculated by the cost to replace the water if the area is prone to drought or has limited water resources.

- Damage to land can be calculated by loss of natural resources (what is a tree worth as wood and clean air and habitat) or loss of hunting (what is the replacement cost of food).

- Road safety can be calculated by the likelihood of an accident times the cost of an accident (property damage, healthcare costs).

- Decrease in air quality or water quality can be calculated by increased health care costs.

- Damage to the local culture leading to a loss of social cohesion can be calculated by the social cost of family support services, increased crime, and healthcare costs.

Once the team has collected the required input data, the process for completing an economic analysis involves building a spreadsheet that allows the positive and negative impacts to be entered for every year of the project, from construction through to end of life and any post-closure impacts. The process involves:

- Enter the economic impact data for each factor into the spreadsheet. For example, for carbon emissions enter the social cost of carbon in $/tCO2.

- For each option, enter the magnitude of the impact for each year of the life of the project, such as the carbon emissions for each year of construction, operations, and restoration.

- Calculate the annual financial impact of each factor by multiplying the economic impact by the magnitude of impact.

- Sum up all of the positive and negative impacts to get the overall impact per year across the life of the project. It can be helpful at this stage to graph the annual impact data to see how the benefits and costs of the project change over time.

- Use a net present value (NPV) function to calculate the overall economic impact of the project. Selecting the interest rate to use in the NPV calculation can be difficult. Organizations may want to use their cost of capital (interest rate for borrowing money), which tends to devalue future costs, but social groups prefer lower interest rates that reflect the longer-term impacts of projects. Performing a scenario analysis with a range of interest rates can demonstrate whether the selected option changes depending on the choice of interest rate.

### Reality Check

Environmental economics is one of the most comprehensive methods of making project decisions, but this makes it difficult for project design teams to complete on their own without the support of an environmental economist who specializes in collecting and interpreting the data required for the input to the calculations. For this reason, it is often limited to large-scale decision making during the concept or feasibility stages of the project or for decisions that will have a major impact on the overall impact of the project.

The process also has a number of challenges that need to be considered when using output from the economic calculations, including:

1. The process will often emphasize short-term impacts over long-term impacts, especially if the calculations use a net present value (NPV) approach that devalues future impacts.

2. The process does not differentiate between winners and losers of a design decision so the selected option might have a high positive economic benefit for the project owner (profits) and the local government (tax revenue) but might have a negative impact on the local community. One approach to understand this is to run the analysis using only the economic impacts to the local community and see if the selected option creates positive local benefits.

3. The process of converting environmental and social impacts into financial indicators (money) can create a negative perception in the local community. Economists and actuaries might be able to put a dollar value on a human life, but it is difficult to discuss this with local communities when it is their lives that are being affected.

Despite these challenges, environmental economics "provides a fully quantitative, objective, and rational way to include all of the social, environmental, and economic issues relevant to a decision into one comprehensive analysis."[5]

## 10.6   Designing for Climate Change

It is difficult to write a chapter about integrating sustainability into project design without paying special attention to the challenges of climate change. Designing for climate change is becoming increasingly important as the impacts of climate change are being felt around the world and the social and political pressure to reduce carbon emissions continues to grow.

Good design should never be built on an optimistic view of the future but on a realistic or even pessimistic view of the future that includes safety factors built into design calculations to manage future risks. Engineering design models that use local weather – wind speed, precipitation, temperature – need to be adapted to pessimistic climate scenarios and not just to historical ranges or published values.

The same applies to financial analysis for design options. Do you select alternatives based on current capital and operating costs or do you evaluate the potential for operating costs to change over time, especially the potential increased cost of greenhouse gas emissions? Following are some things that design teams and project decision makers should consider when considering options for the project.

## Safety in Design

Safety in design principles can be applied to climate adaptation that includes how local weather events like natural disasters and rising temperatures can have an impact on human health and safety. This can include a broad range of topics from the safety of employees during extreme weather events to the health of employees and the local community that can be impacted by disease spread due to flooding or poor air quality from forest fires near the project.

## Weather During Construction

Climate change is causing an increase in the frequency and severity of storms and rising temperatures that can directly affect project construction. Construction planning needs to include emergency response and health and safety plans that incorporate extreme weather, storms, and heat events. This could include scheduling construction activities to avoid the riskiest times of year for weather events, including scheduling of work crews that are being flown to remote sites and could be stranded by bad weather.

The design of construction equipment like cranes and scaffolding needs to take into account potential weather events so that equipment will survive extreme storms or can be taken down quickly if an extreme storm is forecast.

## Weather During Operations

The same principle applies to the design of structures and equipment for full-scale operations. The project design needs to incorporate resilient infrastructure that can withstand more severe storms, wind, increased precipitation, and flooding. Many regions have rules to protect waterways that require infrastructure to be built a certain distance from the high-water mark, but increased flooding is changing the high-water mark. If your project is located near water, the design needs to evaluate if increased flooding will put infrastructure at risk or change the high-water mark on nearby streams and waterways that will limit where you can locate infrastructure.

## Sea Level Rise

Similar to flooding risks, docks and near-water infrastructure on or near oceans could be impacted by rising sea levels and extreme storm events that increase storm surges and damage project facilities. Design work should include conservative predictions of sea level and storm damage to ensure that infrastructure is resilient and safe for workers.

Impacts to port facilities can also have an effect along the project supply chain. Logistics plans for both construction and operations should include contingency for extreme weather and rising sea levels that might impact shipping for equipment suppliers and product shipments.

## Water Shortages and Droughts

With rising temperatures and changes in precipitation, increasing areas of the world are being impacted by drought and water shortages. If your project is located in an area that is currently facing these challenges or is predicted to face these challenges in the future, then the project design should incorporate water management strategies not just to manage the project's water supply but also to consider how the project could have an impact on the local water supply either through damage to existing water resources or through competition for scarce water resources. Protection of the local community's water supply is one of the areas where projects can face the strongest local opposition to the project development. So a well-developed water management plan is critical not just for creating a successful project but also for maintaining community support for the project.

## Biomimicry

One field of study that project design teams are investigating to help build more resilient projects is biomimicry, where concepts from nature are used to improve designs that often have a lower total cost of ownership as well. These concepts have led to buildings designed with termite mound structures to provide natural air flow and cooling to stormwater management systems that use natural streams instead of culverts and pipes.

## Nature-Based Solutions

A related approach is to use nature-based solutions (NBS), also referred to as ecosystem services, which recognizes that the natural environment is a resource for project development and operations. NBS is defined as "actions to protect, sustainably manage and restore natural or modified ecosystems, which address societal challenges effectively and adaptively, while simultaneously providing human well-being and biodiversity benefits."[6]

These concepts have typically been used for the development and restoration of natural resources for public infrastructure for water management and managing severe storms. But they can also be used to improve the design of any major project. The concepts of NBS can be applied to a number of project design areas, including:

- Improved water management and security to support facility operations
- Disaster risk reduction by providing natural buffers for flooding and extreme weather events
- Mitigation of increased temperatures by using natural surfaces to reduce heat-island effects around project facilities
- Improved ecological restoration as part of progressive reclamation or closure requirements (see Chapter 14)

## Logistics Footprint

Projects often limit the assessment of their environmental footprint to the boundaries of the project and do not consider the impact of transporting materials to and from the site. The design and project planning should consider where equipment, materials, and supplies are coming from and how they will reach the project site. Transporting materials by rail or ship has a lower carbon footprint than transporting by truck. Buying local can reduce the footprint for transportation and support the local economy.

## Carbon Pricing Scenario Analysis

The cost of carbon can have an impact on the design and operation of a project and the range of possible carbon pricing should be included in feasibility studies and design options analysis. The current average carbon price is approximately $US 16/tCO_2$ (in 2018) but economists have determined that carbon pricing as high as $200/tCO_2$ may be necessary to control carbon emissions.

The project team needs to establish a project forecast based on a standard set of assumptions that can be used for all decision making. This will help ensure that informed decisions are made that will protect the project and the organization from future risks.

One example is from the International Finance Corporation (IFC), that provides funding for global projects, and has developed a range of carbon prices that start at $30/tCO_2$ and increase to $80/tCO_2$ by 2050:

> The International Finance Corporation (IFC) has operated a carbon pricing pilot since November 2016 using price levels of $US30/tCO_2e$ in 2016, increasing to $US80/tCO_2e$ by 2050. The price is applied to the economic rate of return analysis of project finance investments in the cement, thermal power and chemicals sectors, and is considered as one of several inputs into the investment decision. The price is applied to gross Scope 1 and 2 emissions. The IFC is moving to full implementation in project finance deals in the three sectors listed above, and plans to pilot the application of a carbon price to project finance investments in other sectors with annual emissions above 25 $ktCO_2e$.[7]

## Future Proofing the Design

Climate change won't just change the weather and the operating costs of the project; it is also driving technological change that will have an impact on operating the project. Project teams need to consider in their design work the rapid evolution of renewable energy, energy storage, electric vehicles, and other technologies that reduce energy use and carbon footprint. These changes are accelerating, and the project should include scenario analysis that looks at the future of energy and carbon management, can help teams to understand potential changes, and to design the project with the ability to adapt to changes over time. These changes could also include the evolution of other technical trends that could impact projects, including the Internet of Things (IoT), electrification, and autonomous vehicles.

## Renewable Energy

One key area of design that projects need to consider is the use of renewable energy to replace traditional hydrocarbon power systems. Using renewable energy like solar and wind power can be more complicated to design than a diesel generator, but recent advancements in energy storage and micro-grid energy management has made these systems much more reliable for facility operations.

Industrial facilities also have the opportunity to adapt renewable energy and energy storage to fit with the requirements of an industrial facility instead of the requirements of the electrical grid. These facilities can find ways of integrating renewable energy and energy storage directly into facility operations by looking at nonelectrical applications. One example is solar thermal systems that can store thermal energy for future electrical generation, operate as combined heat and power (CHP) plants, or provide thermal energy for industrial processes such as heating, drying, or distillation.

## Climate Impacts versus Project Impacts

Another reason to look carefully at the potential impacts of climate change is to understand that climate change could have an effect on the local ecosystem, which adds to the environmental impacts from the project. The combined impacts could create unexpected consequences that could be viewed as the impact of just the project. The design of water use, emissions controls, and environmental footprint for the project needs to incorporate the potential for climate change impacts to be additive and for the project to become responsible for the combined effects of project impacts and climate impacts. If your facility is near an ecologically sensitive area or an area that is expected to go through major changes due to climate change, then it may be necessary to manage the project's impacts more carefully than required under regulations.

# 10.7  Summary

Project design is becoming more complicated as local communities become more aware and more actively engaged in project development. At the same time, increased scrutiny on environmental impacts and the rapidly changing response to climate change are making project design more challenging because it is harder to predict what the future will look like.

Integrating sustainability concepts into design provides project teams with the ability to better assess future scenarios, meet regulatory requirements for project permitting, and engage with local communities to develop better design solutions and build better projects.

Decision-making tools also need to be modified to allow social and environmental issues to be incorporate into decision making for design options. The tools we have discussed in this chapter can also be used in other areas, especially procurement decisions, as discussed in the next chapter where social and environmental issues can be used to select equipment, suppliers, and contractors who will help the project meet its sustainability goals.

# Endnotes

1. Bill Lennertz and Aarin Lutzenhiser, "The NCI Charrette System™ for Transit Oriented Development," Federal Transit Administration, March 2013, accessed on December 2018 at https://www.transit.dot.gov/sites/fta.dot.gov/files/NCI_Guide_8-14-13sm_0.pdf.
2. Transportation Research Board, "NCHRP Report 480: A Guide to Best Practices for Achieving Context Sensitive Solutions," 2002, accessed December 2018 at http://onlinepubs.trb.org/onlinepubs/nchrp/nchrp_rpt_480.pdf.
3. Sustainable Aviation Guidance Alliance, "Sustainable Aviation Resource Guide: Planning, Implementing and Maintaining a Sustainability Program at Airports," 2009, accessed December 2018 at www.airportsustainability.org/sites/default/files/SAGA%20Final2.pdf.
4. McPhee, W., and Powell, J., "A Practical Approach to Sustainable Decision Making," *Environmental Management*, May 2011.
5. Paul Hardisty, *Environmental and Economic Sustainability* (CRC Press, 2010).
6. Cohen-Shacham, E., Walters, G., Janzen, C., and Maginnis, S. (eds.). "Nature-based Solutions to address global societal challenges" (Gland, Switzerland: IUCN, 2016).
7. World Bank and Ecofys. "State and Trends of Carbon Pricing 2018 (May)," World Bank, Washington, DC, 2018. DOI: 10.1596/978-1-4648-1292-7.

# CHAPTER 11

# Procurement

We have thus far discussed how to integrate sustainability into project management, stakeholder engagement, and design, but the place where all this good work becomes reality is during procurement. Procurement starts the process of converting ideas into reality by purchasing the key services equipment, materials, and contractors that will build the project.

When we talk about sustainable procurement, we are really talking about is smart and strategic procurement. The World Bank presents this very clearly:

> It is said that sustainable procurement is "smart" procurement, as it takes a three-dimensional life cycle approach versus the traditional one-dimensional, economics-focused approach. Three-dimensional thinking (economic, environmental and social) does not mean it takes three times longer, nor is the outcome necessarily more expensive. Sustainable procurement is strategic procurement practice at its optimum.[1]

Integrating sustainability into procurement practices requires a clear set of objectives for project procurement and strategies to meet these objectives, and then integrating sustainability into how the project requests quotes from vendors, how decisions are made, and how contracts are managed. Managing sustainable procurement on major projects cannot be done with checklists or standard templates because each major project has a unique set of challenges, risks, and opportunities that need to be understood. Each project will need a procurement plan that reflects the unique project design, geography, environment, society, regulatory issues, and local supply chain.

There is a tendency to assume that integrating sustainability into procurement will increase the price of the project, but this is not typically the case. Procurement teams, working in conjunction with the rest of the project team, strategic suppliers, and the local community, will often find creative solutions that reduce costs, manage risks, and lead to better projects.

This chapter will look at the planning aspects of procurement, including developing a procurement plan and a local economic development plan to guide procurement activities. The planning leads into detailed discussion of the key elements of procurement for major projects, including equipment and materials, supplies and services, logistics to the project site, and working with contractors.

# 11.1  Procurement Plan

Like the project execution plan (discussed in Chapter 5), the project's procurement plan should be integrated with the project's sustainability goals and objectives. Establishing up front what the values and objectives of the procurement program will be and providing the team with tools and resources to incorporate sustainability into the procurement of equipment, materials, and contractor labor is necessary to ensure that the planning and design work can create a better project.

## Establishing Values

A key element to the procurement plan is to establish procurement values. These values should build on the overall values established for the project, while also focused on the unique challenges faced by the procurement team. Some values that align with sustainable procurement include fairness and transparency, inclusiveness, and active engagement.

Fairness and transparency are important for the project team to ensure that local communities understand the procurement process and feel that they are being treated fairly. Building trust with local communities is critical to maintaining community support for the entire project. Many projects have lost that trust when promises of good paying jobs made during early engagement and the approvals process did not become a reality during the procurement and construction phases. A focus on fairness and transparency could lead to procurement activities that include:

- Establishing clear requirements in job descriptions and bid documents
- Wherever possible, using plain language bids and contracts and translating documents into the local language(s), if needed, to improve communication
- Appropriately sized contracts so that smaller local firms can compete for contracts
- Structured decision making to clearly show how bid decisions will be made
- Ethical procurement standards to avoid the perception of bias

Incorporating inclusiveness into procurement plans helps to establish programs to ensure that all groups have an opportunity to be involved in the project either through contracts, employment, or skills development. Reaching out to diverse groups and developing plans that could include a wide range of participants including:

- Local communities
- Indigenous groups
- Women

- Youth
- Disabled persons

Procurement teams will often visit large suppliers to assess their capabilities and see new technologies, but equally important is visiting the project site and spending time with the local community and local suppliers. Even better is to establish a procurement office in the local community to build relationships and support local suppliers and potential employees. A locally engaged procurement team can help to identify opportunities not only to reduce costs by using local suppliers, but also help build local relationships and strengthen the community support for the project.

Engaging with local businesses and community leaders can help to expand local supply chains by assessing:

- What types of work can be done locally?
- What skill sets are available?
- What local businesses could be expanded or created to support both construction and future operations?
- What barriers exist for local businesses to bid on contracts or subcontracts?
- What training is required for local businesses to successfully bid on project contracts?

Documenting procurement values and the activities that will be taken to achieve those values can provide a foundation for the procurement team and provide alignment with the other sustainability programs, including the sustainability framework, as discussed in Chapter 8.

## Setting Objectives

Traditionally, procurement objectives were limited to meeting minimum technical specifications for the lowest possible cost. Over time, quality requirements were added, and safety became a key requirement. Procurement objectives have now expanded to being able to de-risk projects to avoid disruption and schedule delays, minimize the total cost of ownership (TCO) in addition to capital cost, meet the project commitments to the local community and government regulators, and build community support for the project.

Risk reduction as a key project objective that requires the proposal team to assess high-priority procurement packages from the perspective of the highest price and by which packages have the potential to create the largest risk to the project. These are not solely sustainability related, but could include long-lead items, logistics routes that are at risk of disruption due to weather or conflict, and currency fluctuations. The risk procedures outlined in Chapter 7 can be used to assess procurement risk and to ensure that risk management plans are in place for high risk packages.

Evaluating TCO requires design and procurement teams to assess the total cost over the life of the project when making purchasing decisions. TCO includes:

- The capital expenditure (CAPEX) of equipment costs, the costs for construction and commissioning
- Financing costs

- The operating expenditures (OPEX), including maintenance, waste management, supplies, and services
- Taxes and royalties
- The cost for closure, decommissioning, or recapitalization, depending on the project being developed

Using a TCO approach to assess bid packages can be a more challenging task for procurement teams, but it can be critical to understanding the full project value when comparing competing bids. This approach does not have to be used for every bid package, but it does provide value when used for equipment that has high operating costs, or where there is a range of differing options that are best compared using full lifecycle costs.

One of the reasons that we mention TCO in a book about integrating sustainability into major projects is that looking at costs over the entire project helps to align typical short-term thinking associated with project delivery with the longer-term thinking of the local community.

TCO analysis can also lead to some more creative procurement strategies where equipment leasing or alternative financing arrangements can be used to expand the traditional view that projects have of buying equipment. For example, installing renewable energy to provide power to a facility will often have a high capital cost and lower operating costs than tradition diesel power sources. Project procurement and finance teams can develop strategies that leverage an independent power producer (IPP) to design, finance, build, and operate the energy infrastructure, and sell power at a set rate to the facility. Not only does this reduce capital expenditures, but it can also provide stable long-term power costs instead of using traditional fuels that come with uncertain future commodity prices and the potential for carbon taxes.

Using IPP strategies can also be done in cooperation with the local community so that the project facility is not the only user of the electrical utility. This approach shifts risk by adding additional customers to the IPP contract, and it helps local communities establish a stable and low-cost energy supply.

In Chapter 8, we presented the process for tracking commitments through a commitment action log. Setting objectives for the procurement plan should, at a minimum, establish that all procurement-related commitments will be met and, if not achievable, that they will be discussed with the project team and the stakeholder group to whom the commitment was made, the objective of which is to proactively reset the commitment to an achievable goal. The procurement team can also go beyond the stated commitments and look to build strong relations with the local community, which can lead to improved performance and a better project. Some of the tools and programs that can help to build better projects are discussed in later in this chapter.

## Supporting Innovation

Innovation can be a key factor in successfully integrating sustainability into major projects. Typically, innovation is seen as a design or engineering function (see Chapter 10), but procurement is also a critical part of project innovation. Procurement teams can:

- Ensure that innovative designs can be implemented and constructed
- Create new solutions for logistics that reduce impacts and improve safety

- Find new ways of supporting the local economy
- Create a structure to promote innovation from suppliers and contractors by shifting from conformance-based specification to results-based specifications

Project design teams typically develop detailed specifications for equipment suppliers and contractors that are based on proven equipment and methods and provide them to suppliers. But this approach does not support newer technologies or methods that do not conform to bid specifications, and so the project ends up with outdated equipment. This can not only impact environmental performance but can also lead to higher overall project costs due to inefficient equipment or construction methods.

An alternative approach is to use results-based or performance-based specifications where the design team provides the required performance or outcomes, and the supplier or contractor is given the freedom to determine how to achieve those objectives. This approach allows equipment suppliers to identify products or technologies that would fulfill the performance requirements and price, and to meet goals for energy usage or environmental impact. It allows contractors to propose methods that optimize construction methodologies to minimize impacts on the local community or suggest training plans to maximize local labor.

Implementing a results-based procurement approach typically shifts the high level of effort and time investment from up front to a high time commitment when bid documents are received and reviewed, which can create challenges for the project team. Detailed review of the bid documents will be required to ensure that suppliers and contractors are meeting the required outcomes. Structured decision methods (described in Chapter 10) that allow proposals to be ranked by a range of objectives can help procurement teams to assess multiple bids that use different approaches to solve the same project challenge.

It may be necessary to use a combined approach that uses the conformance-based for core design items and the innovative results-based specifications for utility or support components like power, water, maintenance, and logistics structures. Building innovation into the procurement strategy and plan can not only help to achieve sustainability goals and commitments but can also help the project to reduce costs and reduce risks by applying the insights of both the design team and the larger ecosystem of suppliers and contractors.

## 11.2   Economic Development Plan

One of the key positive benefits that major projects have on local communities is to promote local capacity building and economic development. It is often one of the key selling points for major projects as they work through government approvals and building community support. So it is critical that the project team and, in particular, the procurement team understand and deliver on the expectations and commitments that the project has made to the local community. It is also important to remember that this is not done just to appease the local community. Creating a strong local economy, including local suppliers, skilled labor, and healthy employees ensures the success of the project and operation over the long run, which reduces operating costs and improves profits.

One way to create a focus on achieving these goals is to create an economic development plan either as an integral component of the procurement plan or as a stand-alone document that supplements the procurement plan. The economic development plan can capture opportunities to help grow the local economy, document initiatives for improving local economic development, establish how the team will meet project commitments, and determine how they will manage these programs and track performance.

One advantage of keeping the economic development plan separate from the procurement plan is that it allows the procurement team to engage with local community and local government representatives to build a stronger plan based on engagement and consultation. Using the working group model for this specific engagement (see Chapter 6), an economic development working group would involve local community members and other key stakeholders to help streamline development of the economic development plan. This approach gets everyone in the same room to develop shared goals, opportunities, and processes for the plan.

Elements to include in an economic development plan will vary depending on the specific opportunities for each project but could include chapters on:

- Supplier development procedure
- Economic development benefits reporting procedures
- Diversity and inclusion processes and procedures
- Hiring and skills development plans
- Indigenous contracting and procurement procedures
- Supplier and contractor prequalification procedures

The economic development plan may also be included in the development of a community agreement, which is discussed in Chapter 6, "Stakeholder Engagement."

## Supporting Local Employees

In most cases, people working on the project consider themselves to be "project" employees and not contractor employees, so any employment issues with a contractor are viewed as an issue with the project. And this would reflect on the organization developing the project.

The procurement team, working with representatives from human resources (HR) and construction management, should ensure that there are clear expectations for all contractors to ensure that they are treating local employees the same way that the project is treating their direct hires. Minimum HR requirements should be identified in all contractor procurement documents to ensure that the project team is able to address issues as they develop during project delivery. Some topics that might need to be addressed, depending the project, include:

- Diversity
- Youth employment
- Training and skills employee development programs
- Safety expectations

- Employee health, benefits, access to health care
- Holidays and vacations

The project team should also develop an employee grievance procedure that applies to direct project employees and to contractor and subcontractor employees working on the project.

## Local Capacity Building

Creating a local capacity building strategy is critical to ensuring that opportunities for local employment is optimized. Projects are often sold based on the ability to create jobs, and procurement teams need to understand what commitments have been made, what the local community expects, and how the project can demonstrate that local jobs are being created.

One key to developing a successful capacity building strategy is to start early in the project to ensure alignment with the local community and the local government. This gives the project time to train local employees and demonstrate commitment to local employment during the regulatory approval process, which helps earn community support and reduce schedule delays for approvals.

The project team might be tempted to train the local community on low-skill-level jobs that require the least investment in training. However, a more strategic approach is to identify skills development opportunities that align with project goals for building community support and lowering overall labor costs for construction and operations.

The first priority should be to align capacity building with requirements for the project and for future operations. The cost savings of a good-capacity building strategy can be evaluated by comparing training costs with the costs of bringing in outside labor (fly-in, fly-out approach) and the reduced risk of travel and schedule disruptions during construction. Disruptions can occur when extreme weather or other events prevent outside labor from traveling to the project site.

A second priority is to look at transferable skills that can support the delivery of the project and support the local community. By building up overall capacity of the local community, the project earns community support as well as establishing a strong local base for the long-term success of the operations. Some of the skills sets that can be useful to local communities might include:

- Safety, emergency response, emergency medical, and fire and rescue services
- Health services
- Business management
- Skilled trades like plumbing, electrical, and welding
- Computer/IT support
- Water and waste water treatment
- Environmental monitoring

The project team will need help identifying the types of skill sets that would benefit the local community. If an economic development working group has been established, then this topic can be raised with them. And if there is not a working group, the team will need to discuss establishing priority skills training programs with community leaders, local businesses, and local educational institutions.

Capacity building should also be discussed with government agencies who have a mandate to provide skills development and education. Depending on the location and size of the project, there may be government programs available to support capacity building training that reduces project costs and improves the overall success of a capacity building program. Other industries operating in the same region may also be potential partners who can collaborate and support local capacity building.

One often overlooked opportunity for building capacity is to examine skills of the local communities that can be transferred to the project team and provide a benefit to the overall project. The local knowledge of environment, animal life, weather, geography, site access, and how to adapt to the local climate can be extremely valuable to the project. Taking the time to ask questions and listen to local knowledge not only can provide valuable insights but can also help build a trust relationship between the local community and the project team.

This approach is not to suggest that procurement teams are responsible for performing all of the capacity building training, but they do need to contribute to the achievement of these goals. The procurement team needs to build a comprehensive plan to incorporate capacity building into supplier and contractor bids. For example:

- Piping and plumbing contractors can be required to provide apprentice opportunities for local employees to gain experience and certification.
- The wastewater treatment system provider can be required to include training and operating manuals in the local language for employees to learn how the system works.
- Medical services providers for the construction camp can provide training to local healthcare workers.

Although every project is different, all have the opportunity to improve skills and capabilities for the local community.

# 11.3   Equipment and Materials

The procurement of equipment and materials can have a significant impact on the sustainability of the overall project. In most cases, large equipment and construction materials suppliers will not be located near the project site and so the procurement team might not need to evaluate local supply options or community impacts. The procurement team can still integrate sustainability into procurement by looking at how the selection of equipment and material suppliers will impact sustainability throughout the supply chain.

## Responsible Supply Chain

Developing a responsible supply chain for equipment and supplies means moving beyond a focus on finding the cheapest price and looking at the broader impacts of the supply chain. Resources to help develop responsible supply chains are typically focused on operations that are producing consumer goods, but the same concepts can be applied to developing major projects.

Selecting what issues to focus on to assess the supply chain can be a challenge. One approach is to take the sustainability goals that have been established for the project and extend them to the supply chain. If the project is striving to reduce the carbon footprint, then ask suppliers how they are managing their carbon footprint in the bid documents. If the project is focused on labor standards in the local community, then ask how suppliers are treating their workers.

Some of the key issues that might be included in a responsible supply chain strategy for major projects are:

- Renewable energy, energy efficiency, and GHG emissions
- Resource depletion
- Chemical pollution and waste management
- Depletion of fresh water and biodiversity loss
- Activities in conflict zones
- Workplace health and safety, worker access to healthcare
- Labor standards including child labor and slavery
- Diversity and inclusion in the workforce
- Bribery, corruption and business ethics

Supply chain risks can also be found a level below the project's primary suppliers. It is important to understand who supplies the suppliers, especially if the supplier is a distributor that just resells equipment or materials. In some cases, the procurement team may need to support suppliers, to help them to meet project requirements through access to resources and training. Engagement with suppliers should go beyond the basic product specifications and price discussion to include how the suppliers can meet the project's supply chain requirements and help the project meet sustainability objectives.

Procurement bid documents should identify clear targets to identify what is expected from suppliers. With the large size of typical contracts for major projects, suppliers who do not meet project requirements will be encouraged to improve their operations and develop the skills necessary to successfully bid on contracts so that they can join the projects responsible supply chain. The bid documents should include a clear indication that the project will be conducting audits to measure performance and determine if suppliers are meeting project requirements.

## Bulk Materials

The procurement of bulk commodities like aggregate and sand, which are often procured locally, needs to be managed carefully. Suppliers of the commodities may not operate their facilities with the same standards as the project. Damage to the environment caused by a commodity supplier can impact the overall sustainability of the project and, if procured locally, could impact the project's reputation and community support.

In particular, concrete sand has been identified in many parts of the world as a scarce commodity and sand suppliers should be carefully reviewed to ensure that their operations are following legal requirements and achieve the project's sustainability objectives.

## Modular Design

Using modular design strategies, where project components are assembled into modular units and then transported to the project site for assembly, is a popular approach for project development. There are numerous advantages from cost savings to safer construction, but there are also disadvantages, including a reduced opportunity for local labor compared to traditional construction methods. The procurement team needs to understand local employment commitments and community expectations when developing bid scopes and evaluating supplier bids to properly assess the potential advantages and risks associated with modular supply.

## Bid Specifications

Bid specifications for equipment and materials need to include energy efficiency and environmental requirements that the project has committed to through both the project approvals and commitments to the local community. If the organization or project complies with international standards, such as the United Nations Global Compact or the Carbon Disclosure Project, then the bid documents can include a request that equipment and material suppliers also become signatories of the selected standards, and therefore follow the required management and reporting requirements.

## Operations and Maintenance

Equipment supply contracts should evaluate total cost of ownership rather than just lowest capital cost. Equipment suppliers may wish to include expensive service contracts that involve the supplier's employees traveling to the site during operations to maintain equipment. Where possible, equipment selection should consider the long-term maintenance of the equipment and whether local employees will be able to service the equipment. Suppliers should be encouraged to include training programs in their bids, as part of commissioning activities, to ensure that local employees know how to maintain and operate the equipment. This will not only create positive benefits from skills development in the local community, but it will also reduce long-term operating costs and improve the total cost of ownership.

## Site Visits

If equipment suppliers will be coming to the project site to install and commission their equipment, then their bid specifications and contracts should include the same requirements that contractors will be required to follow when they attend the site. The contractor requirements could include the project code of conduct, onboarding training and other requirements for working on site that are discussed later in this chapter and in Chapter 12, "Construction Management."

## 11.4 Supplies and Services

In addition to project employment, one of the key project benefits for the local community is the local procurement of goods and services. This can provide employment outside of direct project employment and helps to create a vibrant local economy that supports economic development and provides tax revenue for governments.

Establishing a strong local economy to provide supplies and services also creates benefits for the project and for the organization. The most direct benefit is that committing to using local businesses helps to strengthen community support, which reduces the risk of schedule interruptions due to conflict or delays in government approvals. Over the long run, using local suppliers lowers the total cost of ownership as local supplies and services are located nearby and do not need to be transported over long distances, thus reducing the costs for shipping and the time delay to get required supplies. The investment in developing local businesses may not have a positive payback during construction but it will provide benefits over the life of the project.

### Developing Local Suppliers

As discussed above, developing local suppliers is a component of good community engagement. The procurement team should take time to meet with the local communities, business leaders, economic development agencies, and business associations to explore opportunities. The discussion should include what opportunities there are for the local community to engage in the supply chain, what the local community is skilled at, and what skills they would like to learn or improve upon.

The procurement team should meet with the local business community to identify gaps in the local capabilities that must be addressed to increase the volume of local suppliers on the project. After identifying gaps, the team can provide support for the local suppliers to improve their capabilities and ensure that they are prepared to work on the project. This could be done directly by the proposal team or could be done by working with training companies or project contractors. One approach is to have established contractors form joint ventures with local businesses to encourage knowledge and skills transfer that would benefit both the project and the local business community.

### STORY: SUPPORTING LOCAL CONTRACTORS

During meetings with local businesses we quickly identified that one of the problems with our contracting procedures was going to be the strict corporate requirement for good safety statistics. The local businesses weren't necessarily working unsafely, but they didn't track safety statistics and so would not even get through the contractor registration requirements to be included in future bids. In order to meet project commitments for local contracting, we would need to train local businesses on our safety requirements and on how to track key safety statistics like their total recordable incident frequency rate, so that they could register and bid on the upcoming contracts.

## 11.5   Logistics

One of the most overlooked topics for sustainable procurement is managing logistics to minimize negative impacts and find opportunities to create additional benefits for the local community. Negative impacts from bringing equipment, materials, supplies, and people to the project site can range from road safety issues and traffic disruptions to environmental impacts (noise, dust, and emissions).

### Road Safety

Transportation safety can be a surprising impact to the project's safety risk. Most project safety programs do not include safety incidents beyond the project boundaries in their reportable safety statistics. Road accidents are considered the responsibility of transportation companies and are not considered project impacts, but this view may not be shared by the local community.

The World Health Organization considers road safety to be a major concern for economic development:

> Road traffic injuries are a major public health problem and a leading cause of death and injury around the world. Each year nearly 1.3 million people die and millions more are injured or disabled as a result of road crashes, mostly in low- and middle-income countries. As well as creating enormous social costs for individuals, families and communities, road traffic injuries place a heavy burden on health services and economies. The cost to countries, many of which already struggle with economic development, may be as much as 1–2% of their gross national product. As motorization increases, preventing road traffic crashes and the injuries they inflict will become an increasing social and economic challenge, particularly in developing countries. If present trends continue, road traffic injuries will increase dramatically in most parts of the world over the next two decades, with the greatest impact falling on the most vulnerable citizens.[2]

When developing routes and planning logistics, the project team should evaluate the risk of an accident, injury, or death due to road accidents. The likelihood of an event can be calculated by multiplying the total distance traveled by each type of equipment by the local road injury and fatality incident rates. Most jurisdictions provide statistics on the frequency of road injuries and fatalities in events per 1 billion kilometers traveled, or statistics from similar areas can be used.

The logistics team can calculate the total expected distance traveled for delivery of equipment, materials, and people to the site based on the distance from the source of the materials (or port facility) to the project site, multiplied by the number of trips required to bring all the required materials and people to the site. For example, a major project site that is located 500 km (one way) from a port facility and requires 1,000 truckloads of equipment, materials, and supplies will have 1,000,000 km of total distance traveled. Using typical road safety statistics of 20 fatalities and 500 serious injuries per 1 billion km, the likelihood of a road fatality is 2% and serious injury is 50%. These numbers would be unacceptable for most construction sites but are not typically considered in project safety or risk discussions.

It is important to take the time to calculate road safety risks and decide if it is an acceptable risk for the project. If not, then it is important to find ways to improve traffic safety through route selection, speed control, driver training, contractor selection, and clear communication with the local community. It is also important to track traffic incidents and make them part of the safety metrics even if they will not be part of the project's official reported total recordable incident frequency (TRIF) rate. Track your contractors and treat every accident as a near miss that requires an investigation and corrective action under the health and safety plan. If there are trends or locations where accidents are happening more frequently, be proactive and engage with the local community to find a solution, such as installing traffic controls or improving communication.

A number of measures can be taken to reduce the risk of injury and to mitigate risks, such as:

- Incorporate local traffic patterns, school schedules, and local events into logistics plans
- Plan for regular communication with the local community on traffic patterns, large equipment schedule, and road closures.
- Evaluate and discuss road infrastructure with local government to ensure that traffic lights or stop signs are present where they can help to reduce incidents.
- Ensure that emergency response plans are in place to respond to accidents, spills, and other events.
- Discuss emergency response and hospital care with local service providers to evaluate whether they have the capabilities to deal with an increase in injuries and whether the project needs to provide support during construction.
- Incorporate weather and other risks into logistics planning.
- Track project vehicles to evaluate speed, especially near communities and high-risk areas like schools and playgrounds.
- Identify vehicles with a project identifier and phone number so that community members can raise issues or call to complain.

## STORY: WORKING WITH A LOGISTICS CONTRACTOR TO IMPROVE SAFETY

As we were developing the logistics plan for a remote site, we became concerned about the potential safety of truck drivers who would be making hundreds of trips along a gravel road with poor communications and no emergency response. Drivers would be away from support for over 10 hours and potentially even longer in bad weather. Road safety statistics suggested that there was a high risk of an accident along the road, including the potential for collisions with cars and pickups driven by the local community.

Given the potential risks, we challenged the three transportation companies that we had shortlisted in the bid process to develop a safety plan that would address this key risk. One firm developed a simple approach that involved establishing a waystation halfway along the route at an old construction site that could be equipped with emergency response equipment, maintenance equipment, communications, emergency fuel, and a driver rest area. The station would be staffed by trained local community members who lived nearby.

Surprisingly, the approach didn't just help reduce community concerns about road safety; it also provided the transportation company with more flexibility in their scheduling, reduced equipment risk, and improved driver experience. The result was a bid that not only met our requirements but was also less expensive than their competitors. Creative problem solving led not just to a safer logistics plan but a cheaper one as well.

## Environmental Impact

Another key topic to evaluate as part of logistics planning is potential environmental impacts associated with moving equipment, materials, and people to the project site. Each mode of transportation has different impacts and potential mitigation strategies, but we will focus on two of the most common modes: shipping and trucking.

Transportation by shipping can include transport of global equipment and supplies that are brought directly to the project site or to a port facility nearby. Potential environmental impacts can include:

- Air emissions from fuels, especially when ships are near shore or docked
- Carbon emissions from transportation
- Transport of invasive species in ballast water
- Dumping of bilge water, gray water, and waste in local waters

Procurement of shipping contractors should address these risks and request that the shipping company provide information on how they manage environmental impacts. This could include looking at the carbon footprint of each transportation option. There are also a number of guidance documents and best practices available for shipping, such as the International Maritime Organization (IMO) rules on clean fuels.

Most major projects have a significant amount of trucking and there can be a number of environmental impacts from the movement of trucks on both public and project roads, including:

- Air pollution from diesel exhaust
- Air pollution from dust, especially on gravel roads
- Carbon emissions from transportation
- Waste management from drivers (food packaging, etc.)
- Waste management from maintenance activities (waste oil, etc.)

The procurement team can request that truck transportation companies have an environmental management plan for the project that describes how they will manage their potential impact, minimize the potential for environmental damage, and manage complaints from communities along the transportation routes.

## Supply Chain Risk

There are number of supply chain risks that are associated with sustainability topics. One risk is that the increase in extreme weather events has the potential to impact a number of project activities, including transportation. The logistics team should evaluate the potential impacts to project schedule from extreme weather events along the entire supply route.

Another risk is the possibility for protests along transportation routes. The local community may be supportive of the project but other communities along the supply route may not want the disruption or risk of the project traffic without seeing any benefits from the project. It is important to identify stakeholders along the route as well as at the project site, as discussed in Chapter 6.

## Connection to Markets

With improved transportation comes the movement of people, ideas, and the connection of marketplaces. This connection creates opportunities for economic development, access to markets, and improved communication with the rest of the world. It also brings the risk of disease, drugs and weapons trafficking, invasive plants and animals, uncontrolled immigration, crime, and a dilution or even loss of local culture and language.

The activities of project teams can have an influence on whether increasing the connection of a remote community to the rest of the world is an overall positive or negative experience. The organization and project team can choose to ignore these local impacts and leave the management of the changes in the hands of the local government. Or they can pursue initiatives that will assist the local community to adapt to the expected changes.

# 11.6   Contractors

Contractor actions are often a source of misunderstood risks for projects. Local communities do not typically distinguish between project employees and contractors. The general perception is that everyone belongs to "the project" regardless of who they officially work for. The project team needs to carefully consider how the actions of the contractors could impact the project and include clear procedures for managing these impacts. Sustainability requirements should be made clear to contractors from the start of the procurement process. Ensure requirements are included in contracts and enforceable in the case a problem arises. Clear rules and metrics should be required so that issues and non-compliances can be easily identified, and actions can be taken to correct the issues.

Integrating sustainability into contractor management should follow a defined process that fits with organizations procurement process. It can include:

1. Alignment and planning
2. Contractor screening and requisition
3. Selecting contractors
4. Contractor development
5. Monitoring performance
6. Contract closeout

## Alignment and Planning

The first step in the procurement process should be to ensure that contractors are made aware of the broad project sustainability goals and requirements as part of early engagement and expression of interest (EOI) processes, by providing them with project information. The contractors should be requested to provide their capabilities to address these requirements as part of their EOI submission. Contractors should also understand that they will be responsible for the performance of their subcontractors and that the sustainability requirements are to be applied to subcontractors.

Planning for sustainable procurement should also include prioritizing bid packages based on the potential for community impacts and project risks. An electrical contractor who is installing wiring in a building will have a much lower set of risks than an earthworks contractor who is building a road base near a sensitive ecological area. High risk packages will need a higher level of scrutiny and attention to ensure that the selected contractor will meet the project's sustainability goals.

Another component of procurement planning is the size of contracts. Using a few large contracts can be a benefit for the procurement team as they can be easier to manage, and the project has leverage to drive down prices. But large contracts will often restrict the ability of local contractors to bid on the work. If the project team has worked with the local community to identify the types of contracts that local contractors can bid on, then the contracts can be structured into smaller packages in areas that the local firms can bid on but maintain larger packages of more specialized work that will require external contractors.

Another benefit of smaller packages is that the team can stage contracts so that the construction management team has leverage over the contractors. If contractors understand that strong performance on schedule, quality, safety, and sustainability metrics will help them to earn the next contract, then they will be more likely to meet sustainability objectives and work with the construction team to resolve issues.

## Contractor Screening and Requisition

The next step is to screen contractors based on their response to the EOI and identify contractors that meet the project's requirements for quality, safety, environmental protection, and social responsibility. Contractor screening can use a scorecard or multi-criteria decision process as discussed in Chapter 10.

Request for proposal documents should include available documents that the contractor will be required to follow to ensure contractor scopes meet project requirements. This also avoids the potential for change orders during construction if contractors claim they were not aware of specific environmental or sustainability requirements.

Contracts also need to include the ability to remove contractors and subcontractors from the project for poor performance and to allow termination without penalty, if required, to protect the project's reputation and support from the local community. The text below should not be considered legal advice in any way but is intended to provide a rough guideline for termination language to give the project team the ability to manage future issues with contractors during construction, if required.

## GUIDANCE: CONTRACT LANGUAGE TO TERMINATE A CONTRACTOR FOR POOR SUSTAINABILITY PERFORMANCE

Maintaining a positive relationship with the local community of _____ (name of community) and maintaining strong community support for the project is critical to the overall success of the _____ (name of project) project. Failure to maintain the project's community support could result in material financial loss, cost overruns and schedule delays for the project.

As a result, _____ (organization name) requires that all contractors, including their subcontractors, employees, and agents, respect and follow the rules and requirements set out in the project approvals and operating procedures, as updated at the time of the work, which include environmental protection plans, permits and approvals, code of conduct, human resources policies, and communication plans as identified in the list of applicable project documents identified in this RFP.

In the event that a contractor, including subcontractors, employees, or agents, fail to properly implement the requirements, _____ (organization name) will have the right to terminate this contract, remove the contractor, associated subcontractors, and agents, from the project site at the contractor's expense, and terminate all existing contracts if the contractor does not take immediate and proactive steps to resolve issues and repair any damage to the project.

## Selecting Contractors

Selecting contractors should follow a structured process to maintain transparency and reduce the risk of complaints, especially from local contractors. The decision process should use a scorecard or multi-criteria decision process (see Chapter 10) that has a pre-determined set of decision factors and weightings. This allows the procurement team to review submissions and score them against the decision factors to determine the best bid that balances cost, quality, environment, and social performance.

It is also important to clarify to the contractors bidding on the project how the submission will be evaluated and how the factors will be weighted. Providing the rules used in the decision process (often called the rubric) ensures that the contractors pay attention to all of the bid requirements and will have a clear understanding of how the project views sustainability issues. Providing this transparency, especially to local contractors, does create a risk for the team if the weighting shows that the organization really does not truly support sustainability issues. If the weighting shows that cost represents 90% of the decision, and environment and social issues are only weighted at 5% each, then the project could quickly lose community support.

## Contractor Development

During the contracting process, the procurement team may have learned that good contractors, especially local contractors, will need support to develop their skills in order to deliver on the project requirements. The bid evaluation should not just look at the contractor's capabilities at the time of the bid submission, but should also consider what their capabilities could be when the work will start.

The procurement process should also include support for contractor development that can help to improve the capabilities of local contractors. Development should include an assessment of the contractor's current skills and implement additional training to bring them up to the standard that the project requires. This could include training on:

- Health and safety
- Environmental management
- Time tracking and reporting of local labor

- Work standards/quality
- Invoicing accounting
- Business management

These topics are discussed in more detail in Chapter 12, "Construction Management."

## Monitoring Performance

The procurement process is not finished once the contract has been awarded but should continue through construction to ensure that contractors meet the performance that they specified in the bid. In Chapter 12, "Construction Management," we discuss the requirements to track contractor performance for environmental performance and meeting the requirements of the code of conduct. The procurement team will focus more on ensuring that contractors meet project commitments related to local employment and local supply.

Procurement contracts should require contractors to report on their performance against set metrics to support project reporting to regulatory agencies for project approvals and the local community for community agreements. metrics might include:

- % local labor (by hours worked or by wages paid)
- % workforce diversity
- Value of local subcontracts
- Hours of training for local employees

To ensure that contractors and suppliers are providing the necessary information to track these metrics, the contracts must include a requirement to supply this data as part of their invoice and that invoices will not be paid without the required information.

Tracking performance also helps the project team to consider the use of incentives to encourage contractors to meet project commitments and exceed expectations, or the contracts can establish penalties for failing to meet sustainability requirements. The incentives could be tied to the contractor's support for local economic development, including the percentage of local employment or the number of training hours provided. One example is that the project could provide incentives in the form of a "recruiting fee" for local employees who are trained by the contractor and then become employees of the organization as the project is commissioned and moves to operations.

## Contract Close Out

The project team needs to work with contractors to develop clear communications with local employees to increase awareness and understanding about project transitions and seek opportunities to work with other contractors. For example, a local employee who is working for a concrete forming contractor and whose job is finished once the building foundations are completed, could be trained on structural, piping, electrical, or finishing work and work for other project contractors.

- Make sure communication channels are well established
- Meet with key regulators
- Meet with local government and stakeholder groups

## Managing Local Impacts

The construction phase of the project is when many of the commitments and agreements made during the project consultation and development stage of the project become a reality. Stakeholder engagement needs to include a process for tracking these commitments, communicating progress to the local community, and adapting commitments to the realities of the construction phase.

For local communities, there are a number of project impacts that can lead to complaints such as construction activities creating noise, dust, traffic disruptions, and light pollution. There are also issues that can arise due to an influx of workers into the community, including impacts to housing, price of food, access to medical services, drugs, prostitution, and crime.

Before the construction activities get started it is important to make sure that there is baseline data in place for all potential project risks and major commitments. For example, if the community is worried about traffic disruption, make sure that you have traffic studies that document the time it takes to travel past the construction area before construction starts so that you have data to show the impact from construction. If the community is worried about the potential for an increase in the local crime rate during construction, work with local law enforcement to get baseline data on crime rates before construction starts, and then monitor crime rates during construction.

# 12.2   Stakeholder Communications During Construction

During project design and development, stakeholder engagement is focused on consultation and incorporating stakeholder feedback into the project development and planning process. As the project moves into the construction phase, the focus of stakeholder engagement moves to maintaining open communication with the local community. Key objectives include:

- Providing timely information to the local community that is clear and easy to understand
- Providing information in the language(s) of the local communities
- Provide a clear mechanism for local communities to provide feedback to the project team
- Ensure timely and respectful response to all complaints and inquiries
- Based on community input, modify construction activities and schedules to minimize social impacts

Major projects will often have an individual or group that is dedicated to managing communications during construction. To be effective, everyone on the project, including contractors and suppliers, need to be aware of the project messaging, communication procedures, and how they can help to ensure good communication with the local community.

## Key Messaging

The key messages that were developed during the design and approvals stages of the project need to be updated to reflect the realities of the construction phase and the changing impact on the local community. Some possible key messages for the construction phase of the project are listed below:

- The project will comply with the commitments made in the project approvals and community agreements
- Construction will meet the requirements of environmental regulations, project permits, and organizational best practices
- Strategies have been developed to minimize impacts on the local community, areas around the project site, and related transport routes, including dust and noise impacts
- The construction workforce will follow the project code of conduct and nonlocal workers will receive cultural awareness training to reduce the potential disturbance to the local communities
- Environmental monitoring will follow permit requirements and industry best practices to minimize any impacts on the local environment during construction
- The project team will continue to work closely with the community during construction to provide updates and respond to inquiries and complaints.

## Communication Tools and Mechanisms

A number of community engagement and communication tools can be used during construction to deliver key messages, keep the community updated, and provide an opportunity for community feedback on the construction (see Table 12.1 and Chapter 6). The communication tools should be developed in the local language(s) to ensure that the community is getting the message and to ensure that the project is effectively communicating risks and activities.

## Communication Planning

Communication with the local community should not be limited to responding to complaints or dealing with the most vocal members of the community. A proactive approach to communication involves developing a construction communication plan that documents who key stakeholders are and their issues of concern. In Chapter 6, a detailed approach to stakeholder engagement was outlined. However, the construction stage of the project requires an update to reflect construction challenges and increasing impacts on the local community.

The updated stakeholder engagement plan should include a stakeholder communications table (see Appendix D) that documents:

- Community and stakeholder groups that will be impacted by construction activities
- Stakeholder interests and expectations related to construction
- What needs to be communicated, including project notifications and crisis communications

Table 12.1   Construction communication tools.

| Engagement Tool | Description |
| --- | --- |
| Public Meetings | Public meetings can be held to present project information to the community and discuss community concerns. Meetings can be held at the start of construction and when there is a change in project activities that would have an impact on the community. |
| Group Meetings | Focused group meetings can provide specific information to groups that are interested in a construction-related topic. |
| Site Tours | Tours of the construction site can provide community members and other stakeholders with a better understanding of construction. The tours can also include the monitoring programs to demonstrate how the project is responding to community concerns. |
| Project Website | The project website should have a page focused on construction phase communications including updates, project activity notices, upcoming events, and monitoring data. The website page should also offer information about job opportunities and contracting opportunities that can be updated regularly. The website should include the ability for community members to comment or ask questions. |
| Social Media | The project should also provide updates and notifications through social media. The project should identify and use social media sites that are popular with the local communities. The project may also be able to coordinate social media with the local government to leverage existing connections to share emergency notifications, for example. |
| Traditional Media (Newspaper and Radio) | Some members of the local community will not be connected to social media, so it is also important to communicate using more traditional methods such as newspaper, radio, local TV, and paper flyers. |
| Access Number and Email Address | A project phone number and email should be shared as another method for individuals to request further information or raise any concerns or complaints about the project. |
| Site Signage | Site signage at the entrance to construction sites should be provided to warn people approaching the site of potential safety risks and construction activities. The signage should also be placed at any location where the local community could encounter construction activities (walking or cycling trails, hunting routes, etc.). |

- Key messaging for the construction activities
- Communication tools that provide timely information regarding construction activities
- The timing of regular communications

Using stakeholder engagement software becomes more difficult during construction as the volume of communications increases significantly from the planning and approvals stages. The communications team should still develop systems and identify which communications will require formal tracking and which are less important. For example, complaints should be documented in a complaints system or in the stakeholder system, but inquiries about potential employment might be better managed by an employment tracking system.

# Project Notification Procedure

A project notification procedure should be developed in order to ensure that the local community is receiving timely information regarding construction activities that might disrupt local events or cause concerns with the local community. The procedure specifically focuses on ensuring that the community is informed and consulted with regarding the project scheduling for activities that might cause disruptions or disturbances, such as impacting local roads or waterways. Notices could include road closures, transport of over-sized equipment, or blasting schedules.

The project notification procedure is an integral part of Permit to Work (PtW) system described below. It is important that logistics, contractors and construction planning understand the requirements to inform the community for certain activities. Advanced notification reduces the risk of project activities being delayed or blocked because of a community event or issue that interferes with the activity. This formal process also reduces the risk that a contractor will take it upon themselves to communicate with the local community and potentially create confusion with potentially mixed messages coming from various directions.

The Project Notification Procedure should include a number of key components:

1. Maintaining a rolling schedule of project activities that require community notification. The schedule should be forward looking 6 to 8 weeks ahead and updated weekly to ensure that the new items are added, and schedule changes are captured. A forward-looking schedule gives the communications team time to assess what communication is required and prepare the required notices.

2. Collaborating with logistics to maintain an updated delivery schedule for all shipments planned for the project especially any oversized shipments that may cause road closures or traffic slowdowns.

3. Identifying key local events that may be impacted by upcoming project activities so that construction and logistics teams can be informed of potential conflicts and adjust schedules accordingly.

4. Preparing draft project notification templates that can be used to for communicating about common project activities to reduce the time required for preparing and getting approval for notifications.

5. If project notifications need to be translated into a local language(s), then including time for translation in the notification procedure and schedule.

6. Identifying the communication media that is most effective for each type of notification.

# Complaints Mechanism

The complaints process described in Chapter 8 provides an overall process for complaints. When the project moves into the construction phase, the complaints process should be modified to and expanded to include incident investigation and follow-up. Most major projects have an incident investigation or incident response process as part of the health and safety plans or environmental management systems. The same process can be applied to investigating community complaints to document the investigation, establish root cause and then plan and implement of the required corrective actions.

The incident response procedure should include a process to follow up with the contractor or team that caused the incident (or incited the complaint), as well as all other affected contractors. Ensure that corrective actions are included in revised work procedures to avoid future incidents. The incident response might include assigning follow-up monitoring to confirm that the issue was resolved and that the corrective actions are being followed The response to a community complaint should include a follow-up with the individual or group that lodged the complaint, discuss the issue and the steps taken to address the problem, and thank them for their feedback.

## Communications Training

It is important for the entire team to be aware of the plans and their roles in communicating with the local community, regulators and media to ensure that the stakeholder communications plans are effective. For most construction employees and contractors, communications training will be part of onboarding program. Onboarding training should include the key messages communicated to the local community and the process for responding to enquiries from local politicians, environmental groups or media. Since many of the construction workers will also be local residents, the key messaging and internal training should reflect accurate and transparent communication with the local community. With the prevalence of cell phones and social media, biased communications or training materials could lead to complaints and a loss of community support.

A higher level of communications training should be provided for construction management teams, contractor managers and any team members who will be dealing directly with the local community or governments. The training should include:

- Key messages and available project communication documents
- Procedures for handling inquiries from the media, government officials, the public or unexpected visitors to the construction site
- Notification requirements and schedules
- Emergency response and crisis communication procedures,
- Complaints procedures
- Requirements for documenting and reporting engagements with the local community

## Social Monitoring

It is important to monitor the effectiveness of the stakeholder engagement program during construction to make sure that the programs are working and to be able to respond to changing conditions, such as changeover of contractors in the construction team. We discussed the overall stakeholder and social monitoring program in Chapter 8, so this section focusses on some of the key issues for the construction phase.

Social monitoring during construction can help to ensure that the planned project activities around stakeholder engagement and support for the local community are implemented and generate the intended results. Monitoring can detect if unanticipated impacts or issues so that the project team can develop mitigation measures and change project activities if necessary, to avoid issues escalating into major problems. Monitoring can ensure compliance with government approvals, community agreements, commitments, and organizational goals, and is also required for reporting on stakeholder and community performance.

Monitoring the effectiveness of stakeholder engagement and communication programs helps ensure that the project is maintaining a good relationship with the local community and maintaining community support. Monitoring can include tracking a number of programs during construction, such as:

- Ensure that proactive communications plans are being followed so that community groups and members are getting regular project updates
- Monitor the complaints program to assess the frequency and severity of complains to ensure complaints are being followed up on, trends are identified, and repeating issues are addressed
- Collect data on local employment and local contracts to ensure that procurement and human resources programs are meeting project targets
- Track worker onboard training to ensure that communication requirements are being taught and documented

As construction progresses, the project team will learn what parts of the communication program are working well and which parts need to be updated. The communication program should be updated as necessary during construction to address areas that need improvement and to ensure that the project goals and objectives are being met. Any major changes to construction activities will also require updates to the stakeholder engagement program to ensure that new community issues don't arise because of changes to the construction planning.

# 12.3 Public Safety

One of the key challenges for construction management is to ensure that public safety is proactively managed and controlled. There is no event that can damage community support as quickly as an incident that results in a fatality or serious injury to someone in the local community. There are a wide range of issues that can impact public safety, including:

- Uncontrolled access to work sites
- Blasting
- Road safety (as discussed in Chapter 11)
- Major spills
- Exposure to hazardous chemicals

Managing public safety should also include how the project responds to storm events or natural disasters where project concerns overlap with community concerns. A proactive, supportive response to a natural disaster is one of the best ways the project has of quickly building community support.

Public safety can be integrated into construction planning by integrating public safety concerns into health and safety plans (HASP), environmental protection plans (EPP), communications plans, and emergency response plans. HASPs and EPPs should include procedures and measures that will be implemented to eliminate or mitigate the public's exposure to construction related hazards. Specific measures for public protection could include air and water monitoring, especially in areas where community members might be present.

In addition to communications tasks related to construction activities, raising public awareness of hazards related to construction could include:

- Specific initiatives to promote public awareness of the hazards present at the site
- Development of highly visible signage in local languages placed on roads, trails, and waterways to warn of hazards such as danger ahead or no swimming/boating signs
- Education programs such as community briefings and public service announcements

## Crisis Communications

Most major projects have crisis management and communications plans that address how the project will respond in the event of a crisis. Working with the local community to share information about crisis management and develop cooperative plans for dealing with a crisis can help to establish trust and build community support.

A crisis is a critical event which, if not managed, could grow into a more serious issue. It is important to distinguish between a crisis that requires the attention of project leadership, and a more serious emergency that requires the implementation of the project Emergency Response Plan. A crisis is not restricted to potential emergencies, but can be caused by a number of events such as:

- Environmental spill or damage
- Severe weather or a natural disaster
- Security incident or criminal activity
- Political disturbance or civil disorder
- Human rights abuses, disrespect for local culture or religion
- Labor unrest
- Public protest or NGO activities
- Disease event or pandemics

Transparent and open communications is essential during a crisis because misinformation and perception during this time can worsen the situation for both the project and the local community. The project should develop a Crisis Communications Plan (CCP) to identify potential events, provide response procedures, and ensure there is effective communication of the events. The CCP should identify roles and responsibilities for the project team so that everyone knows what to do and who should be included in the crisis response.

The CCP should also be developed in cooperation with the local community. Discussing the communications and response plans before construction starts gives local officials and groups (such as police, fire, and hospitals) the opportunity to provide input to the plan. When or if the time comes to respond to a crisis, then this upfront collaboration has helped ensure that all parties are aware of and understand their roles in executing the response.

## Emergency Response

Similar to crisis management, major projects will have an Emergency Response Plan (ERP) for Construction that outlines the types of potential emergencies, and the associated procedures and measures for each to provide an immediate and effective response. The ERP should also outline the roles and responsibilities, and chain of command that will come into effect in the event of an emergency.

Like the CCP, an ERP should be developed in cooperation with the local community. Most project emergencies will also affect the local community. To formalize this discussion, emergency response planning can be an element of the Community Agreement and include a statement of mutual-cooperation for emergency response. The ERP with the local community might include communications materials to clarify the types of emergencies that could occur during construction or operations. Communications should outline how an emergency response might occur, how they will be notified, and any requirements for the community to react to an emergency. For example, if the project involves the transport of fuels or dangerous chemicals, emergency response might require evacuation along transportation routes.

Discussion of an ERP should also include the equipment and supplies each group can bring to an emergency and what skilled resources are available. This might be everything from firefighting equipment and medical supplies to back-up power and water treatment equipment. In some cases, the project will need to draw on local community resources, and in other cases the project may need to provide support to the local community to ensure that an emergency is effectively managed.

## Emergency Response Training

The key to a successful emergency response is to have well-trained emergency response personnel available and for everyone on the project team to be trained on what to do in the case of an emergency. Basic emergency response training should be included in orientation training for all site personnel to ensure that the ERP is well structured for a successful emergency response and that the project team can respond effectively.

Emergency response training is also one of the most valuable skills development activities for local workers. Emergency response skills can be used to support the local community and continue to be valuable once the project is finished. A local employee trained in emergency response can help with crisis communication with the local community, build connections to local first responders and provide support for both the project and community response efforts.

## 12.4   Environmental Management

Managing environmental performance during construction is best achieved with an Environmental Management System (EMS) that follows the structure of the ISO 14001 EMS Standard. Using a globally recognized standard not only provides a structure that is recognized and accepted by most government regulators, it also makes it easier to align the project system with the EMS for the organization and the project contractors.

One thing to keep in mind when developing a project EMS is that the traditional ISO 14001 Plan-Do-Check-Act (PDCA) structure was designed for operating facilities with consistent operations over many years. The PDCA cycle assumes that operations can be adapted over time to improve environmental performance and includes the following steps that would be updated regularly (typically annually);

- Plan: Establish objectives and processes required
- Do: Implement the processes
- Check: Measure and monitor the processes and report results
- Act: Take action to improve performance of EMS based on results

But for construction projects, each phase of the construction (land preparation, civil works, mechanical, electrical, piping, etc.) can be shorter than one year so there is only limited opportunity to 'Check' performance and 'Act' to make improvements. For construction projects, the 'Plan' phase needs to be done very carefully so that the 'Do' stage can be completed with a high degree of environmental performance. This is especially true where the local community is concerned about the potential for impacts. The project team will not have time to put in place corrective action to fix a major problem before there are negative impacts and a loss of community support.

This section discusses the main components of a traditional EMS with a focus on areas where special care needs to be taken to adapt the EMS for the challenges of constructing a major project.

### Environmental Management System

The Environmental Management System (EMS) provides a structured and systematic approach to manage environmental issues on a construction project. An EMS helps reduce project risks from environmental impacts and ensures that the construction activities are carried out in compliance with applicable permits and regulations, project commitments and industry best practices.

The system will include a number of specific plans and procedures that apply to different areas of the environment or specific work activities. The EMS will also include;

- Procedures for collecting and managing data
- Corrective actions to take in the event of that work is out of compliance
- Inspections and monitoring that will take place to keep the project on track

- Audits for the project team to check on contractors and work teams to ensure that the correct procedures are being followed
- Change management procedures to adjust the EMS to fit with changing construction plans or regulatory requirements
- Roles and responsibilities for activities within the EMS

Given the complexity of construction activities for a major project, the EMS can sometimes grow to be unmanageable. So, it is important for the EMS to have a clear structure so that team members know where to find the right information and what guidelines to follow. Some of the major plans that are included in an EMS are shown in Table 12.2 below.

Table 12.2    Environmental Management Plans

| Plan and Procedure | Description |
| --- | --- |
| Permitting Plan | Identifies the regulatory permits that apply to the construction activities using a permit register (as described in Chapter 9). Helps to ensure that teams understand all the permits that apply to the work that they are doing and where to find copies of the permits, if required, to confirm activities, data collection and reporting requirements. |
| Environmental Protection Plan | Identifies the environmental concerns for the project and general protection measures that are to be considered in developing mitigation strategies. The plan should be updated and modified to fit the project phase, and if site-specific conditions change over time. |
| Waste Management Plan | Identifies handling, recycling and disposal locations for waste materials. Waste management practices should include preventing environmental incidents, avoiding wildlife interactions, protecting human health, and preventing long-term liabilities from waste disposal. |
| Water Management Plan | The plan outlines water management around the project including waste disposal areas, work areas, and roadways. The plan should address how storm water on site will be diverted, collected, stored and treated to maximize water re-use, conservation and protection. |
| Air and Dust Management Plan | Identifies project areas and activities that are likely to generate dust and air emissions, especially where emissions could impact the local community. The plan will include methods for dust suppression and monitoring of dust impacts. |
| Spill Response Plans | Identifies procedures to use when handling fuels and chemicals (including (lubricating oils and hydraulic fluids). The plan will include spill avoidance procedures and areas where fuel and chemicals should not be handled. The plan will include how spills will be managed, cleaned-up and reported to regulators. |
| Progressive Reclamation Plan | Identifies how areas disturbed by the construction will be reclaimed as part of the construction activities rather than waiting till the end of operation to repair the environmental damage. |
| Wildlife Management Plan | Identifies the potential for wildlife interactions with the project site and the construction team including species at risk. The plan will include construction activities that are most likely to encounter animals and how those interactions can be managed by changing a project location, shifting construction schedules to avoid breeding seasons, or moving animals out of the way of the construction. |
| Energy and Green House Gas (GHG) Management Plan | Identifies requirements for GHG tracking and reporting either as part of regulatory requirements or organizational goals. The plan should also address energy efficiency plans that provide opportunities for reduced energy usage or reduced emissions. |

# Data Management

The amount and diversity of data that can be collected during construction is significantly higher than during operations and data can be located across a large geographic area. Operations may look at monitoring data from a set number of air emissions points or water discharges, but a construction EMS will be collecting data across the entire project development area. Data will include monitoring at every stream crossing, wildlife impacts and interactions, impacts from numerous pieces of construction equipment from trucks to electrical generators, and releases from camps and support infrastructure for hundreds of construction workers.

The EMS should include a robust environmental data management system that will allow the team to collect, store and report on environmental data to communities, regulatory inspectors, and auditors. It is strongly recommended that the EMS use a modern electronic data management system that can track environmental data using GIS capabilities, and upload field forms and photos directly from hand-held devices to reduce data entry requirements.

Having the environmental data in electronic form can also facilitate sharing the data with the local community and regulators. The expectations of local communities are growing and soon it will become a requirement to share monitoring data in near real-time so that the community can monitor the construction activities and ensure that the project is meeting their commitments and regulatory requirements. Voluntarily sharing data with the local community can also help to build trust that the project has nothing to hide and will work to transparently meet its promises, as shown by the story below.

## STORY: SHARING AIR QUALITY DATA

When we proposed putting all of our air quality data up on the project website as part of the weekly project update, a lot of people on the project team thought we were crazy.

Our project was to remove an old hazardous waste disposal site located next to a residential neighborhood with a very concerned group of local residents. They were happy that we were removing the hazardous waste but had serious concerns about how the work would be done. During community planning meetings the residents raised dust issues as their biggest concern because the dust could carry toxic chemicals into the community. We spent a lot of time explaining how our extensive dust control procedures would manage the problem, but the community didn't believe that we would be able to manage the dust problem. Eventually we committed to putting real-time dust monitoring in place and to publish the data on a weekly basis. I wouldn't say that the residents were happy with the solution, but they agreed to let us proceed with the project.

When we put the program in place and explained the process to the project team, our main contractor was very concerned about the approach. As the project got started, the contractor paid extra attention to dust and had their crews focus on good housekeeping and dust control measures so that there wouldn't be any issues. We were able to report in the weekly project update that the dust levels were well below the levels that we had expected.

After a couple of weeks of reporting no dust problems, we noticed that the number of views of the weekly updates dropped to zero or one view per week. The fact that we had listened to the community concerns and followed through on our promise to report weekly on the data had built enough trust to lower community concerns. We didn't tell the contractor that no one was paying attention to the dust data, so they kept up the good work and continued to keep dust levels well below acceptable levels. After 4 months, the work with the hazardous materials was finished and we were able to present to the community that there had been no dust exceedances. We went from very confrontational, angry community meetings to getting thank-you cards for responsibly removing the hazardous waste.

## Corrective and Preventative Action

The EMS should provide procedures for investigating and correcting problems and preventing the re-occurrence of issues with the construction activities. Issues that require corrective action could be those that do not conform with the project's permits, commitments or environmental plans and procedures, and are often referred to as non-conformances. Non-conformances can include;

- Minor non-conformances: an isolated issue that has not led to an impact yet, such as a team member re-fueling a truck without the required spill containment equipment, but no spill occurred, or

- Major non-conformances: a serious issue that has led to an incident such as a spill.

Non- conformances can be self-identified by construction teams, EMS audits, regulatory inspections or community complaints. A minor non-conformance can typically be dealt with through a conversation with the construction team in question and training in the correct procedures to use. A major non-conformance may require an investigation to document the details of the incident, evaluate the root cause, and ensure that action is taken to correct the issue and prevent future occurrences.

## Inspections and Monitoring

Inspections and monitoring are conducted to ensure that the Project is meeting its commitments and regulatory requirements. With so many people involved in major projects and the variety of activities that will be completed throughout construction, it is important to develop inspection and monitoring programs that are flexible and adaptable.

Site inspections involve members of the project team conducting periodic tours of work sites to verify that work is being performed in conformance with plans and procedures. Site inspections should focus on activities that have the highest potential for significant environmental impact or risk, including:

- Storage and handling of hazardous materials (fuel and chemical)
- Control of dust and noise from equipment
- Erosion and sediment control near water bodies
- Control of air and water emissions

- Preparedness for spills and emergencies
- Waste management programs are being followed
- Ensuring teams are keeping proper documentation including monitoring data, toolbox records and Permit to Work procedures

Environmental monitoring could include daily, weekly, and monthly monitoring of the environmental condition at the site. Depending on the project-specific regulations and commitments, monitoring could include:

- Water use volumes
- Water discharge volumes and water quality
- Surface water quality
- Levels of dust and air emissions
- Noise levels
- Light pollution
- Wildlife interactions

Depending on the type of work involved, contractors may be required to monitor their own work to ensure that their work procedures and mitigation measures are effectively managing the issue. The monitoring program would include inspecting the work and performing occasional checks of the contractors sampling.

## Audit Program

One of the requirements of a good management system is to audit performance to verify that proper plans and procedures are being used to ensure the project meets environmental performance expectations. Audit results can be shared with construction teams to improve performance, and with project management to evaluate overall sustainability performance.

Audits can be conducted by internal team members to provide a general assessment of the effectiveness plans and procedures. The project can also invest in external audits, conducted by certified third-party auditors, to assess the performance of the EMS program against industry best practices and other major projects. During construction, internal compliance audits can take place on a regular basis to ensure that individual construction teams are proactively managing environmental impacts. External audits typically occur less frequently but address the overall performance of the entire construction EMS, rather than the performance of a single team or contractor.

The scope of an audit program should include adherence to relevant environmental regulations and permits, as well as how the activities meet the requirements of project commitments and community agreements. The audit should determine the level of adherence to project plans and procedures and construction contract requirements and determine if corrective actions are being followed through on.

## Change Management

The EMS should include a clear process for change management and continuous improvement. As construction progresses, the EMS can be updated based on the experience of the construction team and as improvements are made by team members or contractors. Change management procedures should include:

- Feedback from construction teams
- Improvements from responding to noncompliance issues, regulatory intervention, or community complaints
- Adoption of industry best practices from other projects or industries
- New information regarding environmental or social conditions at the project site

## Roles and Responsibilities

Construction teams for major projects include many organizations and large numbers of people, so there is a clear benefit to defining roles and responsibilities for each group. The EMS should identify the roles and responsibilities for the organization's project team, the construction manager's team, contractors, and subcontractors.

The roles and responsibilities should include specific responsibilities for key team members within each of the organizations onsite like project managers, environmental managers, health and safety managers, logistics, and scheduling teams. The responsibilities should also be outlined for support roles like technical experts, local community liaison staff, environmental auditors, and government relations staff.

# 12.5   Working with Contractors

Most construction projects are built by a team of contractors, each with their own set of skills and areas of focus on the project site. Integrating sustainability into construction management requires that each contractor be aware of the project requirements and that they understand how their actions both on and off of the project site can have an impact in the overall success of the project.

Working with contractors on integrating sustainability into the project is most important when there are construction camps or a large influx of construction workers into the community. Such an influx of workers can create significant problems with crime, drugs, gambling, and cultural conflicts. It is critical in these situations to carefully plan how the project will be delivered and how the risks of negative impacts on the community can be managed. Many of the contractors will have their own experience and expertise in managing these issues, so the project team can engage contractors with a problem-solving approach to identify and implement best practices.

## Kick-off Planning

A major challenge when working with contractors is that the contractor's site manager and the rest of the contractor's team may not have been involved in developing the proposal that described the work plan or been involved in negotiating the contract for the work. The contractor's business development team may have written sections on environmental management or sustainability integration that the contractor's site manager and the rest of the team have not been trained on or have had time to be prepared for.

One of the first steps when a contractor is ready to mobilize and start work on the site is to have a kick-off meeting to discuss the work, mobilization planning, and project requirements. Part of this review needs to include a discussion of the project goals to maintain the support of the local community and the sustainability requirements that are required for everyone working on the project. A standard agenda or set of topics to discuss with each of the contractor teams is required to ensure that they understand the project expectations and commit to working with the project team to deliver on these objectives. The agenda should include a review of relevant project commitments, any cultural issues that need to be addressed, sensitive environmental areas that need to be protected, and requirements for onboarding training. The agenda should also include a review of procurement contracts, and any actions the project team will take in the event that a contractor has disregarded the project rules and code of conduct (see Chapter 11 for more information on contracts).

## Code of Conduct

The purpose of a code of conduct document is to provide a set of guidelines for how project team members should behave toward each other and toward the local community. It can become an integral part of sustainability training efforts and provide the project team with the ability to follow up on any issues being raised. The code of conduct can help to establish a common set of goals and objectives for the entire project team because everyone signs the same document. The code of conduct should include language from the project charter on what the team is trying to achieve and how they will achieve it. This will give everyone on the team a sense of being part of something bigger than just their individual piece of the project.

The code of conduct should include not just expected behavior for work on-site but also address behavior off-site. Construction workers are not just responsible for their conduct when they are working on site but are also responsible for their conduct off site, especially when engaging with the local community. This can include rules about not hunting or fishing around the project or the local community, for example, or not disturbing archeological or traditional sites.

The code of conduct is not intended to be a legal document, although in Chapter 11 we discussed how failure to follow the project code of conduct could result in contracts being cancelled. When drafting the code of conduct, consider that the document should be easy to read and follow but could also potentially end up in legal proceedings.

Some advice for developing an effective code of conduct:

1. Keep it short and in plain language. Remember that you are writing for a team that has a wide range of experience and educational background, so do not use legalese.

2. Have each individual sign, including managers, as part of onboarding training. For individuals who will be on the project for more than one year, an annual refresher is recommended.

3. Translate it into the local language so local workers can understand and the local community can see what expectations you have for the construction project.

4. Use active language, not passive language (like "You are required to follow the … ").

The code of conduct should be part of the onboarding training and should include examples and stories to better explain what acceptable and unacceptable behavior looks like. Helping construction team members understand why negative behavior might impact their coworkers from the community or the families that live near the project site. This can help to keep team members focused on positive behaviors.

## Onboarding Training

It is standard on construction projects to have onboarding training that covers health and safety, emergency response, and day-to-day activities like washrooms and where everyone eats and sleeps. It is also important to integrate sustainability aspects into the onboarding training so that everyone has a common understanding of the project objectives and how they should behave. While this will increase the time required for onboarding training, the benefit of having a project that runs more smoothly and avoids issues creates an overall benefit for the project.

Some of the topics that should be included in onboarding training are:

- Project goals and objectives including sustainability goals
- Code of conduct training
- Cultural awareness training
- Environmental training for waste management, spills response, and wildlife interactions
- Permit to Work (PtW) system requirements
- How to raise an issue or report a problem
- The project's complaints mechanism

# 12.6   Permit to Work System

Construction activities are often rushed as construction teams push forward to get work completed as quickly as possible in order to meet project schedules, and contractors push to minimize unit costs and maximize profits. Permit to Work (PtW) systems are used on construction and maintenance projects to manage high-risk activities where project managers feel that a more structured process would require construction teams to take the time to assess and manage risks.

PtW systems have traditionally been used to manage project safety risks but integrating sustainability into this system can help to capture sustainability issues that can have an impact on project success. The system will help ensure that work teams are taking the time to understand where the risks are and halting the work until they have demonstrated that they are properly prepared for the work.

The basic PtW form should document the work activities, location, schedule, contractor(s), hazard assessment, and safety information (i.e. required personal protective equipment). Some of the key sustainability issues that can be captured in the PtW system can include:

- Training: Do the workers assigned to the work team have the required skills and training to complete the work, are there opportunities for skills development for local workers?
- Environment: Do the work plans comply with the environmental management system, are the required regulatory permits in place and understood by the work team, are there any monitoring requirements for the work, will activities include near-water works, will refueling be required?
- Archeology. Could activities impact on known archeological or culturally important areas and what are procedures if the work encounters artifacts?
- Emergency response. Are there any work activities that could result in an emergency response, and if so, does the project team have all required response equipment in place and have emergency response teams been notified?
- Commitments. Does the work team understand any commitments made to the local community that might be impacted by the work, like noise, dust, or traffic constraints?
- Community impact. Will there be any impacts to the local community that need to be managed?
- Community notifications. Are there any requirements to notify the local community and, if so, have plans been made to notify within the required notification schedule, are traffic management plans, and required signage in place?

The PtW system should include clear rules about who should develop PtW documentation and who from the project team can authorize the work. As part of contractor management, the PtW process should also include procedures to inspect the work being completed and provide a system for putting work on hold or canceling permits if there are changes or problems with the work.

Developing and approving PtWs can be time consuming, so it is important to develop a system that allows approval for large pieces of work so that teams do not spend too much time on planning and developing PtW paperwork. Each PtW should be limited to a set geography, schedule, work team, and work breakdown structure definition. If there are changes to any of these, then a new PtW should be developed. Ideally the PtW is aligned with procurement contracts so that a series of PtWs can also be used for tracking contractor performance.

The PtW should also be reassessed at key stages of the construction work. For example, the installation of camp buildings for construction crews might be covered in a series of PtWs to address key stages that have different risks and different requirements, such as:

1. Land clearing that requires environmental permits, monitoring, and, depending on location, community notification

2. Installation of prefabricated camp buildings, which might require building approvals, waste management, and notification of traffic disruption for the movement of large modules

3. Commissioning and occupancy, which could require permits for electrical, water and waste water treatment, and an inspection and occupancy approval from the local fire department

The PtW should include a completion follow-up document that confirms that the work has been completed and inspected, that any safety, environment, or social issues have been documented, and that the work area has been left in a clean and safe state. Completed and signed-off PtWs can be used to provide support for approval of contractor invoices and tracking of contractor performance.

## 12.7 Construction Sustainability Metrics

We have discussed in other chapters how to create project sustainability metrics that can be used to monitor and manage a diverse range of sustainability issues, from energy use to local employment. A large number of these metrics apply to the construction stage of the project, but often that large number can make it difficult to focus and gauge how the project is doing. One way to manage this complexity is to create a composite metric that captures a number of detailed metrics and allows the project team to track and compare performance across different contractors and construction teams. The same approach was used in the early days of the safety movement to create the Total Recordable Incident Frequency (TRIF) rate. TRIF captures all types of serious safety events into one performance metric that can be used to understand performance and drive improvements. The TRIF rate has helped to change construction projects from counting deaths per project to striving for zero harm.

### Environmental Incident Frequency Rate

A number of firms have started to use a comparable metric, the Environmental Incident Frequency Rate (EIFR), in order to track and create continuous improvement with respect to environmental performance.[1] The definition of EIFR was developed to directly compare to the TRIF rate for safety, and it is the number of "recordable" environmental incidents per 200,000 hours worked.

Unlike safety, where definitions of a "recordable" incident have been well developed over the last 30 years, the definition of a recordable environmental incident does not have a standard set of events that are classified as "recordable." Each project might have a different set of issues and risks that need to be considered but, in general, recordable environment incidents should include events like:

- A noncompliance finding, fine, penalty, or action by a regulatory agency
- A confirmed complaint about the environment from the local community (i.e. noise/dust)
- A spill/release that requires reporting to the government or requires the use of spill containment equipment or resources
- A wildlife incident that results in the death or injury of an animal
- A release of air pollutants at levels above permitted or agreed upon levels
- A release of pollutants, sediment, or other materials into a water body

## Social Incident Frequency Rate

An equivalent metric can be used for tracking social performance for the construction project. The Social Incident Frequency Rate (SIFR) captures the number of "recordable" social incidents per 200,000 hours worked. SIFR provides the project team with a simple way to track performance and compare the performance of construction teams and contractors. Tracking a social metric can allow the project team to assess which contractors are performing the best, which contractors need improvement, and how to capture and share best practices. Tracking a social metric can also allow the team to understand that the construction work could be creating an issue with the community before there is a loss of community support.

Identifying what a "recordable" social incident could be is even more challenging than identifying a recordable environmental incident. Each project will have a unique set of issues and challenges and the community will have a very different response to these issues depending on their previous experience with construction projects.

Events that can be included as social recordable incidents in a SIFR metric might include:

- A confirmed stakeholder complaint
- A grievance, complaint, or report of discrimination or harassment by an employee
- Negative press coverage
- Traffic accident involving project equipment or a project team member
- An unexpected or uncommunicated disruption of services or road closures in the community
- A crime by a project team member in the community or on site
- Property damage involving project equipment or a project team member

Construction sustainability metrics like the EIFR and the SIFR can help to improve sustainability performance during construction when used effectively. They provide a simple, composite metric that can be used to track and compare contractor performance. Similar to the effectiveness of the TRIF rate for safety, the EIFR and SIFR have the potential to improve overall environmental and social performance for the contractors and for the project as a whole.

## 12.8   Creating a Sustainability Culture

Over the last 10 to 15 years, safety programs in many organizations have evolved from prescriptive rules-based systems to behavior-based systems that focus on developing a safety culture. The safety culture emphasizes that each team member is responsible for their own safety and the safety of their co-workers. This same approach can be used to create a culture of sustainability on the construction site where work teams are responsible for the environmental performance of their work crew and for the social and community impact of the project.

Integrating sustainability into a safety program requires expanding on many of the existing systems to broaden the topics covered to ensure that workers and teams understand the environmental and social commitments and opportunities for the project.

Building a sustainability culture requires leveraging change management techniques that help to change behaviors and create better outcomes. Three building blocks of change management are:

1.  Education to ensure that workers understand what behaviors are expected
2.  Evaluation to provide feedback on performance
3.  Encouragement to reinforce good behavior and provide incentives for meeting performance targets

### Education

The core of building a sustainability culture is to ensure that project team members (employees and contractors) understand what is expected of them. The training and support should make it easy to understand and follow the expectations. Good practice should also include connecting behaviors with something that the workers already care, about as discussed in the story below.

Education to create a sustainability culture can include:

- Daily "toolbox" topics with social and environmental topics (see tip box at the end of this section)
- Orientation training
- Code of conduct training
- Cross-cultural training with local residents
- Work crews with local and non-local employees
- Photos of best practices
- Change management checklists that include sustainability checks

## Evaluation

Evaluation processes can be implemented to track performance and provide feedback. The focus of evaluation should not be to create penalties for poor behavior, but rather to create incentives for good behavior. One of the most common forms of evaluating and communicating safety performance is the large sign at the entrance to the construction site that says, "It has been X days since our last lost time injury." This provides a clear evaluation of the performance of the entire team. For sustainability, the team could add two more statements to the sign to communicate performance: "It has been X days since our last environmental incident," and "It has been X days since our last formal complaint,"

Evaluation can assess performance against key sustainability metrics as well as key leading indicators or "near-miss" metrics that show how the team is working to avoid environmental and social incidents, such as:

- Frequency of environmental and social topics in daily toolbox talks
- Equipment inspection frequency
- Number of skills development and on-the-job training events
- Adherence to speed requirements on local roads

## Encouragement

Encouragement takes the feedback from the evaluation and makes good behaviors desirable through incentives and peer pressure, such as creating competition between construction teams on who gets work done on schedule and on budget, as well as safely and with care for the environment and the local community. Encouragement could include:

- Spot awards for good behaviors
- Conversation/intervention cards for positive as well as negative behaviors
- Posting contractor performance scores for environmental and social metrics

## TIP: DAILY SUSTAINABILITY "TOOLBOX" MEETINGS

A common practice on construction sites is to have a daily safety briefing or "toolbox" meeting where the work crew discusses the work that will be happening that day and any safety concerns that they may be facing. This same structure can be adapted to allow sustainability topics to be added to the daily briefing to ensure that environmental and social issues are also captured and discussed with the team.

An effective daily toolbox briefing could have 4 components:

1. Operations topics
   a. What work are we doing today?
   b. Who is doing what?
   c. Are there any changes from the original plan?
2. Safety topics
   a. What are the safety issues we are facing today (weather, work activities)?
   b. Who is working nearby?
   c. Completing daily Job Hazard Assessments (JHAs)
3. Environmental topics
   a. What controls are or need to be in place?
   b. What monitoring and inspections will be required?
   c. Keeping the site clean
   d. Wildlife interactions
   e. Waste management
4. Social/community topics
   a. Code of conduct reminders
   b. Cultural awareness
   c. Have there been any complaints?
   d. Communication and notification requirements
   e. Social media rules

The intent is not to cover each of these suggested topics every day, but to touch on different issues that are applicable to the work and address any issues that have come up during the project. For example, if a complaint has been raised about how workers are behaving in the local community, then a reminder about the code of conduct could be included in the daily briefing.

## 12.9　Summary

The construction phase of a major project is when sustainability planning is the most critical. Every project is unique and the tools that work on one project might not work as well on another project. Different industries, locations, cultures, organizations, and team members can all influence the success of integrating sustainability into construction.

Project teams also need to be ready to adapt. It is usually not effective to force people to follow a management system that is not working. Instead, the team should go back to the project objectives and goals to see if there is another way to achieve the goals or refocus on education and training rather than enforcing rules that are not creating the desired outcomes.

It is also important to remember that very few construction projects have been delivered with a fully integrated sustainability program, so you will encounter team members and contractors who do not yet have experience, and it may take some patience and extra attention to get them on board with the sustainability program.

The requirements for sustainability are also changing rapidly, so plans developed at the beginning of the project development process may no longer meet the requirements of regulators and the local community. It is important of keep track of the changing landscape and available best practices to help adjust to new issues, challenges, and requirements.

The goal of integrating sustainability into construction is to get projects built on time and on budget without losing the support of the local community. That support will be very valuable to the operations team as they take on the project and start operations. In the next chapter, we discuss how to manage a smooth transition from construction to operations.

## Endnote

1. McPhee, Wayne, "Introducing the Social Incident Frequency Rate," *PM World Journal* 5 (no. 2, February 2016).

CHAPTER **13**

# Commissioning

Commissioning is the final phase in project execution, the primary goal of which is to ensure that the project has been completed and to set the operating team up for success. When sustainability has been integrated into a major project, success also means that the operation has been set up for the best possible environmental and social performance.

During commissioning the project team should focus on coordinating a smooth transition with the operations team to:

- Protect and continue the strong stakeholder relationships that have been developed.
- Maintain commitments to sustainability, environmental and social management systems, and monitoring programs (modified accordingly for operations).
- Ensure that construction work is finished properly to minimize environmental damage.
- Maximize the benefits of local capacity building by continuing to employ as much of the trained local employees and utilizing the local supply chain for operations.

Several factors are required to achieve a successful transition to operations. Commissioning must include systems to ensure that the facility will have sustainability built into its core operational procedures and processes. The investments and resources allocated to optimizing social and environmental performance during project execution phases will be lost if the commissioning strategy does not address the conscious transitioning of sustainability systems over to operations. This will provide operations with the ability to reach its targets and generate the greatest return on investment for the organization.

In this chapter, we explore the key resources and systems needed to preserve the project's sustainability systems through commissioning and into operations. We start with the sustainability expertise needed on the commissioning team, explore the transitioning of management systems, and look at the sensitive approach needed to hand over stakeholder relationships, particularly with the local community. We also felt it important to highlight that there is a significant reduction in local employment and local procurement as construction winds down. This can create a significant challenge for the commissioning team and requires preparing local stakeholders in advance to minimize the risk of losing community support for the operations.

## 13.1 Commissioning Team

The commissioning team will typically include representatives from project management, construction management, and the operations team. It is important for the team to be brought together as early as possible in the initial planning stages of commissioning to ensure that everyone understands the sustainability successes that have been achieved during project execution, and the value that sustainability can add to commissioning and to operations.

The commissioning team will include a broad range of skills and responsibilities, and should include:

- Members of the project team who can help preserve knowledge and experience gathered during project development, including from engineers, procurement, and construction teams
- Operations staff who will need to understand the history of the project and know the sustainability requirements
- Sustainability-related resources, including sustainability management, human resources, local procurement, communications, regulatory affairs, and stakeholder engagement
- Representatives from major original equipment manufacturers (OEM)
- Contractors involved in commissioning

All team members should be provided with training on the main sustainability documents and systems so that everyone understands their responsibilities. As discussed earlier in the book, sustainability is a team sport, and everyone has a role to play in creating a better project. The training should include:

- Commitments that apply to commissioning and operations
- Community agreements and economic development plans
- Major permits and approvals
- Stakeholder engagement plans

## 13.2 Management Systems

During commissioning, most of the project management systems will be transitioned to support operations. Examples include health and safety, and environmental management systems that are required for running a smooth operation. Some management systems, like the construction management plan, will need to be significantly modified to shift from major construction activities to ongoing maintenance activities during operations.

Sustainability management systems, including stakeholder engagement and economic development plans, will all need to be modified appropriately for the operations phase. Sustainability management tools developed during project execution, such as the commitments register, permit register, and complaints mechanism, also must be transitioned carefully during commissioning.

The environmental and social monitoring programs will also need to be transitioned to operations. The amount of monitoring will likely decrease, and the metrics tracked will change as the project moves to operations. However, there should be consistency between baseline studies, construction monitoring, and monitoring during operations.

Each department lead should work with the relevant internal stakeholders from the broader project team, members of commissioning, and future operations teams, to coordinate the necessary modifications to their respective management systems.

## 13.3   Stakeholder Engagement

Over the course of project execution, local stakeholders and community members can become accustomed to dealing and working with the project team – for example, getting project updates from the project director and the project's community relations team or community liaison officers. Typically, once the project is completed and handed over to the operations team, these project team members leave and a new team arrives with a new general manager and, sometimes, new community relations team members.

If the transition is not managed well, the nurtured relationships and trust that were built over time could exit with the project team. It is important to transfer stakeholder relationships with care and sensitivity. The outgoing and incoming teams should set up meetings with key stakeholder groups and individuals to consciously introduce the new general manager or community relations manager. Handing over relationships is far more complex and unpredictable than handing over physical assets. One simple way to help the transition is to mark the project's end with a celebration to show appreciation to local communities, businesses, and other stakeholders for their support.

### Managing Expectations

The end of construction and transition to operations creates a lot of changes for the project and for the local community. The invasive and disruptive impacts of construction activities, such as noise and dust from haulage trucks and traffic disruptions, will decrease with the end of construction and the start of operations. The associated human activity will also reduce dramatically with a reduction in the number of construction workers living and working in the area. Consequently, the surrounding communities and local regions will experience a reduction in traffic, noise, people, and economic activity.

The commissioning team will need a comprehensive engagement plan and communications plan to manage community expectations so that surprises are minimized, and the project can maintain community support.

A stakeholder engagement plan for the transition should be developed well before construction is finished and the project begins transitioning to operations. The plan should review the key project stakeholders and evaluate if there will be different stakeholders during operations or a change in the issues that the stakeholders might be concerned about. If there are new stakeholders, then the team should anticipate what their concerns might be and reach out to start the engagement process.

For key stakeholder groups, the commissioning team should actively engage to explain the changes that will be coming, listen to concerns, and, if necessary, revise plans to adapt to stakeholder concerns. A few of these key stakeholder groups are listed here:

- Local communities, including working groups
- Local businesses, suppliers, and service providers to the project (transportation, materials, etc.)
- Project workers who are from the local community
- Government agencies that are responsible for operating permits or economic development
- Academic institutions that have been engaged in local skills development that can help to maximize the local workforce during operations

## Economic Development

Local economic development is often a significant positive influence of major projects and we have discussed the value of developing a local working group and an economic development plan with the local community in Chapters 6 and 11. The plans should address strategies to build local capacity and create opportunities for positive benefits for the local community during project development and construction.

As the project approaches commissioning, the project can reconvene the economic development working group to discuss the transition to operations and the potential associated impacts to the local economy. The working group may be expanded to include other potential employers in the region that would benefit from being informed of the soon-to-be available labor and skills pool when construction ends.

Seeking input from local stakeholders would also inform the design and outcome of the demobilization program, including the potential for reusing construction facilities or equipment. For example, if roads were constructed to access the project site and are now being used by the local communities, an opportunity may exist to leave the roads in place but transfer ownership and maintenance to the local community.

## Local Businesses

The reduction in construction activity can be a welcome relief for some local stakeholders but will have an impact on local suppliers and service providers, who will experience a reduction in sales. Unless there is another industrial project starting up, these businesses may experience a decline. This will also impact other small businesses in the area who have been enjoying the regular patronage of construction workers with money to spend and who will also experience a drop in activity.

One way to help prepare these stakeholders for commissioning is to establish a communication plan well in advance to give business owners the opportunity to prepare for and manage the impact on their business. This will give them time to modify their business strategies, establish partnerships, and evaluate opportunities to work for the operations of the facility.

## Local Workers

As construction nears the end, the construction workforce will begin to demobilize in a phased approach. Demobilization of the external workforce who have been flown in and housed onsite in temporary camps is fairly straightforward. The workers are flown home and the camps dismantled.

The demobilization of local workers can be more difficult to manage. Once construction ends, only a fraction of a large construction workforce will be able to stay on for operations. Unless there are plans for these employees to transfer to other companies or industries in the area, a significant number of the local workforce could become unemployed. Managing this change requires foresight and planning during early project phases. A good economic development plan may help to alleviate the impact.

The commissioning team should work with the local community to develop alternatives that can help minimize the impacts of a decrease in employment opportunities. These may include:

- Financial planning for local employees and their families
- Extension of medical and dental benefits for applicable employees
- Family counseling for the transition
- Job retraining, including support for starting a new business
- Training for other family members so that they can find employment

## 13.4    Communications

Preparing local communities and other key stakeholders for commissioning and the transition to operations is important in order to manage expectations and prevent speculation. There are many ways to let people know that project construction is approaching completion and that the facility will be ready for use or operations very shortly. Some tips on managing communications during commissioning include:

- Prepare standard project messaging related to commissioning that is communicated to the commissioning team and other project employees to ensure consistent communications.
- Keep the project website updated on project progress. It should also have contact information, a community hotline, and an email inquiry account for community members to ask for more information.
- Prepare specific newsletters or brochures to highlight the upcoming shifts in project activity, such as the decrease in construction activity and reduction in employment.
- Keep social media accounts updated with real-time information.
- Issue media statements proactively to address any changes in the commissioning schedule.

## 13.5    Completion and Demobilization

There are many other aspects of commissioning that major projects incorporate into the commissioning plan, including demobilization of equipment and facilities like camps and equipment, cleanup and waste removal, and progressive reclamation (discussed in Chapter 14). Integrating sustainability into project delivery can help ensure that there are plans and systems in place to track and manage the environmental and social impacts of demobilization.

The use of a Permit to Work (PtW) system that tracks how each construction scope of work is executed and completed helps ensure that construction does not leave unfinished work or messy construction sites. The completion portion of the PtW system should include an inspection of the work site to confirm that the work is completed, and that the area has been left in a clean and safe condition. By maintaining clean work sites throughout the construction process, the level of effort to clean up the site before demobilization will be reduced.

The demobilization of construction infrastructure, including camps, temporary utilities (power, water, and waste water), construction equipment, and excess warehouse and maintenance space, needs to be completed in a sustainable manner. Waste and sewage should be treated and disposed of responsibly at approved facilities. Equipment and facilities that will not be needed by the operation should be dismantled and the area reclaimed or, if possible, transferred to a local community that may be able to use the facilities for their own purposes. For example, road building equipment no longer needed by the project could be transferred to the community to support their infrastructure development and maintenance needs.

The demobilization and shift to operations will also create changes to traffic patterns and access roads, which can have an impact on safety in local communities. There should be clear communication regarding the timing of these changes, what the community can expect to experience, and how the impacts will be managed.

## 13.6  Summary

Commissioning a major project is a complex process. Ensuring that all the good work achieved up front to integrate sustainability into the project is continued through to the operations phase is important to the operation's success and to protecting the project's community support and capital investment.

Effective stakeholder engagement is as important at the end of the project as it is at the beginning of the project. It is critical to engage with the local community to review project impacts, revisit economic development plans, and manage the associated impacts on local employees and local businesses.

This chapter has provided a very broad overview of key issues for integrating sustainability into the commissioning of a major project. The right sustainability expertise on the commissioning team and collaboration between members of the project and operations teams help to ensure that sustainability efforts are transitioned effectively. The commissioning team must also manage the demobilization, cleanup, and reclamation of construction areas so that environmental damage from the construction is minimized. Treating the land around the facility with respect will not only help to maintain community support, but it can also help the facility operate safely and successfully, as will be discussed in Chapter 14, addressing progressive reclamation and closure activities.

CHAPTER **14**

# Closure

The closure of a facility is in itself a major project and must be managed with the same attention to community engagement and sustainability as is paid to the design and construction of new facilities. This can be a huge challenge because the closure of a facility is typically accompanied by job loss, potential legacy environmental damages, and poor relations with the local community. Project teams can be proactive by discussing closure openly with the local community, exploring opportunities to repurpose facilities and infrastructure, establishing long-term monitoring, and supporting job retraining.

The challenge of managing closure can be made easier if the project team planned for closure during the design and construction phases. Then closure issues would have been addressed from the start of the project and integrated into project design, delivery, and operations.

Infrastructure developed under a design-finance-build-own-operate (DFBOO) or other similar project structures may have a contract end for the operator, but not an end of life for the asset. Project teams involved in DFBOO projects should take the time to understand how sustainability issues will be managed as the contract comes to an end. Closure planning should also include transfer of relationships and employees to the new organization taking over operation of the facility to minimize disruption and maintain community support.

This chapter will explore how project teams can understand closure, develop plans to manage project closure, and manage the transition to closure through stakeholder engagement and proactive environmental management. We will also discuss how project teams can incorporate design for closure and progressive reclamation into the delivery projects and operations of facilities, in order to reduce the challenge and cost of future project closure.

## 14.1  Closure Planning

Project planning and impact assessments often look at short-term benefits of a project, such as job creation and tax revenue. Communities, however, are looking at additional, longer-term impacts as the project ages and eventually moves to closure. Anticipating and assessing long-term impacts can help improve community acceptance and engagement with project development by demonstrating that the project team understands the local community's long-term view of the project, rather than focusing only on the short time it takes build the project (as discussed in Chapter 2).

One way to think about this concept is to understand the life of project and the project's impact on the local community over time. Most projects create a positive impact during their construction and operating life as jobs, contracts, taxes, and royalties help to create prosperity in the local community. But, as the project moves into closure, the negative impacts will become apparent, and the economic benefits will diminish, leaving only residual project impacts.

This concept is demonstrated in the diagram in Figure 14.1, which looks at the impact to the local community at any one time in the life of the project. In a sustainable project, the expectation would be that the impact on the local community (community health and prosperity) will stay positive throughout the life of the project. This is a different approach than a traditional lifecycle analysis (LCA) model that looks at the summation of impacts across the project and often uses net present value analysis to calculate an overall impact of the project. The LCA approach allows the calculated overall impact to be positive without necessarily being net positive at the end of the project. In sustainability terms, this means that the current generation receives the benefits and future generations inherit the negative legacy.

In the life of a project diagram, we have proposed that sustainability of the project to the local community can be measured as community well-being (or community health and prosperity). This is a conceptual framework but can be understood as a balance between positive community impacts (like health, wealth, education and skills, culture, community infrastructure) and negative impacts (like environmental damage, loss of culture and social cohesion, and poor health).

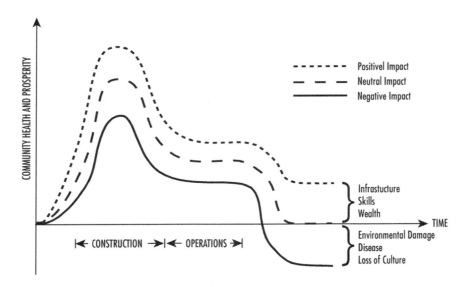

Figure 14.1   Sustainable life of a project.

There is a hypothetical baseline where the positive and negative impacts remain at the same level as they were at the beginning of the project, which would occur if there were no project. There is also a negative impact version where the negative impacts accumulate over time and leave an overall negative impact when the project is over. This is often the case with natural resource projects where the project ends and leaves behind waste and environmental damage, while the jobs and resulting wealth are not sustained past closure.

In the positive impact version of the model, the positive impacts are maintained throughout the project and not only in the construction and operating phases. The community would still experience a loss of jobs at the end of the project, but the skills training and economic development supported by the project is capable of maintaining a local economy that is able to adapt and innovate to create new opportunities.

The life of a project diagram shows how benefits change throughout the project lifecycle and encourages project teams to examine long-term impacts (both positive and negative) to the local community. A well-managed project seeks to minimize negative impacts, like environmental damage and social disruption, and to maximize positive impacts like infrastructure community health and skills development over the life of the project.

## 14.2  Transition to Closure

Like other transitions between project phases that we have discussed in this book, the transition from operations to closure requires a focus on sustainability to ensure that environmental and social aspects are well managed. Transition to closure typically involves a decrease in the number of employees and the potential to lose vital information regarding community commitments, environmental data, and engineering data that can support future uses of the site.

The transition team should take the time to review all of the project commitments by checking the commitment register for any commitments that apply to closure. Depending on the life of the project, closure commitments were probably made many years ago and commitments may no longer be applicable. Or they may represent an old way of operating and need to be updated to reflect best practices.

If the project does not have a commitment register or community agreement, then it will be necessary to find old approvals documents and permits to understand closure requirements. It will also be necessary to work with the local community to understand what their expectations are and if there are any perceptions regarding commitments that have been made throughout operations.

### Stakeholder Engagement

Stakeholder engagement for closure can be more difficult than engagement when the project is being developed. In the early stages of a project, the community can see the project as a new opportunity for jobs, income, and infrastructure, which creates optimism for the future. During closure, the realities of the project have sunk in and community support may have declined during operations. This can happen toward the end of operations in instances where an organization has stopped investing the time and effort required to maintain community support because they will soon be leaving the region.

In preparing for closure, stakeholder engagements will be focused on losses rather than gains: loss of jobs, loss of income, loss of medical benefits, loss of opportunity for youth who may choose to leave the community for opportunities elsewhere. Early engagement and closure planning well before closure of the facility can help to manage the sense of loss and allow the community to look forward and prepare for the future. Communities can work with the project team to find new opportunities for the project's infrastructure, collaborate on renewing traditional skills, or innovate new futures, or all of the above.

The project team should also engage with the local government to get support for retraining, opportunities for reuse of infrastructure, and plans for the future. The project team can use a community working group to bring together all of the parties to get input, plan for closure, and manage transition plans. See Chapter 6 for guidance on working groups.

The transition planning should look at key topics across the range of sustainability issues, including economic, environmental, and social transitions. Economic topics might include:

- How the local community can develop new economic opportunities
- Transition of skills and jobs to other opportunities in the local economy
- Financial planning for employees who will experience a decrease in available income
- Transfer of infrastructure to the local community, if it makes sense
- Reuse of facilities and infrastructure (roads, ports, etc.) for future economic opportunities

    Environmental topics might include:

- Clean up of the facility
- Recovery and potential reuse of equipment
- Removal of waste and hazardous waste
- Re use of water and waste-water utilities

Social topics are related to the social impact of the facility closure and how the local community and families can manage the transition, including:

- Social and family disruption due to loss of income and changing social dynamics
- Pensions and benefits (medical and dental support) that families may no longer have access to once the facility closes
- Loss of opportunity for youth in the community, resulting in out-migration.

## Engineering and Infrastructure

Another key area to manage during the transition to closure is to ensure that engineering design information for any facilities that will remain in place is collected and stored in an accessible location, such as local library or government office. The engineering data should include as-built drawings for the facility that have been updated to reflect any upgrades or maintenance activities. Design information can be used in the future if the facility will be redeveloped and the utilities and buildings are repurposed.

The engineering data should include underground structures or utilities that could become important resources or liabilities for future site redevelopment. Pipelines, sewers, tanks, vaults, wells, and other structures can leave behind pathways for residual contamination to move through the soil and can create future community safety risks due to land subsidence.

# 14.3   Design for Closure

Design for closure is an engineering approach that considers the end of life of the facility and how the areas will be decommissioned and restored. One key issue of designing for closure is to understand how closure security will be managed by the local government. Historically, project design would either ignore closure costs or would evaluate closure costs as part of the project financial calculations. But when you put closure costs into a typical net present value (NPV) calculation, closure costs would essentially have a zero cost to the project as expenses that occur 20+ years in the future are discounted by interest calculations, and therefore have a very low present value.

After many years of facilities being abandoned by organizations (especially in the natural resources industry), governments have started to apply closure bonding or closure security to ensure that sufficient money is allocated to decommissioning, rehabilitation, and closure. Governments assume that closure could be required at any time throughout the life of the project lifecycle and are therefore requiring financial security that is large enough to cover the closure costs, so taxpayers or governments do not inherit this burden. As a result, closure costs are now becoming a significant upfront cost for many major projects.

Design for closure takes into consideration these new requirements, seeking to minimize capital and operating costs and minimize potential closure costs so that financial security requirements can be reduced. For some organizations that are large enough to self-finance or secure a financial bond to cover closure, it can be viewed as a component of operating costs where the interest on the security or the annual cost of the bond is applied against the operating costs. For smaller organizations, the closure costs could be a direct and upfront cost that would increase the capital cost of the project and increase the amount of financing that is required to construct the project.

Design teams should work with the project finance team to understand how the closure costs will be incorporated into the project financing and cost analysis. When they are considering design options, they can then be sure to use a full cost analysis and make decisions that include the full cost to the project.

Design for closure that integrates sustainability can include:

- Develop project components that have a potential future use so that they can be reused instead of decommissioned.

- Design for decommissioning so that the design team has some idea how the facility will be taken down at the end of life rather than just being left to rust.

- Minimize the project footprint and construction footprint to reduce the area that will require reclamation and closure.

- Minimize waste generation during the project so that landfill design is smaller and requires lower closure costs.

- Design for recycling so that components can be taken apart, recovered, and recycled rather than just being landfilled.

- Determine what assets can be recovered (trucks and mobile equipment) instead of being disposed of in a landfill.

- Perform life-cycle assessment (LCA) on project components during design and decision making to determine the full impact of the design.

One strategy that can help with reducing closure costs is to identify project components that can be developed in cooperation with the local community. Typically, this would be project utility or infrastructure components like roads, ports, energy facilities, water supply, and wastewater treatment. If infrastructure is developed in cooperation with the local community, then it can be more easily transferred to the local community, rather than be decommissioned. Shared infrastructure can also be developed as a separate joint-venture organization with the local community, potentially using people-public-private-partnership (P4) structures (see Chapter 2), so that the project can demonstrate that the transfer of utilities will take place in the future. Every project situation is different but integrating infrastructure into a separate partnership or including utilities transfered into a community agreement may allow the organization to avoid or offset closure financing requirements.

Another key strategy for reducing closure costs is to incorporate progressive closure strategies into the project execution plan and construction plan, thereby dealing with closure tasks throughout construction and operations instead of leaving them all to the end of the facility life.

# 14.4   Progressive Reclamation

Progressive reclamation takes advantage of opportunities to repair and reclaim damaged areas of the project site as part of construction or operations, rather than waiting until the end of the project to complete permanent closure and reclamation. There are a number of key advantages to planning for progressive reclamation as part of the project delivery, including:

- Reduced closure costs and reduced financial security requirements

- Helping to build support with the local community

- Improved regulatory approvals

- Enhanced environmental protection

- More resilient facility operations

## Reduced Costs

Progressive reclamation helps to reduce closure costs by taking advantage of the construction equipment, utilities, and personnel expertise that are still onsite. If all closure activities wait until the end of facility operations, then it is likely that you will need to bring in additional equipment as well as new workers who may need to be trained. Any reclamation that can be completed during construction should be planned and incorporated into construction planning. For example, construction of new roads requires land clearing around the road for access and construction activities. Reclaiming these areas while constructing the road minimizes the footprint at the end of the project, reuses stripped cover material to revegetate the areas around the access road, does not require the mobilization of new equipment, and provides an overall cost savings.

## Community Support

As discussed above, community support for a project requires that the community experiences a positive impact throughout the project phases, including post closure. Planning for progressive reclamation and discussing these options with the local community helps to demonstrate that the project is interested in both the short-term and long-term impacts of the project.

Conversations with the community might also include reusing infrastructure and facilities and learning from traditional and local knowledge about the natural environment and how it will respond to being disturbed. Leveraging local knowledge to improve reclamation plans and identify knowledgeable resources in the local community to support will strengthen your reclamation strategies.

## Regulatory Approvals

Progressive reclamation strategies can help to gain regulatory support because it demonstrates to the local government that the project is planning for reclamation, that it will reduce the environmental impacts of the project and aim to avoid long-term liabilities. Successful follow-through on progressive reclamation strategies during construction and operations can also help the project achieve regulatory approval for future expansion plans.

## Environmental Protection

Progressive reclamation of the facility can help to minimize environmental damage over the life of the project. Disturbed lands that are not reclaimed during construction can continue to erode and degrade, which can lead to additional damage. Acting quickly can reduce overall costs by minimizing the area of land requiring reclamation.

Proper management and reclamation of waste management facilities will prevent the spread of contamination and reduce future reclamation costs. Proactive clean-up of spills or leaking tanks can also reduce overall costs by limiting the migration of contaminants and reducing the amount of soil and groundwater that requires clean-up at the end of the facility life.

## Resilient Operations

Progressive reclamation can also have direct impact on the operations by reducing operating risks. Repairing damaged land and managing wastes can improve safety on the facility by reducing potential worker exposure to toxins and by reducing dust exposure during operations.

Reclamation becomes especially important with the increase in extreme storm events due to climate change. A facility that has progressively reclaimed disturbed surface areas, recovered vegetation, and restored natural drainage patterns will be more resilient to erosion and damage from extreme weather and drought.

## STORY: INCORPORATING PROGRESSIVE RECLAMATION INTO THE DESIGN OF A TAILINGS IMPOUNDMENT

Our project engineering team was facing a difficult challenge with the design of a tailings impoundment for the mine we were developing. The local community and government regulators were pushing for a progressive reclamation strategy to reduce the long-term risk and minimize the potential for air impacts from tailings dust to health in the local community. But the owner was pushing for the lowest cost option to get the facility built.

The initial tailings design included an impoundment with a single large cell that would be filled over the 20- to 30-year life of the mine, and would have no closure until the end of the mine life. This used the tradition design strategy that had the lowest capital cost. The engineering design team wanted to use a multicell design approach, which they considered safer because it would reduce the risk of tailings impoundment failure, but they were facing resistance from the owner.

To manage the issue, our sustainability team brought together a multidisciplinary design team that included dam design, hydrology, water treatment, closure design, construction, and finance to brainstorm and evaluate options. The options analysis showed that the multicell design looked more expensive than the single-cell design when it was evaluated in isolation. But the multicell design ended up being much less expensive when you included closure security, reuse of surface material as cover material, and the overall water balance. In particular, the water balance showed that using the multicell design would result in a smaller amount of rainwater falling onto the open tailings, which reduced the volume of water leaching from the tailings and eliminated the need for an expensive water treatment system.

The new design, which used progressive reclamation strategies, allowed us to create a win-win-win for the owners, the community, and the regulators. Once we presented the new approach with the full financial analysis, it was easy to get the owners to change their mind and approve the multicell tailings design.

# 14.5  Summary

Project teams may not see the future closure of the facility as a core problem that they need to address. Their focus is usually on creating something new and not on how that new facility will degrade over time, need to be replaced, or closed down. Integrating sustainability into a project requires that the team starts thinking about the long-term impacts of the project, and how that fits with the long-term requirements and needs of the local community.

Integrating the sustainability of closure into project management, design, and delivery can create advantages not only for the local community and local government, but also for the project owner and project team. Advantages include contributing to a smoother approvals processes, earning and retaining community support, and reducing financial security requirements.

CHAPTER **15**

# Wrap-Up

We have worked on sustainability management on many different major projects, and in our experience, we have found that there were no practical guides to help with the integration of sustainability into project delivery. The academic literature provides some help, but it does not address the boots-on-the-ground realities of managing sustainability that we have experienced. The tools and processes that are used by corporate head offices or operating plants do not address the short-term, intense level of activity and complex risks of a developing major project. The upfront, one-off engagements and impact assessment processes typically end once the project is approved. And these processes do not provide further guidance on how to turn the expectations and commitments into reality during project delivery.

We have collected tools and processes from the front lines of sustainability management. Using our experiences and lessons learned, we intended for this book to be a useful resource for other project professionals engaged in major project delivery who are looking for new ideas to help them address sustainability challenges and create better projects. We also hope that it can be useful for everyone else involved in the delivery of major projects, including project owners, consultants and contractors, financing organizations, governments, and local communities, who can gain an understanding of the challenges that major projects face and the best practices available to proactively manage these challenges.

## 15.1   It's a New World for Delivering Major Projects

Developing major projects is becoming increasingly complex. Local communities expect social and environmental responsibility, financing is tied to environmental and social performance, and government regulators require more diligence in project design to manage emissions, energy use, and closure requirements. Project teams must manage not just the project budget, schedule, and quality, but also the project's sustainability aspects, such as sharing economic benefits with local communities, eco-efficient design, and environmental protection and impact mitigation.

Managing sustainability on major projects like mines, pipelines, wind farms, ports and airports, offshore and onshore oil and gas, military installations, waste facilities, and other large infrastructure developments poses unique challenges. Each project requires its own customized approach to ensure that social and environmental impacts are managed, and potential benefits are maximized.

## 15.2   So, What Can Project Teams Do?

Managing sustainability as a standalone function outside of the main project is no longer an acceptable approach. In order to effectively manage sustainability, project teams must embrace sustainability as a team sport. Everyone on the team is a contributor and can help to integrate sustainability into each part of the project delivery. In this book, we presented tools and processes for integrating sustainability that fit into three main themes:

1. Understanding what is important
2. Planning and project management of sustainability
3. Delivering a more sustainable project

Understanding sustainability involves examining the unique aspects of major projects that make them challenging from a sustainability perspective. We have discussed how the perception of space and time are different for project teams, governments, and the local community.

Once you understand the unique challenges and opportunities that your project must address, the team can develop the required planning and project management approaches to coordinate activities and track performance. We have discussed the need for strong leadership from a sustainability steering committee, techniques for integrating sustainability into standard project management and risk management processes, how stakeholder engagement fits into the project, and some specific tools that can help manage sustainability, including a commitment action log and complaints processes.

Project planning becomes reality when the project moves into delivery with detailed design, procurement, and construction. We have provided tools and resources to support design and procurement teams with community engagement, decision making, and dealing with growing issues like climate change. The tools and advice for integrating sustainability into construction help to address environmental management, community engagement, and managing suppliers and contractors. We also looked at commissioning and the transition to operations, as well as eventual closure of the facility with a focus on ensuring stakeholders are engaged throughout these transitions and environmental impacts are managed.

Integrating sustainability into major projects requires a practical approach that is not focused on philosophical principles. Rather, it is focused on specific activities that the project team should start doing, do differently, or simply stop doing. If integrating sustainability does not change behavior, then it will not change how the project is delivered or the outcome of the project.

## 15.3　Managing Complexity

Sustainability is a very complicated field and the best-laid plans will not always work. Integrating sustainability means dealing with human emotions and complex social structures, as well as the already complicated technical requirements of delivering major projects. In many ways, sustainability is more difficult and requires a more diverse set of skills than traditional project delivery. Sustainable design is more challenging than traditional engineering design. Sustainable procurement requires more thought and planning than traditional procurement. Sustainable construction that gets the project built without losing community support takes a more sophisticated and thoughtful project team that can balance complex requirements better than traditional construction teams. Meeting these challenges is very satisfying and allows project teams to finish projects with the knowledge that they have done the best job possible – that they have created a positive impact for the project owners and for the local community.

Integrating sustainability requires knowing how to do your job in addition to understanding the environmental and social impacts of doing that job. But that should not be viewed as an insurmountable challenge, nor something that another team member should look after for you. Tackling sustainability head on creates innovative solutions, reduces risk, improves financial performance, and creates better projects.

## 15.4　What Does It Cost?

People often ask, "This looks complicated. How much does it cost?" There are a number of different approaches that can be used to answer this question:

1. Wrong question. The right question is "How much money will integrating sustainability save us?" Every project we have worked on has seen project cost savings from integrating sustainability that are many times higher than the cost of the program due to collaboration, innovation, and lowering project risks.

2. Treating sustainability management as an extra cost is like treating project management as an extra cost. Good sustainability management is like good project management. Sustainability is critical to project success and adds value to the project.

3. Integrating sustainability into project management and delivery means that you do not need a significant increase in the size of the project team. It just means that the existing team needs to learn how to do their job differently in order to manage sustainability as part of their roles and responsibilities.

4. Sustainability management is a small overall cost and is usually less than the rounding error on the overall cost of the project.

5. Sustainability has become a necessary part of every project. It is better to proactively manage these issues as part of project management than to ignore them and deal with the consequences.

## 15.5  Getting Started

Integrating sustainability into major projects can help to improve project management, reduce risk, and build long-term community support. However, it can seem like a difficult challenge for project teams that have not developed sustainability programs and are unsure where to start.

We find that it is important to understand that the journey to create a more sustainable project is a marathon rather than a sprint. Teams need to get started as early as possible in the project to be successful. Take a look at the project you are currently working on and ask yourself and your team: What are we currently doing to integrate sustainability and where do we need to improve? And then take a first step toward that goal. It may be something as simple as identifying your sustainability concerns or introducing sustainability shares into team meetings.

Even if the project as a whole has not embraced an integrated sustainability approach, individuals and departments can still make their part of the project a little bit better. Procurement teams can find ways of reducing project risks and encouraging contractors to work in an environmentally friendly and socially responsible way. Design teams can use structured decision tools to balance cost and technical specifications with meeting environmental goals and reducing impacts on the local community. Construction teams can implement permit-to-work systems, open communications and other tools to manage sustainability commitments, and keep the support of the local community.

Check out more information on our website www.integratingsustainability.com. We have provided templates of some of the tools and tables discussed in the book. From these you can develop custom tools for your project and get started quickly and confidently.

## 15.6  Sharing Your Stories

Integrating sustainability into major projects is still an emerging field of practice. No two projects are the same, and the usual score cards and checklists will only get you so far. Sustainability teams need to explore all the tools and processes, and you will need to create custom solutions that fit your project location, technology, industry, stakeholders, and owners of the project.

These tools and processes will require ongoing development, more testing, and more sharing of best practices from other practitioners working on the front lines of major projects. If you have experiences, stories, tools, or other best practices that would help fellow project professionals, we invite you to send us an email or share them on our website at www.integratingsustainability.com. Some things we would love to hear from you:

- What is your favorite "success" story?
- What is your favorite "failure" story?
- What lessons have you learned?
- When have you overcome resistance to change in your organization? What approach worked best?
- What challenges do you see emerging over the next 5 to 10 years?

- Are there specific tools or models that you like to use?
- Do you use a specific piece of software and would you recommend it?
- Where do you get your information from about advances in sustainability management?

## 15.7   Final Word

We have covered a lot of ground in this book and dealt with a wide range of sustainability topics. Many of these topics, like local procurement, are distinct fields of practice and already the subject of publications. Here, we have attempted to stitch these project delivery topics together into a comprehensive approach for project management and delivery.

Integrated sustainability is now a critical part of delivering a major project successfully. We hope that this book provides value to you and your team; that it helps elevate the general understanding of how sustainability fits into major project development and inspires new ideas for creating better, more sustainable major projects.

# APPENDIX B

# Stakeholder Summary Template

| Stakeholder profile | Details |
|---|---|
| Category of stakeholder: | |
| Stakeholder name: | |
| Group or individual? | |
| If group, name of key contact: | |
| Contact information: | |
| Date of first engagement: | |
| Describe engagement history, if not first or early engaged: | |
| THEIR KEY ISSUES OF CONCERN: | |
| What is their objective for engagement? | |
| Preferred method of engagement: How do they want to be engaged? | |
| How often do they want to be engaged? | |
| What is their preferred language? | |
| What are their expectations of the project/operation? | |
| How could this person/group affect the project negatively? | |
| How could this stakeholder affect the project positively? | |
| What is their scale of operating? (i.e. global, local, regional, if a group)? | |
| How are they supported or funded (if a group)? | |
| Other stakeholders with whom they are aligned (formally or informally): | |
| Other stakeholders with whom they are in conflict (formally or informally): | |
| What are the cultural considerations, if any? | |

# APPENDIX C

# Stakeholder Engagement Plan Sample Table of Contents

6. Identifying Stakeholders
   a. Communities of Interest
   b. Community Groups
   c. Indigenous Peoples
   d. Vulnerable Groups
7. Stakeholder Mapping
8. Engagement Strategy
   a. Town Hall Meetings
   b. Perception Surveys
   c. Focus Groups
   d. Working Groups
   e. Design Workshops
   f. Individual Engagement
9. Communications Strategy
10. Issues Tracking and Management
11. Document Management

## TIP: USEFUL APPENDICES OF AN SEP

The main body of the SEP can be updated far less regularly than the appendices. Appendices are where the key information will be stored and updated as needed, and, for the most part, should be kept confidential. They may include:

1. Stakeholder list with contact information
2. Stakeholder map
3. Stakeholder summaries
4. Engagement log
5. List of issues, risks, and opportunities
6. SEP schedule
7. Roles and responsibilities
8. Templates: stakeholder meeting minutes, meeting sign-in sheets

# APPENDIX D

# Stakeholder Communications Planning for Construction

| Stakeholder Group | Interests and Expectations | What Needs to be Communicated | Key Messaging | Communication Tools | Timing/ Frequency |
|---|---|---|---|---|---|
| Environmental Regulators | • Comply with permits<br>• Transparency (no surprises) | • Permit applications<br>• Compliance reporting<br>• Construction schedule<br>• Spills and incidents<br>• Archaeological finds<br>• Complaints from local community | • Environmental monitoring will be undertaken to minimize impacts on the environment.<br>• Continue to work with the community during construction. | • Regulatory/ permitting reports<br>• Project updates<br>• Spill/incident reports | • Prior to major milestones<br>• As required |

*(continued)*

| Stakeholder Group | Interests and Expectations | What Needs to be Communicated | Key Messaging | Communication Tools | Timing/ Frequency |
|---|---|---|---|---|---|
| Local communities | • Local employment<br>• Incidents communicated<br>• No dust or noise, light, visual aesthetics, etc.<br>• Business opportunities<br>• Community safety<br>• Site tours<br>• Minimize disruptions<br>• Schedule of events<br>• No stress on social services or infrastructure<br>• Good conduct from workers in town | • Job/business opportunities<br>• Regular updates<br>• Traffic disruptions<br>• Incidents/ emergency response<br>• Major events<br>• Process for communicating with the project<br>• Feedback on complaints<br>• Proper signage | • Commit to hiring local workforce.<br>• Commit to safety of the community.<br>• Notify the community when major disruptions, emergencies, or major project events take place.<br>• Take complaints seriously and provide an initial response within 48 hours of submission. | • Social media<br>• Radio<br>• Town hall meeting<br>• Employment/ Procurement updates<br>• Project activity notifications<br>• Incident reports<br>• Site tours | • Prior to major milestones<br>• Monthly<br>• As required |
| Local governments | • Manage the project with few serious complaints<br>• No surprises<br>• Maintain a safe environment for their population<br>• Avoid stressing local services/ infrastructure | • Schedule<br>• Inflow of workers<br>• Regular updates<br>• Disruptions<br>• Incidents/ emergency response | • Provide regular updates in local language.<br>• Respond to concerns in a timely manner.<br>• Implement all environmental mitigation measures.<br>• Coordinate with local traffic management agencies. | • Project website<br>• Community visits/ presentations<br>• Site tours | • Prior to major milestones<br>• As required |

# Index